# HOW TO PROFIT FROM THE COMING BULL MARKET

### Dow Jones Industrial Average 1965–1980

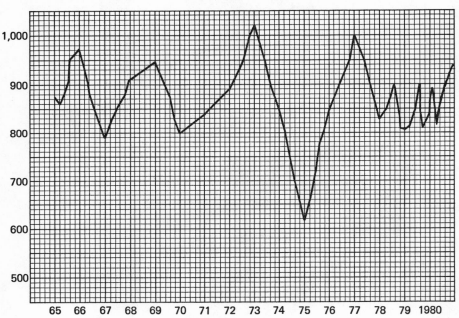

This chart, which is so familiar to most investors, shows the Dow Jones Industrial Average for the fifteen years ending in 1980. In some years it was up and in other years it was down, but like a chart showing annual rainfall in Boston for the last century, it ends up pretty much where it started and certainly shows no upward trend. For another less commonly viewed perspective of the Dow Jones Industrial Average which can lead to a strikingly different conclusion, see Chart 3.

# HOW TO PROFIT FROM THE COMING BULL MARKET

## MAX G. ANSBACHER

Prentice-Hall,Inc., Englewood Cliffs, New Jersey

The author wishes to express his appreciation for
the use of the following:
Chart 1. From the 7/31/78*Fortune* magazine, p. 76.
Fortune Magazine Art Department/Bob Weiss Associates.
Chart 2. From the 8/27/79 *Fortune* magazine, p. 93.
Jean Held/Luis Perelman, Fortune Magazine.
Chart 3. From the 1979 Annual Report of Affiliated Fund.
Reprinted by courtesy of Affiliated Fund, Inc.

*How to Profit From the Coming Bull Market* by Max G. Ansbacher
Copyright © 1981 by Max G. Ansbacher

Address inquiries to Prentice-Hall, Inc.,
Englewood Cliffs, N.J. 07632
Printed in the United States of America
Prentice-Hall International, Inc., London
Prentice-Hall of Australia, Pty. Ltd., Sydney
Prentice-Hall of Canada, Ltd., Toronto
Prentice-Hall of India Private Ltd., New Delhi
Prentice-Hall of Japan, Inc., Tokyo
Prentice-Hall of Southeast Asia Pt. Ltd., Singapore
Whitehall Books Limited, Wellington, New Zealand
10  9  8  7  6  5  4  3  2  1

**Library of Congress Cataloging in Publication Data**

Ansbacher, Max G
  How to profit from the coming bull market.

  Includes index.
  1. Stocks.  2.  Investments.  I.  Title.
HG6041.A57    332.63'22    80-26511
ISBN 0-13-429381-9

# CONTENTS

# PREFACE

An anguishing dilemma faces Americans today as they worry about how to invest their money. With the current inflation rate, their money is shrinking at the alarming rate of 13% a year. This means that $25,000 today will have the purchasing power of only $12,460 in five years. What can concerned people do to prevent this disappearance of their hard-earned money?

There are now bank savings certificates which pay an amount comparable to the current rate for treasury bills, 11.3% in October 1980, and there are also money market funds which have a similar rate. Thus, anyone investing in these cannot hope to keep up with the rate of inflation. But it is even worse than this.

The investor must pay federal income tax on all his interest, and depending upon where he lives, he may also have to pay state and local income tax. The result is that if the investor is in the 40% tax bracket, which doesn't take much of an income these days, he would actually be receiving net after tax income of only 6.8%. With inflation eating away up to 13% of his money each year, he is locking in a loss of purchasing power instead of a profit. The longer this goes on, the poorer the investor becomes.

Is there anything else that can offer a more cheerful prospect? The stock market was supposed to keep up with inflation, but fourteen years of gyrations which at the time of this writing left the market down 5% from where it was in 1966 have convinced most investors that the stock market is certainly not the answer. The bond market has done better, but also has not kept up with inflation.

That leaves only one other area: tangibles. The only investment which has done well for most Americans in the past decade or more is their biggest single investment, their home. Prices of homes and real estate in general have more than kept up with the rate of inflation. And so have the prices of most other tangibles. In an annual review of the returns available from tangibles as opposed to financial investments, Salomon Brothers reported compounded annual gains for the period 1968 to June 1, 1979, of from 9.6% up to 19.4% for various tangibles, whereas the return on bonds over that period was 5.8% and for stocks a mere 3.1%—and all of these gains were from the dividends which were reinvested rather from any growth in the prices of the stocks.

Gold appreciated 55% in the 1979 period alone, stamps 60%, and silver 62%. Clearly these were the investments which were successful not only in staying ahead of inflation but in achieving the real goal of investing, which is to actually make money. And since June 1979, the acceleration of prices in many tangibles has continued. Gold then was still to make its major move, and paintings have moved up substantially since then.

Is the answer to the investor's problem then to invest in tangibles and forget about financial investments?

There is one big gamble in investing in tangibles. It may already be too late. Prices of tangibles have gone up so much already that it is difficult to believe they will continue to go up at the same rate in the future. In fact, there are indications that some may already have reached their peak. Take houses. When the Federal Reserve Board increased the discount rate by one full percentage point in October 1979, the cost of mortgages went up and, more important, the availability of mortgage money began to dry up. The result was that many would-be buyers of houses just weren't able to purchase them and the markets began to slow down, with a resulting downward pressure on house prices.

The star performer of the tangibles in recent years, gold, also hit its high just before the Fed made its announcement, and since then it has been substantially lower. But even those tangibles which are still going up in price may not be good investments.

For example, an auction of American paintings from the eighteenth through mid-twentieth centuries held in New York City at Sotheby Parke Bernet on October 25, 1979, produced prices for some works were ten times the presale estimate of what they were worth. In explaining the astonishingly high prices received for many of the paintings, one gallery director was quoted in *The Wall Street Journal* as saying: "This is pure speculation. People are buying paintings instead of stocks." There might appear to be nothing wrong with that except that the American paintings curator of the Boston Museum of Fine Arts was at the auction, and he said, "A lot of mediocre pictures went for twice or three times what they were worth." Do you want to be one of the buyers who just bought a painting for two or three times what it is really worth?

Diamonds also have done very well. So well that they have spawned a whole mini-industry of so-called "Gem dealers" whose sole function is to high-pressure investors into buying second-rate stones at highly marked up prices. When everyone and his brother begins to buy, it is often time to start selling.

There is one rule, and perhaps only one rule, with which no one can argue, and which applies to any type of investing in any age and for any investment. Often quoted but less often observed, that golden rule of the marketplace is BUY LOW, SELL HIGH. Today tangibles are high. Stocks are low.

Buyers of tangibles at today's sky-high prices could face major losses as prices return to more natural levels. It has happened before and will happen again.

What then is the answer for the serious investor who is looking for a place to invest his money with a low risk and a good chance of having an appreciation which will outperform inflation?

Don't look now, but could it be that the old stock market, so often kicked, maligned, and abused by everyone who has gone near it for the last thirteen years, could be the answer? To find out, just read on.

# INTRODUCTION

January 18, 1966, is just a brief moment ago in terms of human history, but it is a giant step back into time in terms of our fast-changing economy and society. The Vietnam War was still in progress, and President Lyndon Johnson had stopped the bombing of the north with a warning to the North Vietnamese that their only choice was "between peace and the ravages of a conflict from which they can only lose." In New York City the new Mayor Lindsay had taken office, and a twelve-day subway strike had just ended amid speculation as to whether the 15-cent fare could be saved.

Suits at the best men's stores in town were on sale at $84.50, and for those who wanted economy, Robert Hall was offering all-worsted suits for $29.88, including alterations. Help wanted columns were filled with advertisements for clerks and receptionists (in the "Help Wanted—Female" section) to start at $65 a week, and a new luxury one-bedroom apartment in the best part of Manhattan's upper East Side with free use of a roof-top swimming pool was only $230 a month. A new Datsun was $1,295, and a full-sized Plymouth Fury with automatic transmission was $2,222.

While prices of almost all goods and services were low by present-day standards, there was one place in America where prices were definitely not low in comparison to today. That place was Wall Street, where stock prices had been going up for about twenty years. On Wall Street, January 18, 1966, was a red-letter day. On that day the Dow Jones Industrial Average made history by touching 1,000 on an intra-day high for a new all-time record high. While Dow theorists did not accept it as a record because the average did not close above 1,000, nevertheless, there was cheering and excitement aplenty as the magical number was reached.

One indication of the enthusiasm can be gained from the fact that the very next day Paine, Webber, Jackson & Curtis ran a large two-column advertisement for new brokers right on the stock market page, with the headline, "Shouldn't you be earning more in your present job after three years? (The ceiling is unlimited for a stockbroker to know.)" The assumption was that the prices of stocks would just keep on moving up, that more and more money would flow into Wall Street, and that another decade of sharply increased wealth lay around the corner for both investors and their brokers.

How wrong they were. That high-water mark of 1,000 on the Dow Jones Industrial Average, give or take a few points, has not been broken more than briefly since. The stock market took a serious beating in 1970 and a more terrible crash in 1974 and 1975 from which it has still not recovered as this book is being written. In fact, when the prices of common stock are corrected for inflation, they have gone down by about 66%, a terrible loss for an investment which presumably was going to be able to keep up with inflation and produce a total return year after year of 9%, as studies had shown it did during the 50 years preceding 1966.

What the stock market has brought since January 18, 1966, was not joy and prosperity but misery and losses to thousands and millions of investors. Brokers have lost their jobs, and their clients have usually said good riddance. Investment managers, including the brightest and wisest, have been made to look like fools. The entire American system for raising money for industry by issuing new common stocks has practically come to an end. Individual investors sold their stock and fled the market, followed quickly by the big institutional money. *Business Week* magazine recently had a cover story summing up the stock market under the headline "The Death of Equities. How Inflation Is Destroying the Stock Market."

This book is an analysis of why the stock market went up so fast and so far in the sixties, why it came down so sharply and for so prolonged a period in the seventies, and where it is going to go from here. It is the emphatic conclusion of this book that the market will now move upward sharply and reward investors with literally billions of dollars of profit. For those who have the courage to buy stocks now when they are unpopular, the payoff will be large. For those who don't, the missed opportunity may not present itself again for decades. The book, then, discusses just what kind of investment in stocks will be the most suitable for you, and how you can balance your interest in making money with your need to reduce your risk of loss.

You may not agree with the conclusion reached, but when you consider the large amount of money you can make if it is correct, you owe it to yourself to read this book and see if you agree or not. If you do, and if the conclusions are right, you will be thankful that you acted on this book, and your children and grandchildren will thank you.

# *1*

# *THE PROSPEROUS FIFTIES*

The end of World War II in 1945 was a jubilant time for America. Who hasn't seen the photographs of the cheering crowds, the sailors sweeping the girls off their feet with kisses, and the troop ships returning with thousands of cheering GI's eager to get back to civilian life. But while on the human level it was a time for joy, on the financial level it was time for deep concern. The reason for this skepticism was that before the war started, the United States had been enduring the agony of the worst depression in the century. From 1930 until right up to 1941, when the United States entered the war, the country was in abject poverty. Many thought that although the New Deal programs of F.D.R. had helped alleviate the worst of the depression, it was only the massive defense expenditures of World War II which had finally and unequivocally brought the depression to an end.

Now that the war was over and government expenses were rapidly being reduced to the normal peacetime rate, wouldn't the depressed economy that prevailed before the war return? This very real concern explains why the stock market was at such low levels during the late forties. With the Dow Jones Industrial Average (DJIA) selling in the 200 range, the average stock was earning about 13 cents a year for every $1 that the stock was selling for. Another way of expressing that is to say that the ratio of the price of the stock to the earnings of the stock was 7.5 to 1, or, even more simply, the stocks were selling at a price/earnings ratio (or P/E) of 7.5.

By historical standards a P/E of 7.5 is a very low figure and means that stocks were selling at low prices in relationship to the earnings of the companies. This made very good sense, because although the companies were making good profits in the postwar recovery period, investors believed that these profits would be short-lived and that, with the return of a depressed economy, earnings would go down. Since prices on Wall Street generally reflect the expectation of what is going to happen rather than the current situation, the low P/E ratio was to be expected. So the stock market waited for the postwar depression to return.

It never did. Instead the fifties proved to be years of prosperity. Corporate profits continued to grow; industries boomed, fueled first by the tremendous pent-up demand for automobiles and housing which had built up during the war, and then by the enormous buying power being released into the economy by the returning servicemen who were back at work. Next came the bumper crop of marriages and births, further increasing demand for homes and all the related products that go with them. Then the large number of babies growing up created a wave of economic demand—first for more elementary schools, then for more colleges, and finally by adding directly to consumer demand as they became wage earners and heads of their own households.

The result was that while the stock market had a P/E of just 7.5 in 1948 and again in 1950, that was to be the last time for over twenty years that stocks would be so cheap in terms of earning power, and it was the last time ever that they would be so cheap in actual dollar cost. In 1950 the Dow Jones average ended the year at just 235. Interestingly enough, that figure was just slightly above the book value of the Dow Jones average at the time.

This means that a share of stock was worth almost no more than the accountants said the assets of the underlying corporations were worth. The prices of the stocks reflected only the depreciated value of the bricks and mortar, inventory, and cash in the till.

No additional amount was added to reflect the fact that in the case of any successful corporation many valuable intangibles are a part of the entity. These include a carefully assembled collection of talented management people, valuable trademarks which usually have no book value, valuable patents and trade secrets, also without any book value, distribution channels, acceptance of its brands by consumers, a chain of dealers, perhaps millions of dollars of advertising already spent which has created a ready demand for its brands, and research which has been fully paid for but which is only now ready to earn money for the company in the form of new products.

None of these is reflected in the book value of a stock. Therefore, to say that a company's stock is selling at book value is to say that in most cases it is selling at far less than any honest appraisal of the value of the company would be.

An indication of the cheapness of book value can be found in a saying which I heard when I was the international counsel to one of America's largest household products companies, whose trademarks for toothpaste, soaps, and detergents are part of the American vocabulary. The former trademark counsel had been fond of saying that if all the assets of this billion-dollar company were divided into two parts, one part being the trademarks of the company and the other part containing all the other assets, he would choose the trademarks, and within a year he would own the entire company. He was indicating that this company's trademarks were worth far more than all its factories, machinery, inventory, and cash. Needless to say, the trademarks of this company have a zero book value. That gives an indication of just how cheap book value can be. And that's what many stocks were selling for in the late 1940's.

During the fifties, two thing happened to affect dramatically the price of stocks. First, the earnings of companies kept rising as America gained its undisputed position as the leading industrial country in the free world. Under the Marshall Plan, American goods were shipped throughout the world, the American dollar replaced the British pound as the universal currency, and Americans reveled in having the highest standard of living in the world, with every prospect that it would continue to go ever higher.

With rising company earnings, it was a mathematical certainty that since the P/E ratio was already about as low as it had ever gone, the price of stocks had to increase. Thus, if a company earned $13.33 per share in 1950, and that stock had a P/E of 7.5, then the price of the stock would be $13.33 times 7.5 or $100. If next year the company earned $16 a share, and the P/E ratio was kept the same, then the stock would be worth 7.5 times $16, or $120, for a gain of 20%. This is exactly what happened. And stock prices began to rise all during the fifties.

The second event which caused stock prices to rise was that investors began to realize that perhaps there wouldn't be a return to a depression after all. Once this realization sank in, it became clear not only that corporate earnings would stay as high as they were, but that they would in all probability keep on rising through the years to come. If this were to be the case, then the investors concluded that it would be worth paying a larger P/E ratio in order to own a stock.

The reasoning was that if a stock was worth 7.5 times its present earnings, and if it earned $13.33 this year, it would be selling for $100; but if you had confidence that it would earn $16 next year, then you would be willing to pay 7.5 times next year's estimated earnings in order to purchase the stock. Thus, an investor would be willing to pay $120 rather than $100 for the stock, without feeling that he had overpaid for it.

Thus began the era of paying higher P/E's for growth stocks. Obviously, this reasoning could be carried on almost ad infinitum. If a company were earning $13.33 this year, but it was estimated that it would earn $16 next year and $20 the year after that, then it would be prudent to pay 7.5 times the $20 a share earnings, or $150 a share. Of course, the purchaser was no longer paying 7.5 times current earnings; he was actually paying 11.25 times earnings. But that was all right, because investors were becoming patient.

Stocks began to bubble up, riding on the twin jets of higher earnings and higher price earnings multiples, as investors dared to look into the future and price the stocks not on what they were earning that year, but on what they were expected to earn in two or more years down the line.

All during the fifties the prices of stocks continued to rise. Not only did earnings go up, but the P/E ratios kept going up, until in 1958 the P/E ratio of the Dow Jones average had risen from 7.5 to just over 20. The result was that the price of the DJIA went from just over 200 at the beginning of 1950 to 600 in 1960. It is hard to imagine today that the prices of blue chip industrial stocks could actually triple in the brief period of ten years, but that is what they did.

Now this tremendous increase in the prices of stocks began to have a profound effect of its own. Fortunes were being made in common stocks, and this fact was not going unnoticed by investors both large and small.

The small investors told their friends and neighbors that they had doubled their money in stocks, and their neighbors soon decided that they really didn't need to keep all their money in the bank but could risk some of it in the market. The more people there were who decided that they could put some money in the market, the more demand there was for stocks, and the higher the prices went. Thus, to a significant extent the rise in stock prices was self-sustaining. Success breeds success, and nowhere is that more true than in the case of the stock market.

In fact, in the period 1950 to 1960, 14 million new investors came into the stock market, bringing funds which had been safely squirreled away in bank accounts or other fixed income securities.

The story of the large investors was much the same. Institutions had always played a role in Wall Street. Insurance companies, for example, had been investors in common stocks for decades. Now the fifties began to see the rise of pension funds as the major purchasers of common stocks. Being careful and prudent investors, these institutional investors generally preferred bonds to common stocks, but as their investments in common stocks began to earn so much more money for them than their investments in bonds, they began to place a larger percentage of their funds in the stock market. Thus, the increase in institutional purchases paralleled the increased individual investor demand, and further increased prices.

Now another factor began to make its presence felt in the market. The stock market had generally been the exclusive investment province of the upper middle class and the wealthy. To purchase stock had always been considered somewhat risky, to be done with money that was in addition to what a person had in his savings account and in life insurance. Furthermore, because of the commission structure of stock brokers, it really didn't pay for brokers to execute small orders. With no way in which a person of moderate means could accumulate stocks by purchasing a small amount each month, and with no one to interest him in doing so, it was no wonder that the little fellow stayed out of the market.

But with the great success that stocks had achieved in the fifties, the little fellow was hankering for a part of the action, and where there's a need, someone will find a way to fill it. The answer was the mutual fund. The fund bought a selection of stocks and then sold shares in the fund to the public. By charging a "load" or commission of 7% or more, ensuring plenty of commission money, brokers and salesmen were motivated to promote the funds. Because small investors were able to purchase small dollar amounts each month, it was easy for people on budgets to subscribe to the funds. Furthermore, because of their diversification, it was said that the funds were not as risky as simply owning a few stocks which one had picked for himself. For all these reasons mutual funds became very successful and provided another source of funds for the stock market. As the really little investors started buying mutual funds, their billions of dollars of buying power also were applied to the purchase of stocks, and helped to pull up their prices.

Thus, at the end of the fifties the situation in the stock market was as follows:

It had been a decade of exceptional growth in the price of the blue chip stocks which made up the Dow Jones Industrial

Average. From a level of just 200 at the beginning of the period, they had grown quite spectacularly to over 600. In 1960 at that level they were selling at approximately 18 times earnings (for a P/E of 18), and they were selling at almost two times book value. Those investors who had had faith in the country and the stock market in the late forties had been rewarded, probably by far more than they ever expected.

The public was coming into the market through increased participation directly and indirectly through mutual funds. The institutions were becoming bigger all the time, and they were committing more of their funds into the stock market. Finally and most important, the stock market had a solid decade of success behind it. For ten years those who had bought common stocks had made money, and made big money. While bonds of corporations were yielding 5%, the stock market had yielded an astounding figure of almost 20% a year for the past ten years. And of course that was for the Dow Jones average; many stocks had done appreciably better. In short, the fifties had been exceptionally good to common stock investors. They had made a lot of money, and what is even more important to our narrative here, they expected to make a lot more money in the future.

# 2

## *THE SOARING SIXTIES*

On this note of optimism and success, the sixties were ushered in with great expectations. The original investors in the forties had been cautious and careful, burned by the depression; they prudently invested primarily in the best, largest companies with good dividends. The investors of the early sixties did not have quite that caution. For ten years they and their colleagues had been making money by buying stocks. They were not afraid. And it had become easy to make money in the market.

Earlier we said that if it were appropriate to pay 7.5 times earnings for a stock, and you believed that it was going to earn 20% more next year, then you could pay 7.5 times *next* year's estimate of earnings and not be overpaying for the stock. If you had an analyst who said that the stock not only would earn 20% more next year, but would also earn 20% more the year after that, and the following year would earn 20% more than that, then what would be a fair value to place upon the stock? There were some companies that were so situated, either because of patents, unique products, or sales channels, that stock analysts felt quite comfortable saying that these companies would be able to grow at a rate of 20% a year for the next ten to thirty years. Once one begins this type of progression, where does one stop? If a company's profits are growing at 25% a year, in five years its earnings will be 305% of what they are this year. Thus, if it were accepted that 8 times earnings were reasonable for a company with no growth at all, what should the P/E be for a company whose earnings will be three times that great in five years? Three times eight seems like a reasonable answer, which is 24 times current earnings.

But why stop at projected earnings only five years out? Weren't there new analytical tools which could enable analysts to project further than five years? Of course there were. If one only had faith that a company was impregnable to competition, that its product was unique, or that its marketing system was superior to that of any other firm in its field, then of course it was possible to project that ten years from now its earnings would be 305% of what

7

they were projected to be five years from now, which means that the earnings per share would be 930% of present earnings. Therefore, if one started with the assumption that 8 times current earnings was reasonable for a stock with static earnings, one had to reach the conclusion that 77 times earnings was a reasonable P/E for a stock with 25% earnings growth, provided only that one was certain the earnings growth would continue for ten years.

It was with this type of thinking that analysts justified high prices during the sixties. If the fifties could be described as the decade in which the wise and careful investors were rewarded for their faith and risk, the sixties can be described as the decade of greed. As prices of the Dow Jones stocks soared, interest in the market soared with them. Mutual funds were able to raise more and more money for investing in stocks. The records of all the mutual funds were posted, and those that did the best were literally inundated with money.

The saga of Gerald Tsai, Jr., is worth noting here. For many years he had been the portfolio manager of the Fidelity Capital Fund in Boston, selecting which stocks were bought and which were sold by that giant mutual fund. For two years in a row, 1963 and 1964, Fidelity Capital Fund had the best performance of any mutual fund. Gerry Tsai decided that while he was earning a good salary plus bonus as the portfolio manager, he would do better by running a mutual fund of his own. So in 1965 he moved to New York City and set up The Manhattan Fund, hoping that he would be able to attract $25 million on the basis of his reputation and thereby make a good living from the management fees of his fund. He did not raise $25 million. The mailman brought him so many letters with checks that before he even began the fund he had received $247 million.

This is simply another indication of the tremendous enthusiasm which people had at that time for the stock market. It didn't matter to them that stocks were selling at 18 times earnings, which is almost as high a P/E ratio as the Dow Jones average has ever gotten except for the depression, when there were no earnings. It didn't matter to them that stocks were selling at two times book value, which was also as high as they had ever gotten. Nor were they concerned with the fact that the prices of the Dow Jones stocks had just tripled. None of this mattered. All that mattered was that here was a man who had made money multiply faster than any other major fund manager. He would certainly do the same again.

But now the decade of the prudent investor was turning into the decade of the greedy speculator. The Dow Jones stocks, which soared up in the fifties, reached a point in the sixties where their sheer size prevented them from growing at an exceptionally fast rate. After all, if you are General Motors with half the U.S. new car market, how fast can you grow? And since the price which stocks would fetch was based upon the P/E ratio, and since the P/E ratio was determined by how fast the company's earnings were growing, the key was obviously to find those companies which had the prospects of the fastest future growth. Since the large blue chip companies, such as General Motors, Dow Chemical, General Foods, and Procter & Gamble, obviously were somewhat limited in their future growth rates, the sharp speculators of the day looked at other companies. And not surprisingly, the smaller the company, the larger its future potential gains could be.

And so the search for good investments gradually shifted from quality (as defined to include a good balance sheet, high dividends, proven earnings record, and demonstrated earnings capability even under difficult conditions) to simply a question of how fast the earnings were going to grow. When followed to its logical conclusion, this meant that the smaller the company the better, and the newer the company the better. If a company had been around for twenty years and during that time had managed to increase its earnings 10% to 15% a year, there was no way that anyone could be convinced that it would suddenly grow by 40% a year. But if a company were only two years old, and the second year the earnings had been 40% better than the first year, why then, eureka! You had discovered a company with a 40% growth rate, and one whose shares were entitled to be priced at an astronomical multiple of current earnings.

Examples abounded. National Student Marketing was one such company. Founded with the idea of selling various products and services to students on college and university campuses, the firm was balleyhooed as the coming wave of marketing in the future. By buying up a large number of other companies, and by using its own inflated stock as the purchase price, it was able to show rapidly increasing earnings, and this, in the logic of the day, automatically translated into a high P/E ratio. In this case the stock actually reached 150 times current earnings. And why not? Gone were the old-fashioned shortsighted days of before. Now a person was free to focus on the future, to project what a company would be earning in a few years and use that figure as the base for determining the value of the stock.

Although a company that goes around campuses putting up posters and trying to sell college rings and vacation cruises to Bermuda may not seem like a hot item to us today, in the excitement of Wall Street in the sixties it was as innovative and exciting as the latest cable TV company or computer printer company today. To give an idea of what the research analysts were thinking of National Student Marketing at the time, here is one description quoted in Adam Smith's wonderful book, *Supermoney:*

*Dynamic changes have occurred in society, at least in part due to the growing force and influence of the current sophisticated campus groups ... student economic power ... overlooked by marketing experts. National Student Marketing is a pioneer in closing the generation gap between the corporate client with a product or service for sale and the youth market with its purchasing power.*

The financial history of the stock is interesting because it shows the tremendous eagerness of the public to swallow any story that promised quick growth of a company, since the concept was that higher growth equaled higher P/E, and thus quick profits from the stock. Sales of the company for its first year, ending August 1966, were only $160,000, and for the second year just $723,000. Underwritten by the then prestigious firm of Auchincloss, Parker and Redpath, the stock came out at 6 on April 24, 1968. On the same day it went to 14, giving the surprised and ecstatic investors who bought the stuff at the new issue price a profit of 133% in just one day! No wonder the sixties became a decade of greed. What did it matter that the company was not yet two years old? Who cared that its business was not even a proven concept, or that it had no balance sheet to speak of and hardly any earnings? If you can double your money in one day, that's all that matters.

And so the go-go decade of the sixties flourished. The company continued to issue glowing press reports showing how it was prospering, primarily by acquiring other companies. The stockholders loved it, the public loved it, and by early June the stock was selling at 30. The company acquired in quick succession three school bus companies, Arthur Frommer's low-cost travel guides, student list compilers, and publishers of campus telephone directories. Such acquisitions were easy to make, since they involved no cash but were made entirely for stock. Yet the absurdity of the sixties was that since the stock of National Student Marketing had such a high P/E, the more stock they gave out in exchange for acquired companies, the more valuable the remaining stock became. That's the perfect life—to give away something and then end up with something more valuable than when you started.

The reason for this apparent paradox was that National Student Marketing had a highly inflated P/E in contrast to the companies it acquired. By making the acquisition, National Student Marketing was actually increasing the earnings per share of its own stock. Since the earnings per share were going up, under the prevailing view of the time this meant that the shares should be worth an even higher P/E. Thus, the more companies that were acquired, the faster the earnings grew and the higher the P/E of National Student Marketing became; and the higher the P/E of its stock was, the greater the increase in per share earnings when it acquired the next company, and so it went.

To understand how this works, let's take a simplified example. Suppose NSM had earnings of $1 per share and the stock was selling for $100. The other company, being in a prosaic business like running school buses, might have had profits of $1 per share and been selling for $8 a share. If the acquisition were made on the basis of an equal value of stock for an equal value of stock, NSM would swap one share of its stock (worth $100 per share) for twelve shares of the school bus company (worth $8 a share). The result would be that NSM gave out stock earning $1 per share and received stock earning $8 per share. Therefore, for every share of NSM tendered in the acquisition, its earnings per share grew by $7. See how easy it was to have rapidly growing earnings per share? And without any real growth of any kind. The school bus company, which may not have had any real growth in twenty years, was now a part of another company which was rapidly "growing" and therefore entitled to a high P/E ratio.

Through such acquisition strategies and logic, by the end of 1968 the price of National Student Marketing had soared to a high of 82. Thus, the original investors ("original" meaning those who had bought it a whole eight months earlier) had a profit of 1,266%. Need one say any more?

The wonderful world of explosive growth and explosive price action on the stock could last as long as the figures on growth kept coming in. And the founder and president of National Student Marketing, Cortes Wesley Randell, predicted each year that the earnings of his company would triple in the following year. Now, if a company which grows at 20% a year is entitled to have a P/E ratio of say 30, then what is the proper value of a company whose earnings are growing at a rate of 300% a year? Who knew? The sky was literally the limit, and it was possible to argue that even at a P/E of 150 the stock was actually underpriced and should go substantially higher.

To tell the truth there were some skeptical souls who wondered whether the earnings could triple every year, and even if they did, did that mean that the stock was really worth as much as it was selling for? But the answer was quick and apparently irrefutable. The people who had bought the stock at 6 were now rich, and getting richer by the week, while those who stuck to the old blue chips were barely making a profit. As Wall Street loves to say, "Don't argue with the tape. The tape tells all." When a stock is up, it's up because the market believes that that is what it is worth. And if you don't agree, then you just don't understand the game.

In other words, the days of looking at value in a stock were fast disappearing. The way to get rich was not to study book values or look for the lowest P/E ratios or seek high dividends. The message which the sixties had taught investors was to say to hell with all these constraints. The way to really get rich was to buy a stock in a company which had a story to tell, which was going to grow, and which was new, exciting, and on the acquisition path. What seemed high today would seem cheap tomorrow, and the rewards belonged to those who would take the risk and forget the so-called fundamentals.

While National Student Marketing was perhaps the archtypical stock of the sixties, there were many more with similar stories of success.

Another class of corporations which did astoundingly well in the sixties was the conglomerates. While there had been diversified corporations before which had resulted from the merging of many companies, these were usually in the same industry. The principle of conglomerates was that they would combine companies from totally different industries, retain the separate operating managements, and provide them with centralized financial, legal, administrative, marketing, and management services which would enable them to grow more rapidly than they could by themselves. The principle of conglomerates naturally involved fast growth via the acquisition trail, and as in the case of National Student Marketing, this led to high P/E and higher stock prices.

An outstanding example of a conglomerate was Ling-Temco-Vought. James Joseph Ling was an electrician who founded an electrical contracting business in Dallas in 1946 with $2,000 of wartime savings. His company grew to have an annual gross of $1.5 million in 1955, and at that time he decided to take it public by selling 450,000 shares for $2.25 each at the Texas State Fair. From such humble beginnings he was able to acquire his first electronics company. Many more soon followed. He was able to buy these companies by issuing bonds to the companies, and he was able to raise cash by issuing more common stock. In 1961 he acquired Chance Vought Corporation, the famous aviation pioneer. His greatest financing tactic was to sell to the public a part of the shares of a company which he had just acquired. His strategy worked, and the company grew rapidly. In 1965 it was the 204th largest industrial company in the country; by 1967 it had moved up to 38th, and in 1969 it had become the 14th largest in the country. A real accomplishment to be sure. But the stock had been doing even better. While net income per share was increasing, largely because of acquisitions, from the beginning of 1965 to its high in 1967, the price of the stock went up by more than ten times. Anyone buying the stock in 1965 and selling at the right time in 1967 would have made a profit of 1,000% in less than three years.

Other conglomerates produced similar growth and similar spectacular profits in their stock prices. Gulf + Western grew from a small auto replacement parts company to one of the largest conglomerates, acquiring Paramount Pictures, for example. The company started the 1960's with sales of $8.4 million and by 1968 had sales of $1.3 billion and net income of $70 million. The stock went up by over twenty times from a low of $\frac{7}{8}$ to a high of $23\frac{3}{8}$.

Instant profits, quick growth, big wealth for those who played it right. No wonder it was the age of the youngster. Anyone over 35 on Wall Street in those years was over the hill. It was only the young, who didn't remember the bad old days of looking at yields from dividends, who could play this game. And on Wall Street there were plenty of young men who could and would play the game.

Many of them, like Gerry Tsai, became successful managers of mutual funds. A successful mutual fund manager was one who could spot a National Student Marketing before it went up and load up on it. And there were a number of men in the late sixties who had the knack. One of them was Fred Carr, not yet 35, who ran the Enterprise Fund, which set the industry record in 1965 by shooting up an almost unbelievable 77.8%. That was the year that Gerry Tsai's Manhattan Fund went up almost 50%. What is even more impressive than the record of these outstanding mutual funds is that they almost *all* did well. The average of 29 leading "performance" funds as measured by the Wiesenberger Reports went up by an astounding 40% in 1965. No wonder people believed that if you picked the right smart young money manager, and he picked the right stocks, you would go on making 40% to 50% a year forever.

While the mutual funds made it easy for the vast public to play the market, there was another form of investment which grew up for the rich only. Some were not content with the restrictions of mutual funds, such as no use of margin, no use of puts and calls, and no method of selling short. For these wealthy individuals hedge funds were organized with the same objectives as mutual funds but without the legal restrictions. They were free to do all of the above. And when the market was booming, if they bought calls on the right stocks, or bought the right stocks on margin, it was easy for them to come up with figures which were at least twice as good as the best mutual funds. In 1965 a hedge fund managed by Alfred W. Jones was able to show that its record was a five-year gain of 325% and a ten-year gain of more than twice that amount.

Nothing succeeds like success, and the result of all this prosperity was that people couldn't put enough money into the stock market, the mutual funds, and the hedge funds. As the public poured money into the new hot stocks, their prices soared. As their prices soared, the assets of mutual funds climbed and more people put more money into mutual funds. The first mutual fund had been founded in Boston way back in 1924, but they were originally conservatively managed like trust accounts in banks and therefore attracted relatively little interest. It was not until the sixties that they began to attract investors' money in a big way, and by 1965 they had grown to a mighty $35 billion.

With more and more money pouring daily into the funds and the market, no one stopped to ask where the next batch of money was going to come from to push stocks even higher. There was no need to ask that question. When money is flowing in from all over the country, from people in every walk of life, one does not stop to ask whether it will end. One gets busy investing and earning those large sales commissions and large management fees which are what made the stock brokers and the mutual funds go round. When everyone was getting rich, there was no need to question the fundamental value of stocks. "Don't argue with the tape" was heard again and again.

And as investors became more impatient and more greedy, their interest in the underlying securities shrank even more. If some companies were growing at the rate of up to 50% a year, new companies with stock just being issued could increase even faster. Why wait a whole year for a stock to double, if you could buy a new issue in a hot company in the morning and sell it out that afternoon with perhaps a 100% profit?

And so the new issue boom was born. At first the companies which issued new stock were small companies which had a record of good earnings growth. Then the companies became new companies. Some didn't even have a full year's earnings to report, and many just recently had been organized with loans from the founders to be repaid from the proceeds of the stock offerings. Finally, in the height of the new issue market, a company didn't even have to be in operation. It was enough if there were officers who had an idea for a company, provided only that the idea was in the right field, such as a franchised hamburger chain. The prospectus would report that if the offering were successful, the officers intended to go into the hamburger business. Maybe one of them had run a McDonald's stand and another had been in advertising. It didn't matter that none of them had any management experience, or that the company probably wouldn't succeed. The people who bought the stock knew that. But the point was that it didn't matter. New issues were going up through the roof. Do you want to make money or don't you? No one was buying this acknowledged "junk" to put away for their grandchildren. This was the kind of stock you bought today and sold tomorrow and who cared what happened to the company in five years.

Now while this type of thinking was captivating the public, you might assume that the professional managers of institutional money were adhering to their role as the prudent investors. And you would be correct in the main. Certainly institutional investors generally stuck to the blue chip stocks which they had always dealt with. But institutions are like everyone else. They want to make money and they can see what is happening all around them. Thus, when the hot new issues like

National Student Marketing began to go up, the institutions began nibbling away. Among those who bought National Student Marketing were Bankers Trust, Morgan Guaranty, The Continental Illinois Bank of Chicago, the State Street Fund of Boston, the Harvard and Cornell endowment funds, the General Mills pension fund, and the University of Chicago. They too wanted to make the fast dollar.

But an even more interesting phenomenon was occurring in the good old institutional stocks, that is, the stocks of the large, proven companies with large capitalization. As the amount of institutional money entering the equities market each year went up and up, a consensus began to develop that there was a certain type of stock which was ideally suited for an institutional investor, and this was the blue chip growth stock. Here it should be pointed out that when operating at their best level, the professional managers responsible for pension funds and insurance company investments do take a different view of their investing than the public. The public tends to be short range in its investing, whereas the professionals try to finance liabilities which may be many years away. They can and should take the long-range view.

So the institutional investors began looking for the ideal stock to hold over the long run. This ideal stock had to be a large, well-financed company with well above average growth and a unique character that gave it some protection from unbridled competition. For example, Polaroid had the only instant camera, and it was a rapidly growing company. Avon Products was the only cosmetics company which was able to sell door to door and make a profit from doing so. Xerox clearly had the lead in the copier field and for many years had something close to a monopoly in this rapidly growing area. IBM did not have a monopoly in the computer field, but it was so big that it dominated the industry and there was certainly no danger that with its tremendous marketing and research advantages anyone would be able to overtake it.

Finally, there was an entire industry which was favored by the institutional investor: the pharmaceutical industry. Sheltered by patents which prevented any other company from manufacturing the drug which a particular company had invented, the drug companies were practically free to charge what they wished for their absolutely essential products. With more and more new drugs coming out of their laboratories, and with enormous markups in their selling prices, the companies were very profitable indeed. It appeared that they would simply become more and more profitable as time went on.

As the institutions concentrated their buying on these and a handful of other stocks, the prices of the stocks naturally went up. And as the prices went up, the yields from their dividends naturally went down, and the P/E ratios went up. Higher and higher. But why should anyone worry? Weren't the high prices of the stocks proof that they were worth so much? And wasn't the fact that the biggest and brightest institutions were buying more and more of the stocks every week an indication that they would continue to go up?

In fact, some of these stocks were considered to be so good that the institutions began to refer to them as "one-decision" stocks. That one decision was whether or not to buy them in the first place. Once that decision was made, they were considered similar to a fine wine, and had merely to be left in the vault to improve and appreciate in value with the passing of each year.

As the sixties came to a close, the institutional investors were delighted with their performances. The stocks they had invested in had done beautifully. The flyers taken in hot stocks were working out, and the bulk of their money was invested in solid "one-decision" stocks which only went up. The proof was in the figures. At the end of 1969 Xerox was selling at 100, which gave it a P/E of 48 and, not that anyone cared, a dividend of exactly 0.6%. IBM was 70 (adjusted for subsequent stock splits), which was 42 times earnings, and its dividend was 1.1%. Avon Products was selling for 85 with a P/E of 57, and Polaroid was 135 with a P/E of 71. The drug stocks were so high that they acquired a mystique all their own, much like a Rolls-Royce. Typical was Merck, selling at 57 with a P/E of 41 and a dividend of 2.2%. Those were good times for the institutional investors. They had indeed carried out their legal obligations to use care and diligence in investing their principals' funds, and their skill had been rewarded with handsome profits.

It is remarkable that so often in the course of human events, just as a movement of any kind reaches its peak, there will come a voice of wisdom from a recognized intellectual leader of the group, proclaiming that whatever has been happening is now the norm, that times have changed, and that people must now accept the fact that the new trend is indeed a permanent change. This is just what happened to institutional investors. During both the fifties and the sixties, when stock prices almost quadrupled, there were always skeptics among the professional investors who urged that a large percentage of funds be kept in bonds. Many institutions listened to these advisers, and of course missed out on part of the large profits to be made in common stocks. Finally, at the peak of the common stock market, the great voice of the Ford Foundation spoke out. Not only was the Ford Foundation the largest charitable foundation by far in the United States, but under the leadership of McGeorge Bundy it had begun to take a role in advising other nonprofit organizations on various matters. Since many other nonprofit organizations were dependent upon grants from the Ford Foundation for a substantial portion of their income, the Ford Foundation carried a lot of weight in financial matters. What did the Foundation say with respect to this new emphasis being placed on common stocks? Here is a quote from Bundy: "We recognize the risks of unconventional investing, but the true test of performance in the handling of money is the record of achievement, not the opinion of the respectable. We have the preliminary impression that over the long run caution has cost our colleges and universities much more than imprudence or excessive risk-taking."

The Ford Foundation went on to say that whereas previously it had been assumed that only the income from investments could be spent and that all appreciation in the price of the securities must simply be allowed to accumulate and increase the endowment, this was not the case with the new investing methods. Since common stocks went up year after year as a matter of course, the capital gains from this appreciation were as much a part of the organization's income as the interest from the bonds or the dividends from the stocks.

Thus, at the very peak of the hysteria in common stocks, when universities were selling out their bonds and getting into the new performance stocks, the voice of the Ford Foundation not only was urging them to do so in the name of prudence, but was even telling them that they were virtually assured of reaping capital gains year after year which should become a very important part of their income. The Ford Foundation followed its own advice and was able to "increase" the income from its endowment substantially.

It was the fourth day at sea on the *S.S. Titanic,* and it was as if the captain had just announced that since the first three days had obviously shown that all the talk about the dangers of icebergs was false, they were now going to increase their speed and take a more northerly course. For the stock market these were beautiful, exciting times. And no one knew that they were about to end. The bands were playing so loudly, and the passengers were so busy getting their deck chair reservations for the next day, that no one saw the iceberg coming closer and closer and closer.

# 3

# *THE DISASTROUS SEVENTIES*

### *The Crashes of the Early Seventies*

Of course, investors should have realized that when a stock is selling at 150 times earnings, it is highly susceptible to downturns in price, especially if the earnings ever slow down from a growth of 300% a year. And other people should have realized that increasing earnings by acquiring companies whose stocks have lower P/E's than your own is not really a way of increasing earnings at all. And people should have realized that the big increase in new investments made by the public represented a one-time shift out of low-paying savings accounts into mutual funds and stocks which could not continue. And others should have realized that the institutions likewise were investing so much in the market not because they had that much in new funds to invest every year, but because they were selling other assets to invest in stocks, and that this also could not continue indefinitely. For example, in 1972 the institutions actually invested 120% of their net new investment funds in the stock market.

When these factors came to an end, as inevitably they had to, the market was going to be deprived of the flow of funds which had enabled it to make such new highs year after year. And when everyone owned the newest high flyer, and it had risen to 150 times earnings, and that seemed like a good point at which to sell, who would there be to sell it to? Such questions as these were not asked by the people who were making a killing in the market. But the fact that they did not ask the questions does not mean that the questions were not there. They were, and the answers were there too. The market had to fall.

The decline of the stock market started in 1968. Appropriately enough, the first place to suffer was where the excesses were the greatest. Perhaps one of the first signs of trouble occurred in January 1969, when Litton Industries, which had become the prestige conglomerate, discovered that a number of its divisions were doing badly and that earnings for the corporation were going to be down; the string of unbroken increases in earnings which had been maintained for so many years would be broken. The reported earnings for the quarter ending January 31, 1969, came in at 21 cents a share versus 63 cents for the same quarter a year earlier.

The announcement hit Wall Street like a bomb. The very essence of a conglomerate was that it had strong central financial controls. One reason for the attractiveness of conglomerates was that they were in so many different types of businesses, so that when one went down, the others were apt to go up. But so many divisions doing so badly that earnings dropped by almost 66% was simply staggering. It made investors wonder if some of their basic concepts about the new performance companies had been incorrect. But more important, for the first time it raised a question which Wall Street was to be forced to ask itself many times in the next few years: If a stock is worth a very high P/E ratio because it is growing so quickly, what is that stock worth if the growth of earnings slows down or even stops? Put more bluntly, what is that stock worth if the earnings actually begin to decline?

This was not merely an academic question. If a good-quality stock is selling at 40 times earnings, which was very common in the late sixties (if it earned $3 a share, it was selling for $120), then how much should that stock be selling for if the company reported earnings next year of $3? The company was still the same company, with the same assets, the same management, hopefully the same prospects for earning more money the next year, only now one wasn't certain. What if the company reported earnings of just $1 a share? Was it now worth 40 times $1 for a value of $40 a share? Or did one reason that since the company was worth 40 times earnings only because those earnings were growing so fast, it must now be worth a lower multiple, such as 10 times earnings, since its earnings were no longer increasing? Those were questions which were difficult in the extreme to ask.

They were difficult questions because the answers were simply too horrible even to imagine. If it were true that a company which was not growing should be selling at approximately 10 times earnings, then a company which had a decreasing earnings record should be selling at even less than that. But in any event, by this process of reasoning, a stock which had been selling for $120 when the company earned $3 a share might be worth only $10 when the earnings declined to $1 a share. Obviously, such reasoning was impossible. It would mean the total destruction of the stock market as investors had come to know it if there were ever a slowdown in the economy, and when has there ever been a period in which the economy went straight up without a slowdown?

But in the late sixties such questions did not arise. Suffice to say that the January 1969 earnings for Litton were disappointing. The stock promptly lost 18 points in the week after the announcement, and within a month it had fallen to one-half of its previous high. Other conglomerates were also hard hit as investors considered that perhaps conglomerates had not invented a new method of attaining perpetually higher earnings.

Litton Industries was a major company with large profitable divisions producing electronic, aviation, and other defense supplies. There was no question about the basic soundness of the company, and yet its stock quickly lost about half its value. What happened to the stocks of lesser companies can be illustrated by the fate of National Student Marketing. In 1968 the stock had been selling at a high of 82, and its president, C. W. Randell, was predicting that earnings for the next year would be triple that.

Earnings for the fiscal year ending in the summer of 1969 fulfilled his promise by coming in at $3.5 million. Buried in a footnote was the somewhat disquieting information that about $3 million of that profit came from the operations of subsidiaries which NSM was acquiring, but *which it did not even own at the end of the fiscal year being reported.* On November 5, 1969, Randell told the New York Society of Security Analysts that earnings for the coming year would be about triple what they had been. The stock jumped up 20 points and hit a high of 140 in December.

To say that the world was not prepared for the announcement of NSM's earnings in February 1970 would be an understatement. Rather than a tripling of earnings, the company reported a loss of $1.2 million, and two days later this was corrected to $1.5 million. The stock had already begun to crash amid rumors that all was not well, and with this news it went down to $50, a loss of $90 in just two months. By July it had plummeted down to 3½. What more can one say? Once again, the concept of ignoring the basics of a company, listening only to future promises, concluding that because a stock has gone up to a certain price it therefore must be worth that much, and assuming that its previous upward momentum will continue to move upward, all proved to be false. And it was a very expensive lesson, not only for the individuals who bought NSM stock, but for the mutual funds and institutional investors as well.

NSM may have been an extreme case, but it was not by any means unique. Scores of other hot-shot companies began running into similar troubles when their earnings failed to live up to the superhigh projections which the purchasers of their stocks had depended upon. Four Seasons Nursing Centers was just such a case. It pioneered the new concept of a chain of nursing homes for the mushrooming elderly population. When the S.E.C. suspended trading in the stock in May 1970, it was already too late. The stock, which had traded as high as 91 just a year before, became worthless as Four Seasons went into bankruptcy.

Numerous other small, new companies failed or came so close to doing so that their stocks were worth almost nothing. The public was taking a bath, and so were the mutual funds and institutions that had invested in these stocks.

Even the large stocks were having their troubles. Having increased to price earnings multiples of 40 or more, they had little room to move further up, but plenty of room to fall down. Between the start of 1969 and the first quarter of 1970, the Dow Jones average fell from 920 to 680 for a drop of 26%. While this is a large loss, it does not begin to tell the story of the loss suffered by those who had bought the real go-go stocks of the sixties. The new issues in many cases simply disappeared. The conglomerates fell to less than half their previous prices, and the high P/E growth stocks did equally badly. A special index published in *Dun's Review* in January 1971, prepared by Max Shapiro, contained thirty of the leading glamour stocks of the sixties. The list contained ten leading conglomerates, among them Litton, Gulf + Western, and Ling-Temco-Vought; ten of the largest computer stocks; and ten technology stocks, including Polaroid, Xerox, and Fairchild Camera. The average decline during the period 1969 to 1970 for the ten conglomerates had been 86%. For the computer stocks it had been 80%, and for the technology stocks it had been 77%. A devastating loss for any investor, rich or poor, individual or institutional.

In a way, however, the tremendous losses of the 1969 and early 1970 crash had a salutary effect on Wall Street. The thinking was that the speculators who had lost the most money in the new, untried stocks were now out of the market, and the institutional and serious investors could now concentrate on the quality stocks. Quality stocks were defined as the growth stocks favored by the large institutions. They were the "one-decision" stocks, and although they went down with the market in the 1968 decline, they did not fall down to the bottom, and most assuredly the companies themselves did not suffer.

So in a way, the decline of the conglomerates and hot new issues served to reinforce the faith of the serious investors in the virtues of the quality stocks. As analysts searched for stocks which met all their criteria, the list of qualifying stocks became ever smaller and smaller. In the end a group called the nifty fifty arose; these were the darlings of the institutional investors. All the best analysts kept recommending them because their earnings were going up, and the concentrated purchasing of the stocks resulted in increasing their prices.

A wide disparity developed in the market between those stocks which were on the chosen list of the institutions and those which were not. The favorites soared to ever new heights, pulling the rest of the market along with them. By the end of 1972 the Dow Jones was solidly above the 1,000 mark. There was not the sense of excitement and near hysteria that had pervaded in 1968 because the new issue market and the hot stock market had pretty well faded into the past, taking with them a large number of investors. But those who remained were confident that their faith in common stocks would be rewarded, that growth in America was inevitable, and that the stocks they owned would appreciate in value now that the excesses of the late sixties had been put firmly to rest.

Once again, the famous names were flying high, but the owners reasoned that more than ten years' experience with this type of stock had demonstrated clearly that they were well worth the price. It paid to buy quality. And unlike the garbage stocks like National Student Marketing, which had collapsed at the end of the sixties, these stocks were leaders of the American industrial scene. They really were quality stocks, and they were selling at prices and P/E's equal to and usually higher than in the early sixties. At the beginning of 1973, IBM was selling for 91 with a P/E of 41, Xerox was at 150 with a P/E of 47, and Merck was at 95 with a P/E of 48, Avon was selling for 140 with a P/E of 65, and Polaroid was 135 with the incredible P/E of 103.

The P/E's may have been high, but investment managers were not concerned. Time was on their side. As long as earnings were growing at the rates they were, the managers were simply valuing the stocks at what they would be worth in a few years. It was like the reverse of buying a future payment at a discount. If someone promised to pay you $10,000 in ten years, you would figure the present value of the obligation by discounting it backwards so that the amount of money it was worth today would be the amount which, when invested at a compound interest rate equal to today's rate, would earn you $10,000 in ten years. Thus, if the current rate of interest were 6%, a payment of $5,584 today would produce $10,000 in ten years. By discounting a payment ten years away, you find that its present value is much less.

The principle of valuing growth stocks was the corollary of this. Here one had a stock which was producing perhaps $5 a share today in income, but since it was going to be producing $10 a share in five years, it had to be worth more today than if we did not "know" that it would be earning twice as much in five years. By extending this reasoning, there was literally no place to draw the line on how high P/E ratios could go on high-quality stocks.

And the proof of the validity of this theory was right at hand, namely the prices of the favored stocks. As Chart 1, reprinted from *Fortune* magazine, so clearly shows, the P/E ratio of stocks took some dramatic changes during the fifties and late sixties. At the end of 1972 a full 6% of the stocks charted were selling at a P/E of 40 or more. And because they included many of the largest companies and each share outstanding was so valuable, far more than 6% of the money invested on Wall Street was in these high P/E stocks.

Another 6% of the stocks had a P/E of 30 to 39.9, and approximately 15% had P/E ratios of 20 to 29.9. Thus, 27% of the stocks were selling at a P/E of 20 or better. The institutional and conservative investors were happy.

In fact, the pension funds were so happy with the performance of their common stock investments that in 1971 and 1972 they put an average of $8.1 billion annually into buying stocks. This enormous amount of buying substantially exceeded their cash flow, which is to say that they were spending more on stocks each year than they were taking in. They did this by selling fixed income holdings to raise the money for stock purchases.

Thus, 1973 dawned on a robust stock market, with both the weak players and the weak stocks out of the market. Instead, as Wall Streeters are fond of saying, the stocks had gone from "weak hands into stronger hands," that is, to investors who were not apt to sell on bad news and hence would act to keep up the prices of the stocks. After all, why should a pension fund sell any stock? Weren't these all "one-decision" stocks anyway? And so on this optimistic note the Dow Jones average rose to its highest monthly closing point to date, closing on December 31, 1972, at 1020.02. The future looked great and predictions arose of a Dow Jones average of 1500 in the not-too-distant future. But it didn't work out quite that way.

## CHART 1

### The Dramatic Changes in Price/Earnings Ratios

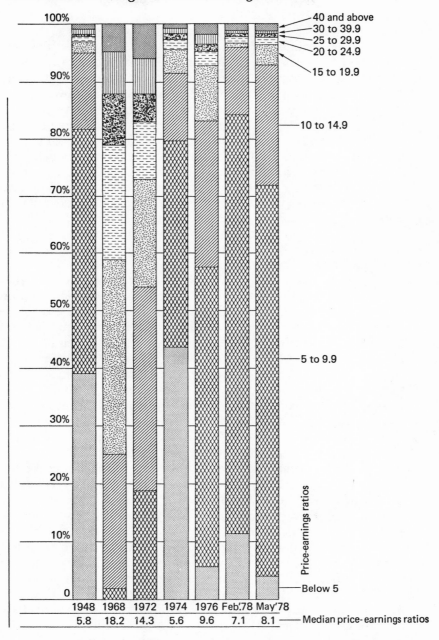

Note that in 1972, 27% of the stocks had P/E's of 20 or higher. By May 1978 only 5% were this high. Conversely, in 1972 less than 20% of the stocks had a P/E below 10, whereas by May 1978 over 70% had such a low P/E.

## THE 1973 MARKET PLUNGE

According to economists today, the 1970–73 business upswing peaked in November 1973. It was a time of roaring prosperity, inflation, and of course a rising stock market. The end of 1973 and 1974 brought a number of economic shocks, the first of which was the OPEC oil embargo followed by a tripling in the price of oil imported into the United States. The effect upon the economy was immediate and severe. First to feel it were the automobile companies, then all the companies which depended upon customers arriving by car, then companies which used fuel. The quick decline in the automobile and related industries produced a rapid decline in other industries, and the most severe recession in the postwar economy was underway. Unemployment rose from its pre-recession low of 4.6% to 6% after a year into the recession, and then on up to a massive 9.1% at its peak, while actual employment declined by about 2 million.

Corporate profits had been at an annual rate of almost $100 billion in the fourth quarter of 1973 (adjusted for underdepreciation and less inventory gains) and then started a deep decline during the entire year of 1974, down to $73 billion in the first quarter of 1975, an enormous decline of 27%. These were totals, comprised of many companies which are not cyclical at all, such as manufacturers of foodstuffs, insurance companies, auto repair, etc. This means that those companies which were in manufacturing and especially those companies which were manufacturing products whose consumption could be postponed, suffered far greater declines in earning. And now Wall Street was forced at last to face head-on the question which it had never really considered before.

If the stock of a company is valued highly because the earnings of the company are constantly growing at a predictable rate, what is that stock worth when the earnings of the company stop growing, or even more dramatically, what happens when the earnings actually decline?

The 6% of all stocks which had P/E's of 40 or more had them because there was a degree of assurance among investors that their earnings were going to increase in the future. A quick look at Chart 1 will show that even in 1972 about 18% of the stocks were selling at P/E's of 5 to 9.9. Why was a dollar of earnings in these companies worth perhaps only one-eighth as much as a dollar earned by the other companies? The only reason was that the earnings of the high P/E companies were constantly rising, and the present price of the stock reflected the higher earnings which were expected to be realized in the future. So, the question returns. What if their earnings didn't increase? Almost no one dared to ask it.

Here were the biggest pension funds and institutional investors in the country, under the guidance of the brightest and most respected banks and professional money managers, loaded up with stocks selling at 40 times earnings, and worth that amount presumably because the earnings were growing so fast. But if the companies suddenly were not growing, but faced with the most severe recession most Americans then alive had ever known, were actually declining, then shouldn't those stocks also be selling for less than 10 times earnings?

At first that seemed unthinkable. One of those things which are just too horrible to contemplate. What, for example, would Avon be selling for? The stock had reached a high of 140 and its earnings for 1973 had been $2.33, but for 1974 they were down to $1.93. If this superstar of the firmament was going to be valued like any common nuts and bolts industrial company at about 10 times earnings, then obviously it would be selling for just under $20. That would mean a loss of 85% of one's investment if one had bought it at 140. And "solid" stocks which banks bought for pension funds just didn't do that sort of thing. That only happened to cheap risky over-the-counter stocks.

Similarly, Polaroid had reached a high of 149. Its 1973 earnings had been $1.58 and in 1974 it earned only 86 cents a share. Should that stock collapse to less than $10 a share? Even mighty IBM had been trading at 365 when its earnings stopped moving up.

As new reports of declining earnings came in at the end of 1973 and during 1974, new waves of selling came into the stock market. The answer to the unanswerable question was becoming clearer every day: The answer was the one that any child could and would have come up with, like the emperor's new clothes. It was simply that when a growth company ceases to have an earnings growth, it is ipso facto no longer a growth company, and its shares will be valued in the market in a manner similar to everyone else's.

And so the absolute collapse of the great and mighty stocks began. It was a collapse that was to last for almost two years. It was to see the Dow Jones decline by almost 50% in a 21-month period from 1973 to 1974, from over 1,000 down to 575 in the fourth quarter of 1974. But the typical pension fund, weighted in the high P/E "one-decision" stocks, did even worse. Data for 3,800 pension and profit-sharing funds gathered by Becker Securities show that, even including dividends received, the equity holdings of the median pension fund suffered a 52.5% decline during the period. Mind you, these were not accounts run by daredevils like the hot mutual fund managers. These were "conservative" investors whose funds were managed by conservative banks and money managers. Corporations which faced fixed pension liabilities to pay their retiring employees realized that the performance of their pension funds had been so bad that they would have to offset the loss by substantially increasing their contributions to the funds, further decreasing their profits.

Mutual funds also saw dramatic losses in their portfolio values. Individuals had been sold the mutual funds in the fifties and early sixties on the reasoning that while their money in a bank was earning only 5%, here was an investment with a record of growth, including dividends, of approximately 10% to 15% a year. No doubt only few of the mutual fund salesmen stressed the fact that the fund could have losses.

The people who had bought the mutual funds were simply unprepared for the losses, and they caused deep resentment and led to two firm decisions by most fund owners: one, they would never buy another mutual fund again as long as they lived, nor would they ever let a friend or relative put one cent of money into such a fund; and two, they would start cashing in their shares now, or at least as soon as they got even with what they put in.

The performance of the stock market had been so bad that individual investors simply stayed away from the market in droves. A whole generation of 30 to 45 year olds, who would normally be investing and trading in the stock market, believed during the seventies that "no one ever made any money in the stock market."

One other category of investor should be discussed to round out the story of the stock market fall of the early seventies. Foreign investors have always played an important role in the American investment picture, ever since the founding of our country when almost everything had to be capitalized by foreign investments. The 1973–74 collapse of the market was bad enough, but it had a double whammy for many foreign investors because of the concurrent fall in the value of the dollar.

Whereas right after World War II the dollar was the international currency without compare, two decades later the German deutsche mark and the Japanese yen began creeping up on it, and by the seventies the dollar was in trouble. This meant that if a

German or Swiss had put money into U.S. investments, and the price of those investments stayed the same, the value to him in his local currency might have shrunk to one-half of its original cost. Since stock prices did not hold their own but went down so substantially, it is easy to see that investments by Europeans in American stocks turned very sour. Many of their portfolios were reduced to one-quarter of their original purchase price. While the foreigners did not become big sellers of stocks, they vowed they would not soon again be buyers.

Thus, the collapse of the stock market to one-half of its former value had many side effects, all of which created the same effect, as we shall see. First, the institutions after two years of gigantic losses in their equities began to make a careful reassessment of their investment policies. This is fancy language for a very simple process. They decided that buying stocks didn't work, and they were not going to buy any more. The bond portion of their investments had done very nicely, and even if the prices of the bonds had gone down with the increase in interest rates, they could simply sit on them until they were redeemed at their full face value.

The institutional investment world is intensely competitive. Everyone is selling the record of his investment results. And the managers who had the best records were generally those who had placed the largest portion of their funds in bonds. So they were out in force, waving their performance charts in the faces of the decision makers. It didn't take long for the message to get across. Soon everyone was deciding that bonds really were the best investment, and the basic reason for going into bonds was to reduce the exposure to the fluctuations and volatility of common stocks.

Now the institutions sharply reduced their buying of common stocks and actually became net sellers of common stocks for a short period. When you recall that they had been pumping $8 billion a year into the stock market in the heydays of the early seventies, this represented a major loss of purchasing power for common stocks. Since the only thing that keeps stock prices up is more buying of stocks, the institutions, by not buying any more, were actually helping to intensify the very condition they were reacting against, namely the decline in stock prices.

A second side effect of the stock market collapse was that the mutual funds almost stopped selling any new shares and were busy redeeming shares as their shareholders cashed them in. The only way they could get the money to redeem these shares was to sell the shares in their portfolios. This selling by the mutual funds also became a significant factor in pulling stock prices down. The net sales by mutual funds during the seventies were truly enormous. In 1972 they were net sellers of $1.35 billion worth of securities; in 1973, $2.2 billion; in 1976 it was $1.53 billion; and in 1974, $1.25 billion. This gigantic drain on the stock market in sharp contrast to the net purchases in the sixties could only be reflected in lower stock prices as this money fled the market.

The third effect had to do with individual investors. They had in many cases suffered more than the institutions or the mutual funds: They did not have the benefit of diversification and, for whatever value it was, the assistance of professional guidance. The individual investor often had only a few stocks, of which perhaps a larger proportion were over the counter. If one or two of them became worthless, his entire portfolio could be decimated, especially if he had been purchasing on margin. So, the individual investor, like the institutions, withdrew from the stock market, taking what was left of his money with him.

And thus the market made its dreary way downward to its low of 575 in December 1974. In early 1975 there was a sharp snap back to the 800 level, but from then through 1979 the market was never really able to pick up steam. No wonder. With the institutions out as far as any serious buying went, with mutual funds continuing to be net sellers of stock, and with the public continuing to sit on the sidelines, there was simply no purchasing power coming into the market to pull stock prices up. The market broke through the 1,000 mark in 1976, but it simply couldn't stay there.

Investors basically did not trust the market any more, and as soon as a little bad news came onto the horizon, they were quick to dump their shares. With no source of large buyers, the result was dramatic drops, like the one in October 1978, which was almost a panic selling. In a brief period of two weeks, the Dow Jones average lost 100 points. And since that average measures only the blue chip stocks, which are generally able to withstand bad news the best, it is not surprising that many lesser grade stocks took significantly larger losses. Nerve-shattering losses of 33% were common. Margin calls inevitably followed in record-breaking numbers. Once again, the absence of any real buying source resulted in a large loss of stock prices, which persisted for months. The decade from the end of 1969 to the end of 1979 saw a loss of 42% in the average of all New York Stock Exchange stocks, and this was the sharpest decline ever recorded for any decade, even more than the depression decade of the thirties.

Thus, the stock market from 1973 through 1979 was simply treading water. There were days when the Dow Jones average would go up or down by less than 2 points, a move of less than two-tenths of one percent. Individual stocks were almost frozen in their tracks, with moves of a quarter point up or down worthy of comment. The market was down and it was going to stay down. And no one cared. People were investing in real estate and speculating in commodities. Institutions were investing in bonds, and mutual funds continued to be net sellers from their portfolios.

But while the stock market floundered and stagnated, no one seemed to care what had been happening to the actual corporations whose stocks made up the market.

The performance of the underlying corporations was in marked contrast to the slow demise of the stock market. You will remember that one of the causes of the plunges of 1968 and 1973–74 was the fact that corporate earnings had not kept up with the high P/E's of the stocks, and when the earnings actually fell, there was no place for the stocks to go except down. But once the recession of 1973 and 1974 had passed, corporate profits came back smartly. They resumed their growth rates in most instances, and went on to make record-breaking profits, much higher than they had been during the height of the bull markets in 1968 and 1973.

But this time Wall Street just didn't care. Too many people had been burned too many times by the stock market. The standard reaction of potential stock customers when told by their brokers that a stock was cheap because the earnings of the company had increased was, "So what? That stock is cheap today and it will be cheaper tomorrow." And since there were no buyers to pull the stock prices up, that is often exactly what happened.

The result was that P/E ratios gradually declined. As corporate earnings moved up year after year during the second half of the seventies and stock prices remained basically stable, the P/E ratios sank lower and lower. At year end of 1976 the P/E for the Dow Jones was 10.4, at year end 1977 it was 9.3, at year end 1978 it was 7.9, and by November 1979 it was only 6.3. Normally this means that stocks are getting to be a better buy. But the market had been so bad for so long, that investors simply ignored the fundamentals of the stock market.

There is a basic human capacity to learn. Perhaps learning is the most fundamental of all human activities, because without it we would be still as uncommunicative and helpless as a newborn baby. Every day we are learning in a thousand ways, many of which we may not even be aware of. You walk out to your car in the morning and stumble on a loose stone in the walk. Subconsciously you remember when you come home not to step on that stone. There are also more forceful methods of learning. A child plays near the stove and burns his hand. The next day he decides to play somewhere else. You have a good vacation at a special resort and resolve to come back next year. You go to a restaurant, get slow service, cold food, and a high bill, and you have learned not to come back. And so it is with investing.

If you make an investment and it works, you decide to do it again, and on a larger scale. This is what happened to stock investments. In the fifties it worked well, and it worked even better in the sixties. But then the big difference between investing and other facets of life was brought rudely home. It is simply this: What worked last year or last week as an investment is not necessarily going to work this year or this week. In fact, quite the opposite may be true when you are investing with the expectation of making capital gains. The very fact that a stock has gone up in the past may mean that it is more likely to go down in the future.

But no matter. People learn from experience. And people in the seventies had learned that you couldn't make money in the stock market. That stocks generally went down. That in any event stocks didn't keep up with inflation. That putting money into stocks was one of the biggest mistakes anyone could make. This learning process is simple, but forceful. It applies equally to individuals and to institutions. If something works, you continue with it. If something doesn't work, you stop it.

If there are no alternatives, you may have to continue with something that doesn't work very well. But if there is a better alternative, you don't have to put up with a disappointment. And there are always plenty of alternatives to the stock market. For the institutional investor there is the bond market, there is the short-term cash market, and there are various types of fixed income investments offered by insurance companies. These investments all performed as they were supposed to. Therefore, just as in the parable in the Bible where the master rewarded those of his servants who had used their talents to good advantage and punished those who had wasted them, so the institutional investors punished those who had served them badly. They cut back on their stockholdings and increased their bond and other fixed income holdings.

Individual investors sold their mutual funds and stocks. For long-term investments, individuals were putting every dollar they could into real estate. If they got a gift of 200 shares of AT&T from Uncle Harry, they would sell it and use the money toward a down payment on a vacation home, or a condominium in the city, or a house in the suburbs. And as real estate prices went up and the real estate investments got better and better, and as the stock market got worse and worse, people simply sold whatever stocks or mutual funds they had in order to purchase more real estate.

For short-term investments, individuals were flocking to the new money market funds, which were a form of mutual fund that invested only in short-term fixed income securities like certificates of deposit. By the autumn of 1979 a number of these funds were offering their investors 12% annually with no commissions to get in or out, and complete liquidity with no minimum length of time commitment, and most important to those who had been burned in the stock market, no chance of losing part of their capital. The amount they put in was the amount they would take out, plus whatever interest they had earned.

Thus there were plenty of attractive alternatives to the stock market in the late seventies. These provided a self-reinforcing argument against going into stocks. And remember that as more and more investors avoided the stock market, there were fewer and fewer dollars available to pull stock prices up.

# 4

# *EIGHT REASONS WHY THE STOCK MARKET "CAN'T GO UP"*

Many investors were aware that on the fundamentals stocks looked very cheap. While stock prices had been going down, the earnings of corporations had been going up, their dividends had been going up, and their book values had been going up. But in the gloomy days of the late seventies these comments were countered by the prevailing view that the so-called fundamentals no longer meant what they once had. We were living in a new age of permanent double-digit inflation, of permanent high interest rates, and of constantly increasing government controls over industry which made the old profit margins impossible to attain.

The stock market languished. The cover of the August 13, 1979, issue of *Business Week* showed a paper airplane made out of a stock certificate crashing onto a tabletop to illustrate its feature story, "The Death of Equities: How Inflation Is Destroying the Stock Market." Mighty strong language for the flagship publication of McGraw-Hill—not that the stock market was in trouble, not that it was sick, but that it was actually dead. And the article had plenty of quotes from well-known economists to back up its title.

Because the stock market was no longer perceived as a hedge against inflation, the article opined that institutional investors would follow individual investors into tangibles such as real estate, commodities, and gold at the expense of the stock market. Robert S. Salomon, Jr., of Salomon Brothers was quoted as saying, "We are running the risk of immobilizing a substantial portion of the world's wealth in someone's stamp collection." *Business Week* noted that the malaise of the stock market had persisted for more than ten years through market rallies, business cycles, recession, recoveries, and booms, and concluded that this "death of equity can no longer be seen as something a stock market rally—however strong—will check." In answer to the position of the fundamentalists that stocks were now a better value than ever, as measured by earnings per share, dividends, and relationship to book value, Dean Alan B. Coleman of Southern Methodist University's business school was quoted as saying, "We have entered a new financial age. The old rules no longer apply."

What he and others meant was that new factors were at work which had not been present years before when the concepts of what made good fundamentals were formulated. The new breed of economists was saying that the apparently low stock prices of the late seventies were exactly where they ought to be based on the fundamentals. The difference was that they focused upon a different set of fundamental economic criteria than the old Graham-Dodd school of fundamentalists. The arguments put forth by these new analysts are worth serious study, because if they are correct, then the stock market cannot rise until there are drastic changes in the economy, or, as *Business Week* concludes, the stock market will not be able to go up for many years if at all. So let's analyze these arguments.

## HIGH INTEREST RATES

The most forceful argument made to explain the level of equity prices was that the stock market cannot go up in the face of high interest rates. The reasoning behind this was that the stock market is competing for investors' funds with fixed income securities, such as bonds, certificates of deposit, Treasury Bills, and commercial paper. When interest rates on these securities rise significantly above the prevailing yield from dividends on common stocks, this argument held, there is no longer an incentive to invest in common stocks. If a person can get 10% on his money in safe obligations which are guaranteed as to principal by major top-rated corporations, why should he take the risk of loss in common stocks with an average return of only 6%, which was the yield on the Dow Jones industrials in July 1980. This argument ran that, because there is such a risk in owning common stocks, the dividend should be higher than the rate on fixed income investments. Furthermore, they noted that this is the way it was years ago. For example, in 1950, common stocks were yielding 7% while top-grade corporate bonds were yielding only 2.8%. That is the relationship which makes stock prices go up. Therefore, the argument went, stocks were now actually overpriced, and they probably would decline in price until their yields exceeded or at least matched that offered by long-term bonds.

Certainly there was plenty of empirical evidence to back up this claim. Both institutions and individual investors were putting money into fixed income securities in record numbers. The fastest growing segment of the investment world in 1979 was the money market fund, and by July 1980 the amount of money in these funds had passed $75 billion. Since many of these funds were run by brokerage firms as a haven for their clients' money, it is clear that a large portion of these funds were diverted from the market by the high rates being paid on these riskless investments. These funds were mainly for individuals, but institutions were playing the same game in their own way. By October 1980 it was estimated that institutions had over $27 billion in short-term investments, most of which would normally have gone into the stock market. The more money that was kept out of the market, of course, the lower stock prices went, and the lower they went, the less inclined any investors were to risk their money in the market when they could get those high rates of interest without taking any risk.

## INFLATION

The second main reason given for the stock market's inability to climb above its existing levels was that the stock market was ineffective in keeping up with inflation. To understand the crux of this argument, one had first to go back to the reason why so many people invested in the stock market in the fifties and sixties. They believed it was an effective hedge against inflation. It was clear that bonds, which in those days were paying from 2.7% to 5.3%, would not be able to keep up with an inflation of any greater amount than that. In fact, since most investors must pay income taxes on the interest, the actual net amount they receive is substantially less than that, and certainly couldn't keep up with inflation.

Common stocks were seen as able to keep up with inflation because the price of the stocks would rise. The assumption was that as consumer prices rose, the profits of corporations would rise, and since the prices of stocks were based upon the earnings of the corporations, those prices would rise as well. Furthermore, with the rise in earnings, the corporations would increase their dividends, and this would also tend to increase the price of the stocks.

The argument now ran that obviously the stock market had not kept up with inflation. The Dow Jones Industrial Average first brushed 1,000 in January 1966. Fourteen years and nine months later, in October 1980, it was 5% *below* that point, and that was measuring the Dow Jones Industrial Average in dollars which are unadjusted for inflation. The real value of the dollar declined precipitously in the intervening years. Even if the DJIA had remained at 1,000, it would have been a disaster in terms of real purchasing power. The fact is that because of the decline in the purchasing power of the dollar due to inflation, the DJIA would have had to be at 2,283 just to be equal to where it was on January 18, 1966, in terms of inflation-adjusted dollars! In fact, at 950 in October 1980, it was actually at a level equal to 382 in 1967 dollars. In other words, the measurement of the best stocks on the Big Board had fallen by over 61% in terms of real money. Those who argued that the stock market could not keep up with inflation had a convincing and powerful argument.

More analytical minds explored further into why the stock market had not kept up with inflation and came up with some very cogent reasons to explain exactly why stock prices had acted so miserably in the inflationary period of 1966 to 1980.

First they pointed out that in a rapidly increasing inflationary period profits did not keep up with inflation. This is because many manufacturers can not constantly raise their prices, but their cost of goods and expenses are increasing constantly. Therefore, they are invariably fighting a losing battle to get their profits up to where they should be. An example of this might be a mail order firm, which has to print its catalogues and prices as much as nine months before the prices expire. Yet in that nine months' period all sorts of expenses can increase, even if its suppliers have contracted to sell the merchandise at fixed costs.

Second they pointed out that much of the profits during an inflationary period were book profits only and did not represent any real economic gain. This was due to two factors: increases in inventory values and underdepreciation of plant and equipment. The argument was that stock prices should reflect only profits earned by companies, not profits which fell into their laps and were no indication that the corporation had learned how to operate more profitably.

For example, when OPEC raised the price of crude oil by 200% in 1972, the oil companies raised the price of their crude which was sold in the international market. The big oil companies immediately began to show enormous jumps in profits because they were selling their oil at the new price, when they had bought it at the old price. But these were just inventory profits; in the following year, with the price of oil remaining at the new level, these inventory profits disappeared and the earnings of the oil companies fell back into the range they had been in before the tripling of prices by OPEC. Thus, the argument went, inventory profits should be excluded from the true profits of corporations in determining their actual operating profits. Once companies do this, they will find that actual profits are not nearly as high as reported profits. Based upon true earned profits, the argument went, stocks are not priced cheaply at all.

A sister argument to the one above was that earnings are not nearly as high as reported because our present accounting rules fail to take into account the fact that the replacement cost of plants and equipment is far higher than the cost of the present equipment. Depreciation is figured on the basis of the cost of the existing equipment, and when that equipment is fully depreciated, there is supposed to be enough of a depreciation reserve to purchase a replacement for the worn-out equipment. But when the old piece of equipment cost $10,000 and the new piece costs $20,000, there is a gap of $10,000. This $10,000 must come out of profits, and thus in this case the profits of the corporation have actually been overstated by $10,000. Therefore, according to this view, a period of inflation vastly overstates corporations' earnings and profits because it does not reflect the true net earnings after charges for underdepreciation.

In summary, the charges against stocks in a time of inflation were twofold. First, the record for the past fourteen and three-quarter years had proven empirically that stocks do not keep up with inflation: Stocks are down 5% and inflation is up 115%. What more need be said? But for those who were seeking a theoretical framework for these results, they offered the second, dual charge of phantom profits of inventory inflation and the underdepreciation of assets which will have to be replaced by far more expensive assets in the future.

Having proved that stocks are no place to find a hedge against inflation, investors naturally have left the stock market in these inflationary times and are investing in tangibles. The list of such investments is literally endless, but it certainly starts with real estate of all kinds, goes on to commodities, includes gold and silver, and finally encompasses works of art and antiques and even postage stamps, which incidentally have done remarkably well.

## TAXES

The third reason given for the more or less permanent decline of the stock market was taxes. While there have always been taxes in the United States, the rate of taxation on income has gotten substantially higher in recent years for two reasons. First, state and local governments have increased their take substantially; and second, while the federal rate tables have remained the same, the rate of inflation has pushed more and more Americans into higher brackets. Thus, dividends are subject to taxation at ever higher rates, and any money made on capital gains is also subject to tax, although in fact the "profit" may simply mean that the stock price has risen as a result of inflation. Thus, you may buy a stock for $50, sell it ten years later for $60, when in fact you should be getting $70 just to remain even in terms of purchasing power. Therefore, in terms of real money you are losing $10, but as far as the tax collector is concerned you have a $10 profit and you must pay a tax on it. No wonder no one wants to own common stocks!

Once again there was hard evidence to indicate that this viewpoint was correct. While stocks languished from lack of any buying, sales of municipal bonds, which enjoy the advantage of tax-free interest, were booming to all-time highs. Mutual funds and trusts which were devoted to municipal bonds enjoyed a tremendous success.

If one compared the 9.6% that was available from some municipal bonds with the return of 5.7% being paid by the Dow Jones Industrial Average in late 1980, and then considered that the 9.6% on the bonds could be completely tax free, once again one could argue that stocks were due for a steep decline to the point where their yields could be competitive with municipal bonds.

## DECLINING NUMBER OF SHAREHOLDERS

Another major argument for saying that stock prices will stay down, and one emphasized by *Business Week*, was that the number of shareholders had seriously declined during the past two decades. This argument was more serious than saying that investors have stopped buying stock. That could be simply a temporary condition. What has happened is that millions of people have left the market altogether. They don't even have accounts with brokers, and they don't follow stock prices any more. They are finished with the market, presumably forever. In short, these people have taken their buying power away from the market and they aren't about to bring it back.

Just how big is the drain? In 1970, 15% of the U.S. population were shareholders of public corporations, and by 1979 that had shrunk to an estimated 8.8%. That is a major decline indeed. What is even more ominous for the future is that the biggest decline has come in the younger age groups. Those owning stock in the 45 to 65 age group have fallen from about 13½ million in 1970 to an estimated 9 million, while those in the 21 to 44 age group have fallen from almost 10 million to an estimated 5 million. The very group which in the past has been the most likely to take a plunge in common stocks has seen the number of stockholders cut in half! The only age group which has remained constant is the group over 65, which has actually seen a slight growth.

What these figures clearly reveal, according to this thesis, is that the stock market cannot go up when there are no buyers for stock. As the older population passes its stocks on to the next generation, they will just sell them off, thus further driving down stock prices. But more important, it is impossible to have a stock rally when there are no individuals around who are interested in buying stocks.

Furthermore, even if stocks begin to go up, they won't cause any buying excitement in the public, because today stocks make up a much smaller part of people's financial assets. Back in 1968 stocks comprised about 43% of individual financial assets. Today it is estimated by *Business Week* that that figure has fallen to 20%. Stocks are therefore less than one-half as important to individual investors as they were. In other words, who is even going to care if they go up?

A host of other more specific reasons were also given for believing that the market will go down long before it ever goes up, and that in any event it will never return to the ridiculous highs of before. Basically these all pointed out that times are different now in fundamental ways and therefore the great growth in profits of the fifties and sixties cannot be duplicated. The changes include energy shortages, government controls, lower profit margins, and fear of recession. We'll list these arguments in detail:

### ENERGY SHORTAGES
In the past the United States always had a surplus of oil products. We had a tariff to keep out the cheap foreign petroleum which endangered a reasonable price for all our domestic production.

Americans loved their big, powerful cars, and when they toured Europe, they laughed at the tiny matchbox cars they saw. Gasoline stations did everything they could to get people to buy gasoline, from giving out free glasses to offering a free car wash. Of course, with low costs for energy, American industrial companies made money and grew.

Now there have been permanent changes. Petroleum prices have quadrupled and control of its price has gone from us to OPEC. Worse, the supply is limited and the shortages promise to get worse. Natural gas is in limited supply, and coal is costly to transport, is difficult to mine, and has severe environmental problems both at the mining and user end. Nuclear reactors were proven unsafe at Three Mile Island, and solar energy is years away from making any tangible contribution to the problem. In short, this argument maintained the United States is in for a new period of slow or even no growth, held on a tight leash by the shortage and expense of energy, and this is a problem which the stock market never had to consider in previous eras.

## GOVERNMENT CONTROLS

When the first laws were passed limiting the number of hours which could be worked by women and children, they were struck down by the Supreme Court as an infringement upon the right of free contract enjoyed by every citizen. How times have changed. Today the government not only regulates the number of hours and the amount of overtime, but controls the price of much of our energy; regulates the precise nature of the exhaust system in our cars and the number of miles they get to the gallon; governs the safety of working conditions in plants and offices; sets the temperatures allowed in public buildings; mandates a federal speed limit; requires massive amounts be contributed to Social Security, unemployment funds, and workmen's compensation; sets regulations on company pension plans; requires various expensive safety features; limits expansion and requires inefficient and expensive means of production in the name of environmental protection; prohibits getting business overseas by paying those in power for it; and in general, stifles the capitalistic drive which enabled this country to attain its great growth in the past. With the crushing burden of governmental regulations stifling future growth, this argument went, of course the stock market is down and will stay that way.

## LOWER PROFIT MARGINS

Whether it is due to inflation, government regulations, increased foreign competition, or whatever, studies by economists have shown that profit margins in the seventies were simply nowhere near as high as they were earlier. Thus, even if sales were able to expand and the economy to boom, profits themselves would not and did not grow proportionally. As Commerce Department figures point out, after-tax profits were about 10% of gross domestic corporate product in 1965, fell all the way down to 2% in the recession year of 1974, but by the recovery year of 1977 they were still only 5%, exactly one-half the level they had been twelve years earlier when the Dow Jones first hit 1,000.

## FEAR OF RECESSION

While this fear is not as permanent as the ones mentioned above, nevertheless by early 1980 the economy was definitely slowing down and there was legitimate fear among economists that it was headed for a major recession. Many figures showed that the economy was in a position similar to what it had been in 1973 just before the worst postwar recession in history. Consumer debt was at an all-time high, inventory was larger than it should have been, and interest rates were being forced up by the Federal Reserve Board in an effort to cut down on the rate of inflation. Since the very purpose of pushing up interest rates was to slow down the economy, it is no wonder that many serious observers believed it would lead to a recession.

In short, the late seventies knew all the reasons why the stock market was down. Double-digit inflation which the stock market could not keep up with, record high interest rates, sluggish profits held down by taxes and government regulations, declining number of shareholders, and a recession on the horizon. Was it any wonder that *Business Week* said the stock market was dead?

Nor was it surprising that the best-selling financial book was *How to Prosper During the Coming Bad Years* by Howard J. Ruff, publisher of the newsletter *Ruff Times*. In his book Mr. Ruff predicted an inflationary depression similar to the one that devastated Germany after World War I. He expected a recession which would be deep but short, to be followed by an apparent rebound beginning in 1981, followed by "runaway" inflation. He then foresaw formal price controls, shortages so bad that necessities would be rationed, riots and the breakdown of utilities and municipal services in big cities, and a collapse of the currency and its replacement with a barter economy.

Eventually, Mr. Ruff said, a new gold-backed currency would be issued, but by then it would be too late for those who did not prepare beforehand. His conclusion was that you should buy a year's supply of food, and not frozen food which would be spoiled when the electricity was stopped, but dehydrated food. To reconstitute that dehydrated food, you would need water, and so he recommended a water-purification system, along with tools, durable clothing, plus guns and ammunition for barter and hunting as well as for self-protection when all those other people started coming after your dehydrated food. He even recommended special "survival homes" which have multiple fuel heating systems, a lot of storage space, and numerous security features. His investment advice? Buy one bag of silver coins per person in your family and an equivalent dollar amount in gold coins, and then invest the rest in small-town income-producing real estate.

And so as the seventies came to an end, they were seen as a decade of great disappointment to equity investors. Discouragement and pessimism were rampant. The smart people were investing in real estate, commodities, foreign currencies and gold, and making small fortunes. The stock market couldn't get out of its own way, interest rates were soaring, inflation was unabated, and there were at least eight good reasons why the market was probably going to go further down rather than up. In the next chapter we will examine each of those arguments and discover that the conclusions drawn from them are far from being as inevitable as they seem.

# 5

## WHY THE STOCK MARKET WILL INDEED GO UP

We are now going to take an analytical look at the arguments in the previous chapter which were advanced to "prove" that the stock market is in a new permanent low level from which it cannot recover in our lifetimes. Before we start, there is one thing which we will accept. That is that the stock market has been a disaster for investors for the past fourteen years. Although there have been periods when stock prices went up substantially, it was only because they were preceded by an even lower drop. On balance, it would have been hard to make a worse investment in 1966 than to buy good common stocks. To suffer an inflation-adjusted loss of approximately 66% of your assets is simply not acceptable. But looking backward is as easy as it is fruitless. Looking to see which way the stock market is likely to go in the future is much more difficult, but it could be a lot more profitable. Now let's reexamine all those reasons why the stock market cannot go up.

### HIGH INTEREST RATES

One of the men on Wall Street whom I most admire told me flatly recently that there was no way the stock market could go up when long-term bonds are paying 10% or more. This man makes his living trading stocks for one of the largest institutional brokerage firms, and he knows how the big institutions are investing their funds. He sees first-hand that when bonds are yielding twice as much as most common stocks, the money managers are not willing to accept that lower return while also taking on the downside risk of owning stocks.

The implicit assumption of this statement is that investors buy common stocks to get a dividend yield. Period. Has anyone stopped to ask if that is really the case? Apparently not, and so we will do it right here and now.

If investors decided whether to put their money into stocks or into bonds on the basis of yield, they would have an easy decision. In June 1980 the Dow Jones Industrial Average was at 870, yielding 6.07%. The Dow Jones Bond Average was yielding 10.61%. What this means is that if investors are buying stocks and bonds for their yields, they are not very smart. Clearly the obvious play is to sell all your stocks, invest the proceeds into bonds, and pick up a gain of 4.54% on your return. (As bond traders say, this would be an increase in yield of 454 basis points, and believe me that is one tremendous increase! A typical bond swap would render 10 or fewer basis points.)

Since we may assume that investors are not *so* stupid that they ignore a simple move which can increase their yield so significantly, we are forced to the conclusion that investors do not purchase stocks solely to get a dividend yield. Obviously they consider something else. There must be some reason why they are willing to take a lower yield.

One reason is that perhaps they believe that dividends will increase in the future to the point where they will exceed the yield on bonds. After all, once one buys a bond there is no way in the world that the interest received is going to go up by even one one-hundredth of a percentage point. But common stocks get dividend increases all the time. In fact, the current rate of increase for common stock dividends is a healthy 8.6% a year. If dividends continue to increase at the 8.6% rate they have shown, the dividend yield on the Dow Jones Industrial Average would increase from its present 6.07% to 10.8% in seven years. So one explanation for the current low yield of stocks in comparison to bonds is that investors are paying now for dividend growth, for the time in the future when the stocks they buy now will be paying more than the bonds they buy now. Thus, to say that stocks cannot go up while interest rates are high is false. One must also take into consideration the rate of increase of dividends. If they will surpass bonds in, say, the relatively short time of seven years, and from then on continue to outyield bonds, then certainly the argument that stocks today do not give the yield of bonds is no reason for stock prices to stay low.

But in fact, one must question further the assumption that stocks are bought for their yield at all, present or future. Is that really why people buy stocks? One way to test that theory is to look back into history and see what the relationship of dividends to interest rates was when the market was successful. According to the relative yield theory, these should have been times of low interest rates, when stocks were paying high dividends and so luring money out of the bond market into the stock market.

Let's start with 1966, certainly a booming year in the stock market. In 1966 the Dow Jones average paid dividends of $31.34 per share, which gave it an average yield of 3.3%. At that time the bond average was yielding 5.3%. Another good year for the Dow Jones industrial was 1973. At its high point that year it was yielding 3.4%. Bonds that year were yielding 7.8%.

But those are the Dow Jones averages, made up of the dull old blue chip companies which have high dividends. What about the stocks which have done really well in the past? Let's take a look at a standout stock over the last 30 years. There is no question that one of the best stocks to own over that period was IBM. The value of its shares far exceeded those of any other company. How has its dividend yield compared with the current yield on bonds?

While it was making its dramatic rise in price during the sixties and early seventies, during no year in that period did its dividends ever get above a 1.6% yield! And this was the stock which the public and institutions were clamoring to buy more than any other stock in existence. Not until the stock began to go down with the market slide of 1973 did its dividend begin to increase slightly until in mid-1979 it was paying 4.8%.

Other successful stocks have similar histories. Avon Products was also one of the best performing stocks of the sixties and early seventies. But its dividend was even worse than IBM's. Not until the crash of 1974 did it ever pay more than 1.4%! But the stock soared from under $25 in 1964 to $139 in just eight years. They must have been doing something right. And while investors were snapping up these shares at ever higher prices, they could have been buying AAA bonds yielding 5%.

Merck was never as spectacular as IBM or Avon, but it managed to go from $25 in 1965 to $101 in 1973, which isn't so bad either. It must have been paying a very high yield indeed to compete with all the bonds and get investors to buy that stock. Let's see. Strange, during that entire period its average yield never exceeded 2.2%. And so it goes. Xerox managed to find enough buyers to bring its stock from $51 in 1966 to $171 in just six years, but it never paid out more than 0.7% as an average yield!

And let's not forget the invention of the instant camera. It also succeeded in producing almost instant profits for its shareholders. Polaroid went from $22 in 1965 to $145 just four years later. That's pretty spectacular. Do you suppose it did this because it increased its dividend way up above what those corporate bonds were paying? Surprise! During these four years its average dividend was 0.3%. So while an investor in $10,000 worth of bonds was getting $560 a year, the fellow who owned Polaroid was getting only $30. Boy, was he losing out! And you should have heard those Polaroid shareholders complain! All the way to the bank in their new Rolls-Royces. In fact, it was not until disaster overtook the stock in 1973 and it plunged 88% that its dividend yield even got over 1%.

What have we shown by all these examples? Very simply that dividend yield is not what makes stocks attractive for investors, and it is clearly not what determines whether stocks are going to go up. The main point it shows is that while some investors may buy some stocks for their yields, e.g., utilities, it is not essential to a rising stock market that the yield on stocks equal or even come close to the yield offered on bonds or any other interest-bearing security.

The only reason for buying fixed income securities is to get the interest. The reasons for buying stocks are many. One is current dividends, and another is expectations of future dividends. But by far a greater reason for purchasing common stocks is the possibility of increases in the price of the stock, caused not by dividend increases, but by increases in the earnings of the corporation. This is the reason why people buy common stocks. And if you don't believe me, just ask any broker. And this *should* be the reason they buy stocks. With earnings increasing year after year and dividends increasing year after year, as we shall see later, investors have every reason to believe that stock prices will also increase. If they bought merely to get a higher yield, then every stock would fall in price until it paid the 8.45% yield currently offered by utility stocks.

How then can one explain the flight of capital from the stock market into the money market funds, and the dramatic change in the institutional mix from common stocks into bonds and other fixed income securities? As the previous examples show, the lack of high yield alone is not the reason that people have avoided stocks.

They are avoiding stocks because they do not want to take the risk of stocks going down further. That is the real motivating force behind the switch. As an explanation for their actions, they can easily use the excuse of higher yields. After years of being buffeted around by volatile stock prices, which went up and down but never seemed to get as high as they once had been, investors simply had had enough. Interest rates on fixed income securities happened to be high, providing a convenient alternative.

Let's look at this interest rate question from another point of view, the point of view of the investor who wants to purchase bonds rather than common stock. Why would someone make such a decision? Let's forget for a moment that he may be buying bonds because he doesn't want to buy stocks. What would be the positive reasons for buying bonds? As we all know, we live in an inflationary era, with the rate of inflation ranging up to 12% annually. To keep things simple we will discuss the purchase of a new bond at par by a person who intends to hold it until it matures.

What is he getting for his money? He is getting a guaranteed interest rate of approximately 12% as of October 1980. Since the inflation rate is equal to this, the interest on his bond will just offset the decline in value of his principal. In other words, instead of making money on this investment, he is going to be breaking even for as long as we continue to have an inflation rate of 12%. There is no possible way that he can make any money through capital appreciation of the bond, because the company has the right in a given number of years to pay him back his $1,000 with $1,000 of currency, no matter how little it is then worth. Therefore, unless the inflation rate goes down, the purchaser of the bond is guaranteed to have a zero profit. Some investment.

Furthermore, the interest in a corporate bond is subject to all federal, state, and local income taxes. If the investor is in the 40% bracket, that 12% interest, after taxes, gives a net of just 7.2% a year. But his principal is still shrinking by the 12% rate of inflation each year! Thus, he is actually losing 4.8% a year. Thus buying a bond is virtually guaranteeing an after tax loss!

If he wants to avoid income taxes, he can buy municipal bonds, but they pay even less interest than corporates—in October 1980 about 9%. This would represent a real loss of just 3% at a 12% inflation rate. Thus, bonds represent an almost certain method for *losing* money. In short, for most individuals and many institutions, bonds are a terrible investment in an inflationary age. The only things they have going for them are guaranteed return of principal, and interest rates which are higher than those of stocks. Now that you understand what poor investments bonds are, you can appreciate why they *have* to pay higher interest rates than stocks. If they didn't, no one would buy them. Thus, the fact that bonds pay a higher return than most stocks is not a reason for not buying stocks, it is simply a reflection of the way things are in an inflationary period.

Finally, it is worthwhile to reflect upon why people buy common stocks in the first place. Certainly current dividends are a factor, but the interesting thing about dividends is that when times are good no one cares; it is only when stocks are relatively cheap and dividends relatively high that people look at them and decide that they are too low. As we noted above, during the boom years of the sixties and seventies, the big stocks paid almost no dividends. And this is what the investors wanted.

Ask the average investor at that time if he was worried because there was no dividend to speak of and his reply would be: "I don't want a dividend. Why should I pay taxes at the high regular income rate on dividends? If a company can't reinvest that money and put it to better use than paying out a dividend, then I don't want to own part of that company. I like a company which is reinvesting its earnings into new plant and equipment so that its earnings will go up faster. That way the stock will be worth more in the future, and I can sell out and pay the low long-term capital gains tax on my profits."

In a way dividends are like the tires on a used car. When you pay $10,000 to buy a two-year-old Lincoln Continental, no one pays too much attention to the tires. You're looking at the condition of the body, searching for any dents or scratches, checking the acceleration, looking at the upholstery, checking the air conditioning and stereo, and so on. But if you're buying a junk car to get you around at your summer place and you don't want to pay more than $250 for a ten-year-old heap of rust, the tires are important. If the car has good tires, that could save you $150, but if they're really bad, you'll have to go out and spend that much. Suddenly the tires become very important. In short, the less value to the car, the more important become the tires. Dividends are a bit like that. The less value people place on the stock itself, the more value they place on the dividends. They are important, certainly, but they are not by any means the only indication of value.

Right now dividends are higher than they have been at any time since 1950, except for the bottom of the 1974 crash. The ratio of dividend yields to interest rates of bonds is much more favorable to stocks than it has been for most of the last thirty years. High interest rates are clearly not a reason why the stock market must stay down.

*INFLATION*

As we saw in the previous chapter, the arguments concerning common stocks and inflation break down into three subarguments. The one that most investors are familiar with first-hand is that stocks have proven they are not a hedge against inflation. Just look at the record. Between 1968 and 1978 prices went up 89% as measured by the Bureau of Labor Statistics Consumer Price Index. During that same period, stocks went down from 840 on the Dow Jones average to 820, an actual decline of 2.4%. And, of course, in other periods the disparity between the CPI and DJIA would have been even greater. In short, this experience convinced many investors once and for all that stocks are not an inflation hedge.

Does the fact that prices went up while stocks went down really prove that stocks are not a hedge against inflation? When one studies logic, one learns the various fallacious forms of logic, that is, conclusions which appear to be logical based on two premises but which may have no relationship to each other at all. One of those false forms of logic is called *post hoc, ergo propter hoc,* which means "after this, therefore because of this." A common example would be that you wash your car and a few hours later it pours. You might jokingly say that every time you wash your car it rains. In this case you are just kidding: You know that washing your car does not affect the weather.

In considering stocks, the break in logic is not so clear. Indeed, if one means by an inflation hedge that every time the consumer price index goes up, the investment will go up by an equal or greater amount, then what happened proved that stocks are not a hedge against inflation. But most people know that buying stocks involves risk and that there is always the possibility that they will go down. So presumably they don't expect stocks to track the inflation rate precisely.

All we can say about what happened between 1968 and 1978 is that stock prices did not go up, and consumer prices did. Thus, the stock market was not a hedge against inflation during that period. But it was also not a good investment during that period, regardless of inflation. Does this mean that we have proven for all time that stocks are not a good investment? Hardly. What we have shown is that stocks are not always a hedge against inflation.

If we go back for a longer span of time, stocks have been an excellent hedge against inflation. From 1950 to 1970 the DJIA went up 281% while the Consumer Price Index went up only 61%. Not only did the prices of stocks grow at a faster rate during these decades, they have been growing at a faster pace than prices for over 50 years.

And it didn't just happen as a coincidence. There is a very basic reason why stock prices go up with inflation. This is because stock prices reflect in general the earnings of a company, the dividend of the company, and the prospects for future earnings and dividends. As prices go up, either causing or resulting from inflation, the profit which a company can earn from the products it sells at these higher prices goes up also. Hence its earnings go up, and when that happens the next normal step is to raise dividends. This brings us right into the next argument on inflation as to why stock prices will not go up: namely that reported earnings are distorted by inflation to appear much larger than they really are.

First, do earnings go up as fast as the inflation rate? The answer depends upon many things. Obviously if the wholesale price of cherries goes up this week by 5 cents a bushel over what they cost last week, a food company is not going to increase its price of frozen cherry pies this week. For that company to change the price of its frozen pies to its distributors each week would create a nightmare of paperwork. The distributor, in turn, would have to change his prices to his wholesalers each week, and the price to the retailers would change every week also. What the retailer paid for a frozen dessert would depend upon the week in which it was manufactured. It would be chaos. And this is not the way American industry works. Prices are changed whenever there is a major shift in costs, perhaps every few months. Clearly, if the price of cherries goes up and there is no increase in the price of the frozen pies that week, the manufacturer will be making less money.

But is that really what happens to food manufacturers? The answer is no. They are quite capable of estimating what their costs are going to be for months in advance, and when they do make one of their periodic price changes, they make it large enough so that it will protect their profit margin not only for the present but for the foreseeable future as well. Thus, if there has been a 5% increase in costs so far, they will raise their prices by perhaps 10%. The result of such a pricing policy is that for the next few weeks at least they are making more profit than normal.

In fact, building in an inflation factor has become routine in industries which have to project costs for any period of time.

Typical is the construction industry, in which cost estimators routinely add a 12% to 15% inflation factor onto their total costs for every year that a project will require.

Nevertheless, the argument remains that profits have declined and that while they were 10% of gross domestic corporate revenue in 1965, they had declined to 5% by 1977. These figures require some analysis, and just such an analysis has been done by Professor Eugene F. Fama of the University of Chicago. In an unpublished study reported in the August 27, 1979, issue of *Fortune* magazine, Professor Fama looked at profits a number of ways. The Department of Commerce, in reporting profitability over a period of years, deducts inventory profits. However, all interest payments are deducted before net profits are arrived at.

Professor Fama noted that during a 27-year period the amount of money paid out in interest had increased from just a few billion in 1950 to over $20 billion in 1977. The reason is that companies were not raising money by selling new shares. Because interest paid on debt is tax deductible while dividends paid to shareholders are not, it was more economical for companies to borrow money. They now had large debits on which they were paying large interest payments. But for every 1% of inflation, the real value of the liabilities is reduced by 1%. Thus, Professor Fama reasoned, most of the interest payments really had the same effect as if they had been a reduction of debt. In other words, the high interest rates are not higher real interest costs, but rather represent a payment to the creditors to compensate them for inflation.

Therefore, part of the interest payments are to reflect the shrinking value of the debt and thus are similar to a repayment of the debt. Since repayments of debts do not appear on a profit and loss sheet, these repayments should not be deducted. Professor Fama therefore added the part of interest which represented compensation for inflation back into the profits of the companies, and came up with an interesting conclusion.

When profits are adjusted for inflation by adding in net interest payments, the picture looks quite different. (See Chart 2.) Cash profits during most of the seventies were just as high as they had been during the fifties. The reason they aren't quite as high as they were during the sixties is that the sixties were a period of remarkable economic growth when profit margins were at a historically high point. The conclusion is that profits and profit margins are now about as high as they normally are.

Finally we come to the third aspect of the argument about inflation. Are the current profits artificially high because they do not take into account the increased replacement cost of assets (which means that deductions from profit for depreciation have been too low) and because they fail to take into consideration inventory profits caused only by inflation?

One of the most respected economists to look at this question is Professor Franco Modigliani of the Massachusetts Institute of Technology. In association with Richard Cohn of the University of Chicago at Chicago Circle, he published a paper in the *Financial Analysts Journal* discussing the point. His conclusion was that it was indeed correct to adjust earnings downward to reflect understated depreciation and phony inventory gains. But this was only one half the adjustment which was needed to

## CHART 2

### Profit Margins

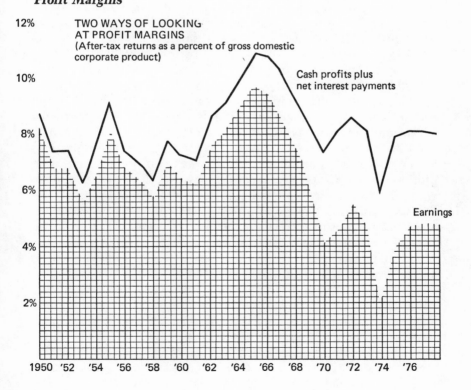

12%　　　TWO WAYS OF LOOKING
　　　　AT PROFIT MARGINS
　　　　(After-tax returns as a percent of gross domestic
　　　　corporate product)

10%　　　　　　　　　　　　　　　Cash profits plus
　　　　　　　　　　　　　　　　net interest payments

Earnings

1950　'52　'54　'56　'58　'60　'62　'64　'66　'68　'70　'72　'74　'76

compensate for inflation, and to correct for only these two items was to grossly distort true earnings.

Modigliani and Cohn point out that there is a tremendous advantage created by the falling value of corporate indebtedness. A rise in the rate of inflation will almost immediately push up interest rates. This will immediately lower the real value or price of any bonds which the company has issued. Let's say a company issued 30-year bonds ten years ago for $1,000 each. Interest rates have risen so much in the last ten years that the bonds have now fallen in value to only $750. Even though the real value of the bonds is reduced by $250, the corporation is not allowed to show this on its books or in its profit and loss statement in any way. Yet if the corporation decided to buy in those bonds at $750 each, it would then realize a capital gain of $250 a bond and would be able to report this as a profit, although perhaps it would have to specify that this was a nonrecurring profit. It was just such a maneuver which produced a profit of $89.3 million for Pan Am in 1976 when it decided to buy in one of its bond issues in exchange for another issue. The point here is that whether the company chooses to actually buy in its indebtedness or not, the actual value of its liability has been reduced. By not permitting corporations to reflect this fact in any way, the present accounting rules arbitrarily reduce the profits of companies.

To get an idea of just how significant a factor this is in the overall picture, Modigliani and Cohn looked at the debt figures for the average company, which in 1977 amounted to about five times its annual profits. But the real burden of that debt fell by about 7%, which was the inflation rate for that year. In order to measure profits accurately it is necessary to increase profits by 7% times the amount of the debt, which equals 35% of corporate profits. The Department of Commerce estimates that understated depreciation and phony inventory gains increased profits by about a third, so the two adjustments cancel each other out. Thus, true adjusted-for-inflation profits even in an inflationary period turn out to be almost exactly what they are reported to be.

Modigliani and Cohn have found that the notion that corporate profits decline sharply during a period of high inflation is just a myth. They report that there is absolutely no evidence of a long-term decline. Apparently the widely held view that profits are not keeping up with inflation comes from the fact that the Department of Commerce gives widespread publicity to the mistakes of underdepreciation and phony inventory profits which reduce stated profits, but it neglects to correct for debt-related gains. The result is that many analysts on Wall Street have been systematically reducing earnings to adjust for inflation. This has brought them to the conclusion that earnings are not keeping up with inflation. With this misinformed opinion they have concluded that stocks are no longer a hedge against inflation, and therefore they value them even less. Not only are they using earnings which are too low, but because the earnings are too low, they are only willing to give them a P/E ratio which is also too low. The result is a compounding of the original error which produces stock prices far lower than they ought to be.

Because of these false perceptions, among others, Modigliani and Cohn have calculated that for every one percentage point increase in the rate of inflation, the price of stocks tends to fall by 13%. Performing their calculation upon the Standard & Poor's Index at the end of 1977, they found that the stocks were valued only at 46% of their theoretical value. In other words, if the stocks were being valued without the errors caused by inflation, the stocks would be selling at over twice their current prices! So much for the argument that stocks should be much cheaper because their earnings are overstated in an inflationary period.

## TAXES

When investors talk about high taxes keeping the stock market down, they are not talking about taxes at the corporate level. The corporate tax rate has remained almost constant for decades, and in fact it was even reduced by two percentage points a few years ago. What they are talking about is the impact taxes have on the individual investors. First, they must pay taxes on dividends at the regular rates. This is certainly a drawback, and as more Americans move into higher tax brackets, it becomes more serious. But most other investments also produce taxable income, and in the end the attractiveness of an investment is its after-tax return to the investor.

Municipal bonds do not produce taxable income, but their return is limited to about 7%. With the average common stock paying about 5.5%, if the investor is in the 50% bracket, he has a net after-tax return of 2.75%. Subtracting this from the 7% of municipals, we arrive at a difference of 4.25%, which must be made up from something else. That something else is the potential capital gains on the stock. With corporate profits increasing each year at about 10% or more, there is sound reasoning which says that stock prices are going to appreciate by about that much, and certainly far more than 4.25%. Thus, the difference between the lower after-tax yield of stocks and municipal bonds should be more than made up for by capital appreciation of the stocks.

And this brings us to the other method by which stock-holders' profits are taxed: capital gains. When stock is held for over one year and is then sold at a profit, it is entitled to be taxed at long-term capital gains rates. Under a reduction in the tax rate for sales after October 31, 1978, the taxpayer is permitted to deduct 60% of the capital gains from the amount on which he must pay taxes. For example, if you buy some stock for $4,000, hold it for over a year, and then sell it for $5,000, you will have a long-term capital gain of $1,000. To determine the tax on this gain you first deduct 60%, or $600; the remaining $400 is then taxed at your normal rate. Therefore, the tax on long-term capital gains is reduced to just 40% of your regular tax. With the maximum tax rate now at 70%, the most tax that anyone can pay on his long-term capital gains is 40% of 70%, or 28%. And that is some tax break. For most investors who are not in the 70% bracket, the tax will be even less than that.

Since the primary income component of stocks can be expected to be capital gains, there are many important tax advantages to owning stocks. The first one was just mentioned: Congress is giving you a 60% reduction on all taxes for profits on stocks held over one year. But there are other advantages. First, there is no tax to pay until you actually sell the stock. Let's compare this with regular bonds, money in the bank, or commercial real estate which is producing a taxable profit. In each case you must pay taxes every year when the money is earned, whether you actually withdraw the money or not. With stocks you do not pay that tax until you actually decide to take out your money. And this can be a valuable consideration.

Keep in mind the old tax planning adage, "A tax delayed is a tax not paid." At today's high interest rates, when you have to pay perhaps 12% to borrow money, that money is doubling in just over six years. Therefore, if you can postpone paying a tax for six years and invest that money somewhere else, you are literally not paying the tax at all (ignoring taxes on the interest). While this is a dramatic example, even postponing the tax one year will result in a large savings to you. So owning stocks gives you the right to postpone paying taxes as long as you want. Furthermore, because not all stocks go up, you have the opportunity to do some tax planning at the end of each year by selling those stocks which have gone down, thus reducing the capital gains taxes you pay, and to the extent of $3,000 you can even reduce the amount of ordinary income on which you pay taxes.

Thus, for the high tax bracket investor, stocks can provide a very interesting tax shelter. No taxes on capital gains until you sell the stock, even if they go up in price every year, and a 60% reduction in taxes when you do sell. Conclusion: It isn't onerous taxes which are keeping stocks down.

## DECLINING NUMBER OF SHAREHOLDERS

How can stocks go up when there just aren't any people around any more to buy them? While this seems like a rhetorical question, it isn't actually because there is an answer. We just have to go back into history a few decades to find out what happened last time. The great depression of the 1930's pretty much wiped out most stockholders. Only a small band of people continued to own stocks during the forties, and it is doubtful whether they could have pushed stock prices up even if they had invested every dime they owned into the stock market. But what did happen? In 1950 there were approximately 6 million Americans who owned common stock. By 1960 that number had increased by 83% to 11 million! In just one decade the number of stockholders almost doubled. And while we do not know how many of the existing shareholders were buying more stock, there is no question but that each *new* shareholder was only a buyer of stocks, since he could not be a seller of what he didn't own. But now, with the shareholder population up to 11 million in 1960, you might suspect that most of the people who were likely stockholders would already own stock, and that it would therefore be harder to attract new shareholders. Wrong. Between 1960 and 1970 the number of shareholders increased by over 127% from 11 million to 25 million people! These were people from all walks of life, rich and not so rich, who decided that they wanted to own common stocks.

The relevance of these statistics to today is that if millions of people in the fifties and sixties could decide that they wanted to become stockholders for the first time, then there is no reason why the same process cannot be repeated in the eighties. It is no harder to open an account with a brokerage firm today than it was then, and the last I checked the firms were just as pleased to get new

customers as ever. Furthermore, the greatest increase in new
shareholders then was in the under-65 age group, which is exactly
where the fewest shareholders are today. In other words, the
opportunities for new shareholders are greatest today in the very
group which showed themselves so eager to become shareholders
from 1950 to 1970.

And what about the people who have given up common
stocks? Did they desert them because they were messy and time
consuming and back breaking like a coal-burning furnace? Did
they leave them because they didn't work very well, like the old
iceboxes which were traded in for electric refrigerators? Those
might be seen as irreversible changes. But getting out of the stock
market can be explained on a much simpler ground. Stock prices
went down, and since people don't like to lose money, they got out.
The process can be reversed just as simply. When stock prices go
up, those in the market will start making money. They will tell
(perhaps brag is a more accurate term) their friends, and their
friends will start to buy. Cautiously at first, then more wholeheart-
edly. They in turn will tell their friends, and so it will go. There is
nothing mysterious, complex, or even unusual about it. And it isn't
even anything new. It has all happened before, and it will happen
again. In conclusion, the absence of stock buyers is not a cause of a
declining stock market, it is the result of it. Let stock prices go up
by any substantial amount, and you will see new investors
streaming into the stock market.

## ENERGY SHORTAGES

It is easy to say that the 1979 increase in OPEC oil prices along
with the shortages of oil and natural gas impose a limitation upon
our growth. Let's remember that this is not the first time that we
were faced with a major increase in oil prices. The 1979 increases
were about 33%, but the first big shock came in 1973 and 1974,
when the oil prices tripled. In other words, the cost of petroleum
went up six times as much in 1973 and 1974 as it did in 1979. So
1979 was really not even in the same ball park as 1973 as far as
impact upon the economy. That was a *real* shock, and serious
economists wondered then whether the country would ever be able
to recover. Indeed, it was one of the major causes of the 1974–75
recession.

But what happened to the economy after that? It rebounded
beautifully with the longest peacetime recovery period in the

history of the United States. The tripling of oil prices was not able to prevent the U.S. gross national product, even adjusted for inflation, from reaching all-time highs, to prevent corporations from reaching record profits year after year, and to prevent dividends on stocks from reaching new highs, all adjusted for inflation. Therefore, it seems highly unlikely that an increase of one-sixth that proportion can permanently affect the expanding U.S. economy in any serious manner. Let's remember that prior to the Iranian political revolution in 1979 there was actually a spot surplus of oil.

Furthermore, oil consumption is much more elastic than had been previously realized. That is to say, as the price of energy goes up, the amount of consumption goes down. This is especially true in the United States, where the price of petroleum had been so cheap that no one paid much attention to its efficient use. Compare the mileage of American cars in the 1960's with that of our European counterparts. In a thoughtful analysis of the energy situation which appeared in *The New York Times* of August 19, 1979, John P. Henry, Jr., a vice president of Booz, Allen & Hamilton's energy division, pointed out that the economy would in all probability be well able to survive the oil price increase. He noted that automobiles account for 20% of all primary energy consumption in the United States, and that even before the latest oil price hikes it was estimated that auto consumption of fuel would be 25% less in the year 2000 than in the 1970's.

Furthermore, the world's demand for energy in the year 2000 has already been reduced 22% to 24% from its earlier estimates. Probably the latest increases will reduce estimated consumption even more. The price hikes in themselves will provide increases to other industries such as insulation; it will also lead to more efficient engines and to more computers so that energy output can be controlled more efficiently. Mr. Henry's conclusion is that the ultimate outlook for the U.S. economy should be good, and that, in fact, because of our enormous reserves of coal, oil shale, and recoverable oil and natural gas, the OPEC price hikes could actually put the United States in a position of relative economic strength.

Our economy is always facing problems. Sometimes it is high unemployment which reduces consumer purchasing power. Sometimes it is old-fashioned plant and equipment which reduces productivity. And sometimes it is high interest rates and inflation. The increase in the price of oil is one such problem, but it is in no way a reason why the American economy will stop growing. The American economy will adapt as it has before to higher taxes, higher minimum wages, and before that to unions and strikes. Anyone who thinks that an increase of 30% in the price of oil is going to permanently impair the growth of the U.S. economy simply hasn't realized how resourceful, adaptable, and powerful our economy is.

## GOVERNMENT CONTROLS

New government regulations passed in the liberal spirit of the sixties and early seventies are certainly costing industry substantial amounts of money. These include safety regulations, environmental controls, pension plan reforms, and increased reporting burdens on a wide variety of matters. Yes, these are burdensome, and yes, many of the new regulations, especially the environmental ones, are restricting industry's growth. But put in the context of history, are these really a major problem of the type that will permanently decrease the growth of profits?

The cost of complying with the various reporting requirements has been estimated by Professor Murray Weidenbaum, a resident scholar at the American Enterprise Institute on leave from Washington University, to be $100 billion a year, or $500 for every person in the United States. But this figure rests on conjectural assumptions and may well be too high. A U.S. Government Accounting Office study concluded that the cost was $38 billion, and a survey by The Business Roundtable of its own members came up with a sharply lower figure. But even if the $100 billion were correct, it represents only 4% of the Gross National Product, and that does not take into consideration the valuable economic benefits from the regulations such as the reduction in death from automobile accidents.

Many of the safety requirements are indeed expensive, but in many more cases it is simply making sure that everyone has earplugs, which cost pennies, or that they are wearing safety glasses or proper clothing. Probably the minimum wage costs industry more than all the safety regulations put together. But we have had a minimum wage since the New Deal almost fifty years ago, and although it is higher now, the principle is the same.

In other words, the many regulations, controls, and reports which are reported in such detail by the nation's business press turn out to be nothing more than an expensive and bothersome nuisance when looked at in the perspective of the total gross national product. The only ones which could cause a real problem are the environmental controls to the extent that they stop new plant and industrial expansion. And there is already the belief that the golden age of the environmentalists, when, for example, they could stop a much needed facility from construction because someone's view would be impaired, is coming to an end.

It is now recognized that a political system of numerous competing agencies and jurisdictions, any one of which can say no but not one of which can say definitely yes, is simply impossible. See, for instance, President Carter's energy message in which he asked for an Energy Mobilization Board which would have the power to approve projects that were in the interest of the nation's energy policy.

Are the recently enacted governmental controls a reason for thinking that America's corporate profits will stop growing or will grow slower in the future? They may slow them down but not by a significant amount.

### LOWER PROFIT MARGINS

Profit margins have indeed been lower in the seventies than they were in the sixties. But as we discussed above in our exploration of the inflation issue, this is partly because of an incorrect view of profits. If retirement of debt due to inflation is considered, then the profit margins of the seventies are almost equal to those of the fifties. What happened in the sixties was simply that there was a period of unusual economic growth which produced unusually high profit margins.

The important point is that there appears to be no fundamental economic change which will result in basically lower profit margins in the future. That would be the only thing which could keep stock prices down.

### FEAR OF RECESSION

When this book was being completed in mid-1980, it was clear that the economy was in a recession. But the point is not really how long and serious the recession was. Economists can argue endlessly about whether it will be followed by a smooth recovery or will give way to renewed galloping inflation accompanied by even higher interest rates.

The big question for us is not whether there is going to be a continuing recession or whether it will be followed by a runaway inflation. There is always a question about the upcoming economic picture. There never has been a time in history when serious people did not wonder where the economy was going and whether it might not be going to hell. The bottom line for those of us who wish to invest in the stock market is that, no matter how difficult it is to foresee the future, and no matter how bleak some people may believe it will be, there are still tremendous profits to be made by buying common stocks when they are cheap.

The problems of today cannot compare to the problems of the Great Depression. And a depression is exactly what many investors believed would reoccur in 1950. Certainly they had good reasons for so thinking. No other than the chairman of Montgomery Ward almost staked the entire future of his company on the proposition that a depression was coming; he was not going to spend a penny to modernize his stores or to open any new stores, until the depression had come and he could do it cheaply. Of course, the depression never came, and Montgomery Ward almost didn't survive.

Yet, the early 1950's, when there was that fear of a depression, was the best time in fifty years to purchase common stocks. Remember that the Dow Jones average tripled between 1950 and 1960! Then the United States was torn by the Korean War in 1955. How could one buy stocks when the country was about to enter a wartime economy? Then there was the question of how it would adjust after the war. Then in 1965 the United States began to get involved more and more deeply with Vietnam. This time we were on our own without the help of the rest of the United Nations' forces, and this time with a president who believed that we could have guns and butter, in effect, wage a major overseas war and not increase taxes. No wonder there was inflation. Was this a time to buy stocks? In 1974 and 1975 the nation entered the worst recession in thirty years. Profits tumbled, unemployment soared, but unlike in previous recessions, prices did not go down. Was this any time to buy stocks?

In short, in almost every period in history the future has presented grave questions, and some observers, with very good reasoning, have concluded that the stock market was about to go down sharply. The present time is no different. If anything, the problems facing us today are far *less* severe than those of the past. The nation is not at war or in imminent danger of going into one.

There may be a recession, but almost no one believes that it will be as severe as the 1974–75 recession. Was the past a good time to buy common stocks? Except for much of the past fourteen years when stocks were overpriced, any one of those times was an excellent one to buy common stocks. So is the present time.

We have now completed our analysis of all the reasons why the death of the stock market is "a near-permanent condition," to quote *Business Week* again, and we find that not one of them is a valid reason for the stock market to stay down. They are, in fact, all versions of the same reason. They are excuses for not buying stock by people and institutions who have lost so much money in the stock market in the past fourteen years that they have "learned a lesson" never to buy stocks again. But the fact that these people bought high and sold low does not mean that the next decade will not see just the opposite result. People buying now are buying low, as we will see in the next chapter. In the chapter after that we will examine the probabilities for believing that they will also be able to sell high within a very few years. And that, my friends, in the words of the greats of Wall Street, is how to make money. Buy low, sell high.

# 6

# THREE INDICATIONS THAT STOCKS ARE UNDERPRICED NOW

Some mighty strange things happened in the late 1970's. Companies were bought out by other companies. One would normally assume that such a transaction would not make the shareholders of the acquired company very happy; they had lost the stock in the company they wanted to own, and now they suddenly found themselves with stock in a company they may never have heard of, in a different industry, and probably with totally different characteristics. Years ago these shareholders would have been mildly displeased. In the late seventies these people jumped for joy as though they had literally discovered a gold mine.

In fact, for many arbitrageurs that was exactly what had happened. The new company usually offered stock of its own worth between 30% to 100% more than the stock in the acquired company had previously been selling for. Trying to buy stock in companies that were thought to be on the verge of being taken over by other companies became the hottest game in a rather cool stock market. In fact, many stock market players in the late seventies believed that it was the only game in town. These takeovers happened so often, and the prices were so far above the current prices of the stock of the soon-to-be acquired company, that no one thought it strange or unusual that the prices were so high.

The advantage of a book like this is that we can look back upon these acquisitions from a perspective unclouded by the details of any one particular deal and ask ourselves a question or two. Under the forces of our marketplace, if a company's stock is selling at $33 a share, for example, that is supposed to represent its exact current value. Any basic book of economics will tell you that in an open market system like the stock exchange, the price of the stock represents what willing buyers are willing to pay for the stock and what willing sellers are willing to accept for it. It is the exact balance between the forces of supply and demand and represents its exact value in the marketplace.

Those experienced on Wall Street will go even further, and tell you that the current price represents the combined judgment of all the experts on the company, including those with special inside knowledge about it and those who make their living by being experts on that particular industry and the value of its shares. In short, the wisdom of Wall Street is that the current price of a stock is something to be respected. It can never be wrong. "Don't argue with the tape" is one of the most basic sayings of Wall Street; it means that if the New York Stock Exchange tape shows that a stock is now selling for $33 a share, that is exactly what it should be selling for. If you believe that the stock should be selling at $44 a share, so the conventional wisdom goes, you are wrong and the tape is right.

When a stock is trading on the New York Stock Exchange, anyone in the world can come along and pay $33 and buy a share of that stock. If they want a lot of the stock, then like some institutions, they may have trouble buying it at exactly $33, so they may be willing to pay $33.50; or perhaps, if they really want a lot of stock and there isn't much traded each day, they will have to pay as high as $34 a share. But anything over that for a stock with any trading volume would be considered excessive.

Under the securities law there are limits to how much of a company one can buy without making a public disclosure. Once you reach the point where you own 5% of the shares of a company, you must so notify the S.E.C. and advise them whether you are buying the shares for investment purposes or whether you plan to take over the company. In a truly perfect economic model, this shouldn't make any difference to the price of the stock. If there were plenty of willing sellers at $34 a share before anyone made an announcement that he wanted to acquire a block of the stock, they shouldn't care to whom they were selling. So in the old days, if someone wanted to acquire a company, he would simply buy more and more of the stock until he owned almost all of it, and then he would make an announcement. The result of all this buying was, of course, that the price of the stock was pulled up. At $34 he purchased from all those who really didn't care about owning the stock, and at $35 from those who were a little more reluctant to sell, and at $36 he was buying from those who were even more reluctant. But it is likely that by the time he got to $37 or $40, and kept buying over a long enough period of time, he would have acquired majority control of the company. And that would be only proper, assuming, as Wall Street does, that the price of $33 really represented the true value of the shares at the present time. By paying 10% to 20% more than the current price, he would encourage those now owning the stock to sell, and he would at the same time outbid anyone else who was thinking of buying the stock.

Now, we return once again to the real world of late 1979. A company decides that it would like to acquire XYZ company whose stock is selling for $33. It makes a filing with the S.E.C. or perhaps holds a news conference to make the announcement. The announcement may be that it is holding talks with the management of XYZ company about taking over the company, because it would not want to take over XYZ unless its present management was in agreement with it, and that they are currently discussing the price at which they will buy all the shares of stock from the existing shareholders.

What do you suppose the price turns out to be? $36? $38? Even $40 for a 20% profit? Could it be $44, as some speculators thought? That would be a full 33% above the current price of $33, which supposedly represents the true value of XYZ. If the purchase price were to go that high, it would make you wonder why another company would be willing to pay so much more than the true value for it? Are they willing to pay more than true value for something? Are they confusing their role in the world with that of Santa Claus? Is there something they know about the company that others don't know? Will it suddenly become more profitable after they own it?

While we ponder these questions, let's go back to that acquiring company and find out what they really offered. It wasn't $36, it wasn't $38, it wasn't $40, and it wasn't even $44. In fact, when the price of the offer came out there were more than a few gasps of surprise. The price was $72 a share. This is a true story. The company making the offer was not confusing itself with Santa Claus. It was paying what it believed to be a fair value for the stock. And that company knew what it was doing. I can say that because it has long been considered one of the best managed companies in American business.

That company was Exxon, and the company which it acquired for $72 a share was Reliance Electric. It is very unlikely that Exxon knew anything about Reliance Electric that was not readily available knowledge to anyone who cared to find out.

Although Exxon mentioned in its press conference that it was working on a new method of saving electrical energy in electric motors, it later turned out that only a very small part of Reliance's business was actually in the manufacture of electric motors; furthermore, Exxon would probably license other electric manufacturers to use its new technology, and there were a number of other manufacturers who were working on similar methods of saving electric energy in small motors. In the final analysis it didn't seem as if Exxon would be able to increase the earnings of Reliance that dramatically. It seemed more likely that Exxon, thinking of itself as an energy company, wanted to diversify into another area of energy and decided to purchase Reliance as a means of accomplishing this diversification.

So the basic question remains. If the Wall Street marketplace had established $33 as the true value of Reliance's shares, why was Exxon willing to pay $72, or a whopping 118% over "true value" for these shares?

Before you spend too much thought trying to unravel this question concerning Exxon and Reliance Electric, here is another one for you. Babcock & Wilcox, the old-line heavy equipment, boiler, and generator manufacturer, was selling at $34¾ a share when a takeover offer was announced by United Technologies. The price? $42 a share. But as it turned out, even that mighty premium of 20% over the current price was only the beginning. Babcock & Wilcox was not altogether happy about being acquired, and it sought to obtain an offer from someone else. So United Technologies raised its offer to $48. Then J. Ray McDermott came in with the price of $55. Now the bidding war began. United Technologies met the $55 bid. McDermott went up to $60 and finally McDermott closed the deal at $62.50. This was 80% above the earlier stock price, which was supposed to represent its true value.

In one of the larger acquisitions, United Technologies acquired Carrier Corporation, the air conditioner makers, for $28 a share. Before the purchase was announced the stock had been selling for $19. The list goes on and on. Fairchild Camera & Instrument was considered an excellent takeover candidate, so much so that after Gould Inc. announced acquisition plans at $54 a share, Schlumberger, the oil industry supply firm, stepped up with an offer that eventually reached $66 a share for stock which prior to the takeover talks had been selling for just $32 a share. Perhaps the most celebrated takeover occurred in the fight for Carborundum, whose stock had been selling for $33 a share. Originally, Eaton

Corporation announced that they were prepared to take over the company for $47 a share. Then Kennecott Copper entered the picture and offered $66 a share. As *The Wall Street Journal* noted, the offer stunned stockbrokers, but Kennecott bought the shares of the company for about 100% more than the market forces had been saying the stock was originally worth.

There were many more takeovers, too numerous to mention. Among them Aetna Life acquired American Re-insurance for $62 a share, when the shares had been selling for $35 prior to any takeover activity. American Credit Corp. shares were selling for $25 a share and Barclays Bank Ltd. purchased them for $50. Dun & Bradstreet picked up National CSS for $48 a share, although the shares had been trading at $28 before the takeover.

In what became a three-way competition, Texas International Airlines got into a bidding war against Pan American World Airways to acquire National Airlines. National's stock was selling at $18.37 before the takeover campaigns began. First Texas International announced its takeover intentions. Then Pan Am came into the picture with an offer of $35 a share. Next Texas increased its offer and Pan Am went up to $41. Then Eastern Airlines decided that it was interested and offered $50 a share. This was matched by Texas and Pan Am, and eventually Pan Am got National at a price of $50 a share. This means they were paying a premium of $31.63 over the previous market price, or 172% more than the stock market had said that the stock was worth.

There were many motivations for these takeovers. One was to use up idle cash of the acquiring company, one was to broaden the acquiring company's product or service base, one was simply to acquire another company in order to prevent being taken over by someone else. The takeovers also were accomplished in many ways: some were for cash, some were for shares; some were friendly, some were carried out over the vehement objections of existing management; some were quick, and some dragged out for months; some were competitive with two or more would-be acquirers, and others were not. Though the methods and means used to accomplish these takeovers were diverse, one common thread stands out. In every case the acquiring company was willing to pay amounts of money greatly in excess of what the shares had been selling for.

It is true that there may be a premium attached to having a controlling interest in a company, and so an investor may have to pay somewhat more to obtain a large block of stock, or majority control of a company. But these takeover prices were not simply a bit more. The fact that a company is willing to pay twice as much as the shares had been selling for raises a few questions. First we may safely assume that the acquiring companies knew what they were doing. They had the time, money, and expertise to analyze the companies they were buying thoroughly. They knew what they were worth. Also, they obviously did not want to overpay for the acquisition. Finally, we may assume that the only reason they were willing to pay as much as they did for the acquired companies was that they believed them to be bargains which were worth more in fact than what they were paying for them.

If we go back to a statement made at the beginning of this chapter, "Don't argue with the tape," i.e., a stock is worth exactly what you can sell it for at that moment, then there is something very strange going on. If Reliance Electric shares were really worth only $33, then Exxon certainly made a big mistake when they offered to pay $72 for them. Assuming again, as we did, that Exxon really didn't have any special way to make Reliance Electric more profitable than it was, only one of two things are possible. Either Exxon, with all its highly skilled financial analysts, made a mistake of unbelievable magnitude, or else the stock market made a mistake in pricing the Reliance shares as low as it did.

The same thing can be asked about every one of the other takeovers mentioned. In each case the acquiring company was more than willing to pay far more for the shares than they were priced by the stock market. Take your choice. Did the companies grossly overpay? Of did the stock market underprice the value of the shares? One of these must be true. We'll reach a conclusion on this issue later.

There were other interesting developments during the late seventies. Corporations started doing something which was almost unheard of in earlier days. In earlier times corporations raised money from investors by issuing new stock. The companies would then invest the proceeds from the stock in their businesses, where they could earn a good return, and they would then pay dividends to the stockholders. Raising money for American industry was the function which Wall Street had served from its inception. But a funny thing began to happen in the late seventies. First one company and then another began to buy stock from investors instead of selling it to them. The reasons were extremely logical, and in many cases compelling.

The corporations had to choose a place to invest their money where it would get the greatest return. Let us assume that, like many companies, a typical company wanted to get a pretax return of 20% on its investments. If it were to invest $100,000 in a new project or piece of machinery, it would expect to get back $20,000 a year on that investment. With the sluggish economy and the roaring rate of inflation, it wasn't always easy to find investments which would pay off at that rate with any degree of assurance. On the other hand, their own stock might be selling at a P/E ratio of 5 and be paying a dividend of 7%. Once a corporation purchases its own stock, those shares are simply cancelled, or perhaps denominated treasury shares, which amounts to the same thing for our purposes.

The results of this were manifold. In the first place it was a wonderful investment for the corporation. It was purchasing an asset which, with a P/E of 5, was earning 20% a year on the investment on an *after-tax* basis. This was the kind of investment which they might never be able to make by investing in bricks and mortar, or a new product introduction, research and development expenditure, or anything else. Of course, the corporation also may have had projections that it was going to earn more in the future. So not only were they getting 20% earnings now, but they probably felt very confident that that rate of return would increase in the future.

Second, the stock may have been selling for less than book value. Let us assume that the stock was selling for $20 a share and the book value was $30, which certainly was not unusual. This means that for every share they bought, they were increasing the book value of the stock that was held by the remaining shareholders. What happens is that after the purchase, the book value of the outstanding shares is reduced by the $20 used to buy in the stock, but it is increased by the $30 which used to be owned by the acquired share. That $30 now belongs to the corporation itself. So, for every share that the corporation buys, it increases the book value of the other outstanding shares by $10. Therefore, purchasing their own stock when it was selling below book value increased the book value of the remaining stock.

Once a company has bought in a share, it no longer pays dividends on that share. After all, it couldn't very well write out a check to itself. Dividends are paid from the company's treasury in after-tax dollars. This means that for the average corporation, it takes almost $2 of earnings to pay out a $1 dividend. By buying in that one share of stock for $20 which was getting a 7% dividend, the company has now saved itself a drain on pretax earnings of $2.80 a year for every share that it buys. That is a big savings on the corporation's till.

Finally, of course, the best effect of all from the shareholders' point of view was that by being a major purchaser of the shares, the corporation was keeping up the price of its own stock. And since every shareholder wants the price of his stock to go up, buying its own stock is one of the more direct ways in which a corporation can support its own shareholders.

In fact, the program of buying in one's own stock made so much sense in many cases that it even paid to borrow in order to make the purchases. With the high costs of interest, that doesn't sound sensible—until one recalls that interest which a corporation pays on money borrowed is fully tax deductible. So, when a corporation borrowed money and paid 12% interest, it was only reducing its after-tax profits by approximately 6%, assuming a 48% corporate tax rate. And if it were paying out a 7% dividend, the corporation showed a profit of 1% on the borrowings. And this was without any risk to the corporation! In fact, most corporations had programs for regularly increasing their dividends. So if they could get a fixed rate loan at 12%, they would be saving more and more money as their dividends were increased each year.

The benefits of a stock-buying program were so strong that many corporations began to initiate plans to acquire really substantial amounts of their own stock. Gulf + Western had a program to buy in 2,300,000 shares of its stock at 15. This represented 4.8% of its outstanding stock and may well have been one of the reasons for the stock price increase in the late seventies. Teledyne bought in 7.3% of its stock, representing 1,065,000 shares, and since theirs were purchased at the price of $88 a share, the value of those purchases was much greater than Gulf + Western's. The brokerage firm of E. F. Hutton decided that what was good for its clients was good for it, too, and it purchased 205,000 shares of its stock for an average price of 16½. Ashland Oil bought a whopping 4,842,000 of its shares at a price of $43 a share, and the biggest purchase of stock in terms of percentage to all outstanding stock was Chris-Craft, which went into a program to buy 31.4% of all the common stock outstanding. Talk about a snake eating its own tail.

These purchases are interesting because never before had so many companies bought so much of their own stock. Companies had always bought small amounts of their stock for specific purposes, such as issuing to employees who exercised stock options granted by the company. But this was a purchase as a normal investment.

To appreciate the unusual nature of these purchases, just imagine a giant corporation set up specifically for one purpose, such as the manufacture and sale of widgets. It has the world's greatest facilities for making widgets and makes an excellent profit from them, and indeed, its business is worldwide and expanding rapidly. It has on its payroll people who are experts in manufacturing, distribution, packaging, advertising, design, and research of widgets; it has bright managers who can make things, top-notch financial people who keep projects on budget—all these hundreds of gifted people ready to take on the next project to make more and better widgets. It has a worldwide reputation which helps it sell to its customers. It has hundreds of millions of dollars of assets assembled so that it is the world leader in widgets. And it has the financial resources to invest in any other type of business which it believes will be profitable.

So what does this company do? Build a new plant? Introduce a new product? Buy out another company? Go into a new line of business? Not at all. It does just what little you or I can do equally well. It decides that the best business it can get into is to purchase its own stock on the open market. And it borrows money from a bank to finance the project, just as if it were opening a new subsidiary in an international market. This is a "business"? Buying in your own stock? But it was profitable.

A third interesting and related development in the late seventies was the small but meaningful number of companies which decided to "go private." This newly created term describes what happens when a company with publicly traded stock decides that the principals of the company and some private outside investors want to buy in all the stock owned by the public and keep it for themselves. This is also known as a "leveraged buyout." Again, this was normally done at prices substantially in excess of the going market rate in order to encourage the existing shareholders to sell their shares. It started slowly with a few companies like Wells, Rich, Greene, the advertising agency, deciding that since the price of their stock was so cheap, they would buy it in themselves.

But it soon went on to much bigger deals. In the spring of 1978 Houdaille Industries, an industrial products corporation with sales of $409 million, was bought by a group headed by Kohlberg, Kravis, Roberts & Co., an investment banking firm. The existing shareholders got $40 a share, more than twice the market price of the stock at the beginning of the year. They were delighted. What is interesting is who would want to pay twice the market price of the stock? Were they a bunch of unsophisticated rubes who were being swindled by some Wall Street sharpies? Hardly. The Kohlberg firm is one of the smartest on Wall Street. The management of Houdaille was a substantial buyer, and they should know something about the value of their own stock. Furthermore, the bulk of the money for the purchase came from large institutions such as Prudential Insurance, which are professional lenders, investors, and risk takers. Presumably they knew very well what Houdaille Industries was worth, and yet these knowledgeable investors paid twice the market price.

In another big leveraged buyout, a group led by First Boston Corp. offered to buy Congoleum Corp. from its public stockholders for $445 million, which was more than twice the value of the common stock just eight months earlier. Until the buyout offer, the stock had been selling at 6 times earnings, and yet the new investors were willing to pay 11 times earnings. An analysis of the cash flow of the company shows, however, that even with the higher price they were willing to pay, they would end up with a payment of about four and a half times cash flow. So, they still appear to have gotten a bargain, even at almost twice the price you or I could have bought the stock for.

The third large leveraged buyout was also started by the Kohlberg firm with an offer to purchase all the common stock of Flintkote Co. for $52 a share, double the value of the stock just eight months earlier. Eventually Genstar Ltd., a Canadian company, made the acquisition for $55 a share. Once again large institutions, which presumably could have bought the stock at the pre-buyout price, preferred to lend money to existing management who would buy the stock at almost twice the price. The point to remember is that the investors behind the buyout had very good reasons for believing that even by paying twice what the stock had been selling for, they would make a great deal of money on the deal. And they are completely professional in their analysis of businesses and where they can make the most money for their bucks.

While all these creative methods were going on to transfer shares of stock from one group to another, another small but noticeable movement was also taking place. Some corporations were simply going out of business by selling off all their assets and paying their shareholders the proceeds. In some cases the corporations only sold off a major part of the business and continued to exist at a much smaller size. In all cases, the amount of money received by the shareholders was greatly in excess of the price of the stock before the announcement of the partial or total liquidation.

The most notable case of this was UV Industries, whose president despaired of ever seeing his company's stock price rise to more than the 2 to 6 times earnings it had been at since 1973. While analysts had been valuing UV's assets as high as $30 to $40 a share, the stock had been selling for less than half of that. The company proceeded to sell off its biggest subsidiary, Federal Pacific Electric Co., representing 60% of UV's sales, for the equivalent of $22 a share, $2 more per share than the whole company had been selling for six months earlier. Then the company liquidated itself. At this writing the final amount of money which will be paid out to each shareholder is not known, but many analysts estimate that it will be between $38 and $40 a share.

An early liquidation was Shenandoah Oil Co., which was liquidated for almost $40 per share, almost double what the stock had been selling for a year earlier.

It isn't easy to liquidate a company, and it certainly isn't popular with most managements. Why should they vote themselves out of a job? What it does do, if successful, is to give the shareholders a lot more money than if they had held on to the stock. Thus, it is usually done only when the management owns a lot of the stock. Also it is not always possible to realize the value of the underlying assets, and so liquidations are easiest with companies that have hard assets, like coal or oil in the ground. Reeves Telecom Corp. owned radio stations and thousands of acres of North and South Carolina real estate. Once the company announced that it hoped to liquidate, its stock went from $2.50 a share to $5.38.

As is the case with everything on Wall Street, there are twenty rumors for every actual liquidation. But it is interesting to note some of the results of the rumors. When *The Wall Street Journal* published a report showing that Vornado, Inc. could be worth $55 a share if it liquidated, the stock jumped 3⅜ the next day to $23 ⅝. Former conglomerator Jimmy Ling and a partner were trying to woo shareholders of Texas International by saying that the assets could be sold for over $20 a share. When they began buying the stock, it went from $9 to $15.

And finally, one of the biggest liquidations never happened. The July 9, 1979, issue of *Forbes* magazine related that when the Canadian firm of Brascan was trying to take over giant F. W.

Woolworth Co., Woolworth's had a plan that if all else failed, rather than give in to the Canadians, the firm was going to announce that it could liquidate for $45 a share. That was interesting because the Woolworth stock hadn't traded as high as $25 for years, and Brascan was offering a generous $35 a share in its takeover effort. The point is that once again, the value which a financially sophisticated acquirer was willing to pay for the stock was 40% higher than the value that the stock market had placed on the shares, and the value which the underlying assets were worth was estimated to be even 28% higher than that.

Strange that a company when dissolved should be worth more than it is valued as a going, profit-making concern. It makes one wonder whether the value of the shares is really reflecting the value of the underlying company. Could it be that the stock market is not really reflecting companies' true value?

Let's go back for a minute to the basic theory of shares in a corporation. A share in a corporation is the ownership of a certain part of that company. The value of all the shares combined represents the value of the company. So if a company is worth $10 million and it has a million shares of common stock outstanding, then each share would be worth $10. If it turns out that the company is worth $20 million, then obviously the shares must be worth $20 each. But what if a company is "worth" $20 million and the shares are still selling for only $10? That is exactly the situation with the companies we have discussed in this chapter.

First is the case of the companies which were bought by other companies. The other companies knew that the takeover candidates were worth far more than the combined value of the shares of stock. And they were willing to put their money where their minds were and put up twice as much as the stocks were selling for in the open market for the privilege of buying the companies. They knew that the price of the stock did not reflect the true value of that stock. They knew that the tape was wrong!

What about all the companies which went private through leveraged buyouts, again at prices up to 2 times the price of the stock? Here we had the best informed people of all, the top management who actually ran the companies, aided by supersharp investment bankers and professional lenders. They also concluded that the stock price was about one-half of what it really was worth. And they also were willing to put their money where their conclusions were. They also paid up to twice the market price of the stock and are convinced that they got a bargain. Once again the price of the stock did not represent the actual value of the stock, and the tape was wrong.

Finally, what about the companies that liquidated? Here we had companies which the stock market valued at certain prices as ongoing money-making corporations. When they stopped making money and simply sold off the various parts of the company, the amount of money received was in some cases twice the price of the stock. Once again, the price of the stock was simply not a true measure of the value of that company. The stock market had made another mistake, and it was not until the ultimate in drastic measures had occurred, the actual death of the company, that Wall Street came to its senses and valued the stock at its actual worth.

Here are three types of transactions which have managed to bring home to investors in dramatic, concrete form that the prices they are paying for stocks are in many cases much less than the companies are actually worth. In the next chapter we will examine in more detail the reasons why stock prices are as they are, and question whether they should be higher. After all, it is only a small percentage of all companies which are ever taken over by another company. And even a smaller number of companies can be bought out by their own management with the help of outsiders. Fewer yet are the number of managements which want to end their careers permanently by liquidating their companies.

So the three types of transactions mentioned in this chapter will never apply to more than a tiny percentage of all companies, and probably not at all to the largest and most important companies. While this chapter has shown instances in which the price of a stock was far less than its true value turned out to be, one must still ask whether this same reasoning is true for all the other companies which are never going to be taken over, never going to be bought out by their managements, and (at least not in our lifetimes) never going to be liquidated.

# 7

# WHERE STOCK PRICES ARE GOING IN THE EIGHTIES

In the first part of this book we saw how stock prices went up in the fifties as investors overcame their fear of a recurrence of the great depression of the 1930's. Prices of the Dow Jones Industrial Average tripled between 1950 and 1960. The stock market success of the fifties led to the excesses of the sixties, which in turn led to the great crashes of 1968 for the lower-priced and small comapnies, followed in 1973 by the collapse of the entire stock market, with the higher P/E stocks leading the dive bombers on their plunge down. Then stocks made a modest recovery, but for the balance of the seventies the stock market just couldn't get anywhere. This chapter will now discuss where the market is going from here.

There is general agreement that by traditional indications of values, stocks are cheap now. The so-called fundamentals are good. That is, the P/E ratios are low compared to historic ratios, dividends are high, and relationship to book values are low. But the arguments cited in Chapter 4 have been raised by many students of the market as reasons why what appear to be cheap fundamentals are really not, once one probes the surface and adjusts the statistics for the many problems facing the economy in the eighties. These problems, many of them never before faced by American industry on such a major scale, include inflation, high interest rates, high taxes, government controls, declining number of shareholders, energy shortages or at least higher energy costs, lower profit margins, and the probability of a coming recession which could be the most severe of the postwar era.

In Chapter 5 we examined these arguments and found that not one of them was a really convincing reason why the stock market had to stay down. High interest rates concern stock market investors only when the market is down, not when it is going up; inflation has been misinterpreted by analysts as being twice as negative for stocks as it ought to be; taxes on many stock transactions have recently been reduced; government controls are not much more onerous than they have been since the 1930's; the declining number of shareholders can easily be reversed if individuals decide that they can once again make money in the stock market; profit margins are as high as they were in the 1950's; worry about a recession is nothing new; and other problems such as the cost of energy are not quite the progress stoppers that some people think.

What the nullification of these negative factors means is that we are now once again free to look at the fundamentals of the stock market to try to determine whether it will be going up or down. That is the only useful method ever found for determining the future course of stock prices. Its basis is as old as the hills and as solid in logic as the rocky Green Mountains of Vermont. The rule is this: When stocks are cheap on their fundamentals, they will go up, and when they are high in terms of their fundamentals, they will go down. The reason that this works is that the stock market contains its own rules of dynamics. After all, stocks do have real inherent value as investments. They represent ownership of corporations which are earning money, which are usually growing, which are often earning more money every year, and which generally are paying their owners more money each year in the form of increasing dividends. This is a valuable feature differentiating stocks from many other "investments," and it enables us to find a measurement of whether they are cheap or expensive.

This type of analysis is simply not possible with some other investments. For example, is an Andy Warhol painting of a Campbell Soup can priced at $4,000 cheap or expensive? The art at first doesn't seem particularly impressive. Anyone can make a stylized reproduction of a Campbell Soup can. Go to an art dealer and he will be able to tell you the price history of those soup can paintings. They may originally have sold for so much, then they went way up in price, and now perhaps they have come down. But in terms of *inherent value,* are they now cheap or expensive at the price which this one is offered to you? What is the true value of that soup can painting as opposed to its current price? There is absolutely no way to find out.

Because the soup can painting is worth only what someone is willing to pay for it, there is no inherent financial value in it. It will never pay a dividend; thus, there is no way of determining its true value. The history of its price during the past fifteen years is of only limited assistance because if that particular style of painting goes out of style, the painting may become worth almost nothing, and there will be absolutely no assurance that it will ever come back into style. In fact, one of the reasons these paintings have been so valuable may simply be the fact that they are expensive and therefore there is a certain snob appeal in hanging one on the wall of your living room. If this theory is correct, then if the price goes down, possession of one of those paintings could classify its owner as passé rather than "in." Suddenly everyone could be trying to sell his old soup can paintings and the price could just melt away like an ice cream cone in July.

In short, there is really no inherent value to a soup can painting in terms of an investment. Any art expert can list for you the number of fads which have come and gone in the art world. A few have come back, like art deco, but many have never come back, and what once were expensive objets d'art are now collecting dust in attics all over America.

The price of faddish art can almost be compared to the level of a great battleship which is in a battle at sea and suffers a hit. The first hit may let in some water and the ship sinks a little lower. As the ship sinks lower, it becomes harder to move ahead, and as the ship slows down it becomes an easier target for the enemy. The lower in the water it gets, the more water comes in, and the more likely it is that it will finally sink. This is exactly what can happen to the price of a modern painting, a Coca-Cola bottle top collection from the 1920's, or anything else without inherent value. It is valuable only when the whims of collectors or speculators at that moment are willing to assign it value. Let the mood change, and presto, the value has disappeared.

Much of the gloom and doom involving the stock market arises from a basic misconception that stocks are like knickknacks and fads, which have value only if someone is willing to buy them at a specific price at a certain time. The basic purpose of this book is to point out that that is not the case with common stocks. Stocks are not worth only what a person is willing to pay for them on the floor of the stock exchange at a particular moment. That may be the current price, but it is not necessarily the value of the stock. And no matter what the current price of the stock is, it still has a true value.

The value lies in the fact that a stock has the potential to earn money for its owner as an ongoing investment, not just by being sold to produce a capital gain. If a new law were passed today saying that it was henceforth illegal ever to buy or sell a stock again, they would still be valuable because of this right to obtain future dividends. What would an Andy Warhol soup can painting be worth as an investment if a law were passed saying that it could never be bought or sold again?

And so we begin to see that stocks are different from many other kinds of investments in that there is an inherent value to them. They have a real worth, independent of their current price, and the only method of determining that true worth is to look at the fundamentals of the company and the stock. As the fundamentals of the stock get better, that stock is selling for less than its true worth. As the fundamentals look worse, the stock is selling for more than its true worth.

What are these fundamentals? Probably the most important is the P/E ratio which we have discussed before. The more earnings you get for each dollar you pay for the stock, the cheaper the stock is. Historically you can plot the price earnings ratios of the Dow Jones Industrial Average and see that for more than four decades, since 1936, P/E ratios have ranged from a high of 25 times earnings to a low of about 7 times earnings. Every time they got below 10 times earnings they came up again. In mid-1980 they are at approximately 7 times earnings, which is almost equal to the all-time low. (See Chart 3.)

Objectors to the fundamental approach to investing argue that this is too simple, that there are valid reasons why stocks should be at a low P/E right now, and that because times are so uncertain and difficult, it does not mean that they are a bargain today. That is why we spent so much time in Chapters 4 and 5 discussing the reasons given for believing that times today are different. Since we discovered that they are not so different at all, we are free to draw our own conclusion. The only conclusion one can draw from this chart of 45 years on Wall Street is that the time to buy stocks is when they are cheap on their fundamentals, and that the most important fundamental of all is the price earnings ratio. After all, the reason for buying stock in the first place is to get your hands on the earnings of the company.

A second fundamental is the relationship of the stock price to the value of the underlying assets of the company. This is called the relationship to book value. Chart 4 shows the high and low closing prices for the Dow Jones Industrial Averages for every year from 1935 to late 1979. It also has a line indicating book value, and another one above it indicating when stocks are selling at 2 times book value. As is readily apparent, for the past few years the Dow Jones Industrial Average has been below book a number of times. A

## CHART 3

### *P/E Ratio of the Dow Jones Average*

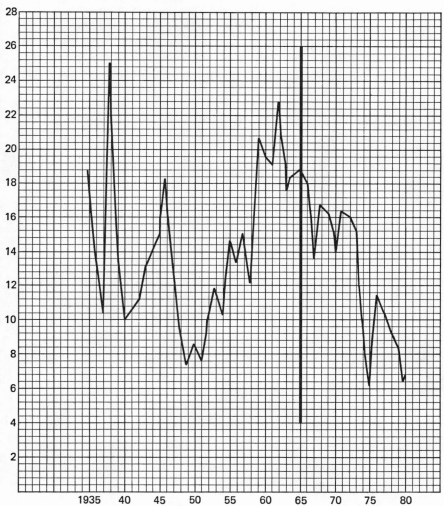

Note that since 1963 there has been a strong trend down-ward until in 1980 it was even lower than it was in 1949. That part of the chart to the right of the vertical line corresponds to the period shown on the DJIA chart at the front of this book.

survey of the chart shows that this has been the case only two times previous to this, in 1942 and in 1949. As a further look at the chart reveals, both of these times would have been excellent times to make purchases. Within three years of 1942 the average had almost doubled, and in six years after 1949 the average went from 160 up to 400 for an increase of 150%. The lows of 1974 and 1975 were the lowest points ever, in terms of being below book value. So far the average has already rewarded anyone who bought below book value in those years when the Dow Jones average was below 750.

## CHART 4

Common Stock Prices Are Low Relative to Book Value

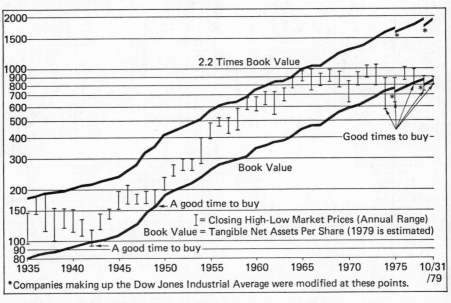

*Companies making up the Dow Jones Industrial Average were modified at these points.

Dow-Jones Industrial Average Yearly High-Low vs. Book Value

The third fundamental indicator which is often useful is the dividend rate. Here Chart 5, based this time upon the Standard & Poor's 400 Industrials, shows that dividends are almost as high in 1980 as they have been at any time since 1951. And of course 1952 was a sensational year for buying stocks.

Based upon these three fundamentals, the real value of stocks has been getting better and better. As stock prices have floundered around for the past fourteen years, the underlying performances of the companies have been getting better and better. Thus, while the prices of the stocks have gotten worse, the actual real worth of the stocks has been increasing. And when the real

## CHART 5

### Dividend Yields

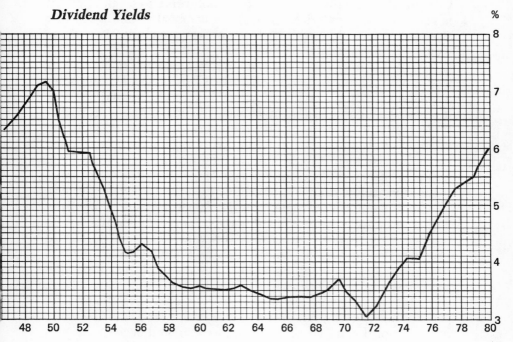

worth, as measured by the three fundamentals mentioned above, are plugged into current prices of the stocks, the results are an indication that now is an excellent time to buy. The fundamental values are there. And when the fundamental values are there, the odds are that prices of the stocks will soon go up. It has always happened that way, and there is no reason to believe that it will not happen that way again. In fact, one of the reasons cited by the bears as to why one should disregard the fundamentals is the very reason why the stocks should go into a near explosive growth within the very near future.

That reason is inflation. In previous chapters we saw how inflation has been incorrectly used as an excuse for low stock prices. Now we are going to learn why inflation itself is one of the reasons why stock prices are going to move up. As we noted from Chart 4, showing the relationship of book value to stock prices, it is very rare for stock prices to be below book value, and when that situation occurs, it generally does not last very long. This alone would be reason enough to buy stocks now.

But in addition, there is an even stronger reason for buying stocks now below book value, and that is that the book value is not a constant factor but is rising inexorably for two reasons. The first is simply that corporations are constantly ploughing a large part of their profits back into assets. For every year that they are in existence and earning a profit, they are increasing their book value by amounts of up to 50% or more of their net earnings. The second reason is that in many cases, because of inflation, the stated book value is far below the real book value measured in current prices.

Let's take an extreme example: a paper products company which owns vast expanses of timberland. That land is valued at its original cost to the company. If the land were just purchased recently, the book value would be a fairly accurate reflection of its true value. But if the company is an old one and the timberland were first acquired in the early 1800's, then it would have a book value of perhaps just a few dollars an acre. And with the price of paper going up each year, the true value of that land could be many hundreds of dollars an acre. But under standard accounting procedures, the timber company is not allowed to increase the value of that land on its balance sheet. No matter how much the land is really worth, it will stay on the balance sheet with a value of its original purchase cost. So with each year of inflation, the book value becomes more and more an imaginary number which bears little relationship to the true value.

The same thing will be true, to a lesser degree, of almost any type of manufacturing concern. The land on which its factories are built has undoubtedly gone up in value many times since it was originally purchased, the buildings are probably worth more, the trademarks are worth more, and yet none of this is reflected on the balance sheet of the company. The point is that as inflation goes on, the book value itself becomes more and more understated, and so if a company's stock is selling below even that understated book value, it must be really cheap!

Another basic way in which inflation works to bring up stock prices is that as long as we continue to have inflation, and provided there is no major recession, the earnings of companies will undoubtedly keep going up and up. I am not predicting here that we will be in a major growth period of the economy or that business is going to pick up. Let us assume that we are in for a very hard time of it and that things get so bad that we actually have zero economic growth for the next ten years.

Accepting arguendo that pessimistic scenario, inflation itself, at let's say 10% a year, will boost the prices which companies charge for their products by 10% a year, and since there is no indication that profit margins are decreasing, that means that corporate profits will continue to increase by 10% a year for the next ten years. Now, if profits continue to rise 10% a year, only two things can happen to the price of the stocks of those corporations. Either the prices will rise by 10% a year, or the P/E ratios will continue to decline. As we noted, P/E ratios are already near historic lows. Any further decrease in the ratios would bring them into new record-breaking lows.

Let's examine this a little more thoroughly. In mid-1980 the Dow Jones Industrial Average had a P/E of just over 7 times earnings, with the average at 880 and the earnings of the average at 125. If these earnings increase by 10% in the next twelve months, they will be at 137.5 next year. If the prices of the stocks stay at the same level, the P/E of the average will be down to 6.4. If profits go up by only 10% again the next year, the earnings will be 150. If stock prices stayed at the 880 level, that would mean that the P/E ratio of the average would have sunk to 5.87, which would be lower than ever in the recent history of the average. If one follows this out even one more year, it becomes almost absurd. Another 10% increase in earnings would bring them to 165, and dividing that into 880 gives a P/E ratio of 5.33.

There is no reason to prolong this exercise. Obviously, if earnings continue to increase because of inflation and stock prices do not go up, the P/E ratio will become so absurd that it will eventually be selling at 2 times earnings, and finally at one times earnings. And if the dividend payout ratio stays where it is now at about 40% of earnings, the dividends will go up to a 20% yield, which is hard to imagine even with the present high interest rate climate.

In short, there are not two possibilities in the face of long-term inflation. The P/E of stocks cannot constantly fall. Eventually it will reach such a low figure that it becomes absurd. This means that there is only one other possible result: The prices of stocks must go up.

Not only will the P/E go up, but the earnings on which the ratio is based will go up. This means that there will be a double whammy which will bring stock prices up faster than most people would even dream.

In fact, the first part of this trend has already started. A look at the Dow Jones Industrial Average (see frontspiece) from 1965 to 1980 reveals no trend whatsoever. Anyone looking at that chart would be correct in concluding that it is merely a meandering line with no apparent direction. It could just as well be the annual rainfall in the Amazon Basin of Brazil. Some years are very wet, and some are not, but after a century of more of keeping records, there is just about as much rainfall in an average year today as there was in 1880. And so those who are pessimistic about the market see only the prices and predict that the market is not going to do anything for the foreseeable future.

But those who know that the market contains its own dynamic forces concentrate on the fundamentals which move the market and provide the powerful springs which will propel it upward. One of those springs is the P/E. So while others are seeing no trend at all by looking at the DJIA prices, we will look at the P/E's on Chart 3. Now if we start with 1968, a trend is clearly visible. This chart has direction. The P/E has been wildly gyrating, but at least we can see that today it is decidedly below where it was in 1968. Clearly, this is the type of trend which cannot continue. The P/E could stay down where it is, but as we discussed above, even if it stayed stable, the increase in earnings due to inflation alone will result in stock price increases of 10% a year.

In fact, as a glance at the long-term P/E chart suggests, it is not very likely that the P/E will stay where it is. Rather, if history repeats itself, and it usually does, the P/E will climb again. A climbing P/E superimposed over climbing earnings can result in only one thing: rapidly increasing stock prices. And this is not even taking into account the fact that we are in a growing economy and that even with all the gloom and doom around we still have a real economic growth of about 2% to 3% a year. There's another boost for stock prices.

So, dividend yields have been going up and are going to go higher in the future. The P/E ratio is down and is going to go lower unless stock prices go up, and the discount from book is going to steepen, even as book values become a smaller and smaller percentage of true value of a going corporation. It is easy to see that none of these trends can continue forever; if stock prices stayed where they are now while income of corporations rose year after year, the P/E would reach absurdly low levels, dividends would reach absurdly high percentages, and stocks would be selling at such a steep discount from actual value that taking over corporations and liquidating them would become the national pastime.

Nevertheless, there is always the doubting Thomas who says: "Sure, stock prices are cheap, but they're going to get cheaper. I don't want to hear about all this theoretical stuff. P/E's can get a lot lower than they are now, dividend yields can get a lot higher as they both have in the past, and the relationship of a stock's price to book value never has sent the prices up in the past. Don't give me theories, I've heard enough of them from my brokers in the past. The only reason stocks go up is because more people want to buy them than sell them, and P/E's, dividends, and book values alone don't get people to buy stocks." So, Mr. Thomas wants to know, what is going to make people buy stocks?

As we admitted, stocks have been the worst investment of all in the past fourteen years, and there don't seem to be any signs that they are getting better. So, until our doubting Thomas sees people rushing into their local brokerage offices demanding to buy stocks, he is going to keep putting his money into real estate, commodities, Chinese porcelain, stamps, diamonds, and paintings by the old masters.

And do you know what? Mr. Thomas is right. Right, that is, about one thing. Stock prices don't go up simply because the P/E is low or dividends are high. That's what has disillusioned investors for the past five years. It is true that stock prices go up only when there is a greater demand for shares by buyers than there is supply available from sellers. In the next chapter we are going to look closely at the supply side of the market and then at the demand side, and you can see for yourself exactly why I believe the market is going to go up and why it will go up much further than most people think.

# 8

# *THE THREE WAVES OF BUYING THAT WILL CAUSE THE NEXT BULL MARKET*

Stocks go up for only one reason. The price increase starts when there are more investors who want to buy the shares at the current price than there are sellers interested in selling at that price. So there is a stalemate, and nothing happens. The specialist on the floor of the stock exchange may quote the stock 37½ to 37¾. This means that there are people willing to buy the stock for 37½, and there are people willing to sell it at 37¾, but since they are one-quarter of a point apart, nothing happens. After a while, one of the potential buyers decides that he has waited long enough for a seller to come along with stock to sell at 37½, so he tells his broker that he is willing to pay 37¾ for the stock. He buys it at that price, and it has now gone up by one-quarter of a point. However, the specialist may still be quoting the stock the same way, that is, bid 37½, asked 37¾.

But suppose that the buyer is a large institution and it wants to purchase 10,000 shares. Perhaps there are only 1,000 for sale at the offering price of 37¾. Since the institution is willing to pay 37¾ for 10,000, it will pick up the 1,000 offered, and it will then make a bid at the higher price of 37¾. This now becomes the bid, and the specialist will look on his book to see if anyone earlier gave him an order to sell some stock at 37⅞ or 40. If so, that will become the new offering price. If there are no sellers on the book, the specialist himself may offer some stock at that price, believing that after the institution completes its purchase, he will be able to buy it back in at a lower price. In any event, the new quote becomes 37¾ to 38.

At this higher quote, some people who wanted to purchase will decide to wait until the price drops back, and some people who had been merely contemplating selling the stock will decide that if they can get 38 for it, it will be a good sale. If the institution decides that it wants to get the other 9,000 shares badly enough, it will decide that it can pay 38 for them and it will purchase some more. So, every time someone purchases stock, he tends to make the stock go up, and the more he purchases, the more the stock tends to go up.

Similarly, if there are no sellers around to sell at the bid price, then the stock will also be forced up. Following one of the most basic laws of economics, the price of stock will always find that level where the forces of supply exactly match the forces of demand. I believe the new bull market is going to come about because of changes on both sides of that equation. First, the supply of stock for sale is going to shrink, and then the demand by purchasers is going to increase. Let's examine the supply side first.

As we have noted frequently in this book, stocks have been the worst investment one could make over the past fourteen years. And for many unhappy investors, the "solution" to this problem was to get out. You don't stick with a sinking ship or pour good money after bad. The mutual funds sold stock, individual investors sold stock, and institutions almost stopped buying stock. But like all trends, this one cannot last forever. Mutual funds cannot go on forever selling stock, because after a while they will have no more stock to sell. When that occurs, there will be a substantial drop in the supply side of the equation.

Just when will that happen? In late 1979 and early 1980 mutual funds became net buyers of stocks once again. Whether this trend will continue we don't know, but in any event, the conclusion is absolutely clear: Here is one large source of selling which is rapidly coming to an end. This drying up of a truly major source of stock will help tilt the balance of supply and demand in favor of higher prices.

The second largest source of stock being sold has been the individual investor. While there are no accurate statistics kept on individual investors as there are of mutual funds, we can make some fairly sound projections. First, it is probably safe to state that many individual investors act in the stock market just as the mutual funds do. After all, mutual funds are owned by individuals, and the funds sell stock only when their individual shareholders decide to sell their shares in the mutual fund. When individuals who own mutual funds decide to sell, there is a large likelihood that individuals who own stock directly also are deciding to sell. They are both individual investors who made a choice at one time to be in the stock market, one deciding to do it through a mutual fund and the other deciding to do it directly. As the redemption of mutual fund shares slows, it is logical to assume that many individual shareholders are also no longer net sellers.

There are some statistics on individuals which suggest that this is happening. The most obvious is that individuals simply don't own as much stock as they once did, and you can sell a stock only when you own it. In 1979, the number of people owning stock had shrunk from 25 million in 1970 down to an estimated 20 million; 5 million people had sold all the stock they owned. That obviously had a depressing effect on the market. But the bright side is that those 5 million people can never again cause the market to decline, because they are no longer a potential selling group, and 5 million people is a pretty substantial selling group.

But these figures do not tell the whole story. The people who sold their stock were those who either really needed the money for some other purpose, or simply were in the market for short-term or speculative purposes, or were simply fainthearted. What this means is that there has been a process of selection at work. Those who sold their stock were the ones who perhaps were not sophisticated and expected too much too fast. There must be a clear demographic profile of those 5 million who sold their stock as contrasted with the 20 million who did not. We know that those who did not are older, and because they have not already sold, they are by definition those who are not as likely to sell in the future. They are the ones who have owned the stock for years, are holding it for its dividends, feel comfortable owning common stock over any other type of investment, and just are not likely to sell, no matter what happens.

The individual stockholder at this point can be compared with the owners of houses in a new development. When the houses are first built, the new owners include those who are transient because of their jobs, those who perhaps never owned houses before and are straining to make the mortgage payments, and those who want to stay there for a lifetime. Let a few years go by, perhaps hard times come and the development is less elegant, and a lot of people will move out. First to leave are those who were transient to start with, then those who never had any real attachment to that neighborhood, then those who cannot keep up the payments, and gradually you have a turnover of owners.

However, if you take a survey of those original owners who are still there ten years later, you will find a hard core of loyal homeowners who are staying for life. They have made this their home, they like the neighbors, they like the houses, and they ain't moving no matter what happens. They have formed a civic improvement association, they are working to improve their homes and the area, and by God they are going to stay!

In far less dramatic ways this is what has happened to the individual owners of stock in the last decade. The ones who are left now are the real loyalists, the ones who fiercely believe in the long-range benefits of owning common stock, and the ones who aren't going to sell no matter what happens. They certainly are not going to sell now if stock prices go down or stay where they are, because these shareholders have seen prices lower before and they didn't sell then, so there is no reason for them to sell now. Thus another source of large chunks of stock being thrown onto the market—the individual—has now been greatly diminished.

Finally, we turn to the institutions such as the pension plans, insurance companies, bank trust departments, and university endowments. As noted earlier, institutions at one time were large buyers of common stocks, but during the late seventies they almost stopped entirely. In fact, there has not been a single year when institutions were actually net sellers of common stock, but as a result of the many lean years of buying stocks, the institutions have now gotten their ratio of common stock down to 50% of the value of their entire investment. This is a low figure, but there is no law of economics that says it couldn't go lower. However, reading the trade press of institutional investors, one picks up the sense that this is about where they want to be, and surveys of money managers indicate that they are happy with the present mix. This means that they do not intend to be great sellers of stock in the near future.

Thus, a survey of three major categories of shareholders indicates that all three are pretty well sold out. Although anything can happen in the future, and probably will, we know for a fact that the mutual funds simply don't have the stock to sell that they once had. We know for a fact that there are 5 million ex-shareholders who don't have any stock to sell, and we also know for a fact that the existing shareholders have been through a lot in the way of tough markets and they haven't sold out in the past, so we can safely conclude that they are in for the long term and are not likely to be big sellers in the future. Finally, we saw the institutions do a massive reduction in the proportion of their assets in common stock, but such a change happens only once in twenty years and is not likely to happen again; they will not be coming nearly as close as they did to being net sellers of common stock. In short, the sellers of common stock are drying up.

I am not saying that there is not going to be stock for sale. Obviously there are tens of millions of shares sold daily. But that is normal, and makes for a normal market as long as there is as much demand for shares as there is supply of shares to be sold. What I am saying is that the days of huge excesses of stock for sale appear to be over. And since there are always buyers of stocks around, when the normal supply of sellers begins to dry up, there is going to be upward pressure on stock prices.

Now let's take a look at the buy side. Even if the sellers do dry up, stock prices can go up only if there are buyers out there. And by "buyers" we don't mean merely lookers, but people who have large amounts of money which they are willing and able to commit to the stock market, now, and at prices which are higher than the present prices. Let's take a detailed look at how the next bull market could come about.

Please understand that what follows is an oversimplification of one possible scenario. I am going to divide the potential buyers into groups, and discuss one group at a time. Actually, in the real world, all the different groups would be buying at more or less the same time, and many buyers would not be part of any group I am going to discuss, such as brokerage firms buying for their own accounts. But what follows is a logical progression which I believe is likely to happen. Please also remember that there are always buyers and sellers of every type, and what I am talking about is the net excess buyers who make the market go up.

First will come the foreigners. Foreigners are going to be large purchasers of American stock for a number of reasons. The first requirement is that they have money. And money they do have. With the decline of the U.S. dollar and the appreciation of the German deutsche mark and the Japanese yen, along with other European currencies, foreigners have plenty of money, especially when translated into U.S. dollars. That they have enough to make a major impact upon the American stock market was dramatically shown in the 80-point rise in the DJIA in April 1978, which was attributed primarily to buying by foreigners. Not only do the foreigners have the money, but there are many persuasive reasons why they will probably become bigger buyers of U.S. stocks.

The first is that while Americans often tend to see this country as leaning toward socialism with more and more centralized government, most foreigners regard the United States as the last major bastion of free enterprise. We tend to forget that in parts of Italy almost half the voters are actually communists, and that in most European countries socialism is already an accepted way of life. Foreigners believe that the United States is the one place capitalism will survive. Thus, there is a very favorable political climate for foreign investment.

Also foreigners know the industrial and agricultural might of America. Those of us who live here tend to take for granted just how important the United States is in the world economy. Travel overseas and you will eat food which may well have been imported from the United States, you will travel on airplanes more likely than not manufactured in the United States, and while you are shopping for local curios in the tourist shops, you may not realize that your sales are being rung up on a computer probably made in the United States. Foreign armies are equipped with numerous American weapons, their television programs are often reruns of ours with translated sound dubbed in, and of course our movies dominate the world. What may be even more surprising, considering the large sales of imported cars in the United States, is that American auto companies provide most of the cars in the rest of the world through plants located in almost every major country. Thus, for foreigners, investing in American stocks is often purchasing shares in companies which they already know and respect.

But there is a more practical reason as well for foreigners to buy American stocks. They are often better values than they can get in their home markets. Let's compare P/E ratios on some major stock exchanges around the world. While stocks in the United States were selling at a P/E of 8.2 and paying a dividend of 5.4%, at the end of July 1980, in Switzerland they had a P/E of 12.3. Norway and Australia were both 11 times earnings, but Japan had a P/E of 17.7 for its average stock. That's 116% more than the U.S. average P/E. So when foreigners with money are looking for a place to buy more stocks, where are they going to buy them? Right here in the good old U.S.A.

There are two reasons why there has not been more buying by foreigners recently. First is the same reason why Americans have not been buying: They lost money when stocks went down. But an additional reason is that foreigners must bear the burden of changing foreign currency exchange rates. For example, if a German buys U.S. stock, he lays out deutsche marks, which are then converted into U.S. dollars to make the purchase. If, after he has bought the stock, the dollar declines in relation to the mark, as it has done in the past, then he will lose money even if the price of the stock stays unchanged. So, as long as it looks as though the dollar is declining against foreign currencies, there will not be buying by foreigners. But let the dollar stabilize as it did in the spring of 1978, and foreigners will come back into the market, because the U.S. stock market offers the political stability, the industrial power, and the values they are looking for.

My scenario is that, as the dollar begins to firm up in foreign exchanges, foreigners will begin to purchase large amounts of stock. In the first quarter of 1980, for example, they were net purchasers of $2.1 billion of stock, a new record. Coupled with the dwindling amount of stock for sale, these purchases will produce an upward price movement on stocks. As the stocks begin to move, the stage is set for the second and major source for the next bull market. That is the institutions.

As history has shown, institutions are not necessarily any better at getting investment results than anyone else. They do most of their buying when the market is high, and they do most of their selling when it is low. You might therefore conclude that they are not any smarter than anyone else, which should be an encouraging fact for the ordinary investor. But one big difference between institutional investors and individual investors is that the institutions are much better informed about what is going on in the marketplace, and they are much more competitive.

Whereas an active investor may call his broker once a day to check up on his stocks, the professional investors are constantly monitoring their portfolios and comparing them with other portfolios. The professional money managers receive a mass of information each day which is a burden simply to digest. Bond portfolios are compared as to safety, yield, and prices; stock portfolios are compared as to volatility, safety, dividend yield, and price appreciation. Portfolios are compared as to how much is in cash or equivalents and how much is invested in stocks and how much in bonds.

Those not familiar with the world of institutional investing would be surprised to learn that there is an entire subindustry which does nothing but compare the performance of various funds, and there is hot competition among a number of companies, each of which claims that they do the best job of measuring the performance of the various institutions. For the individual investor who simply multiplies the number of his shares by the last price and adds up the results, it seems perplexing that there can be any problem in measuring the performance of investments. But the professional investors want to be compared not just on how well they did, but on how much risk they took, on how well they are likely to do if the market goes up, and on how much income they are getting annually. So, it gets pretty complicated.

But the result of all this emphasis on measurement is that each portfolio manager knows each week exactly where he stands in relationship to other money managers. If other funds begin to do better than he is doing, he knows about it fast, and he takes action fast. The reason that he takes action fast is that in addition to being well informed, the professional money managers are extremely competitive, and there is not a great deal of loyalty among the institutions which have the money to invest.

Typically a large pension plan will have a number of money managers, perhaps twenty or more. The plan sponsors, whether they are unions or companies, are monitoring the results of the various managers, and frequently decide to drop the managers with the worst record. At the same time, those managers with superior investment records are sending out their salesmen to all the investors and showing what a wonderful job they did in investing money. So it is an easy switch for a company, union, or university to dump any manager who is not doing well and hire one who is. Therefore, doing well for a professional manager is not just a question of making more money, as it is for most of us, but truly a question of actual survival. If he doesn't do as well as his competitors, and there are hundreds of competitors in this business, he is not going to be in business very long. Hence, the pressure to perform well is intense and never ending. Relative standings of various money managers can change overnight, and everyone knows what everyone else is doing.

Now into this fluid type of situation we have the present investment posture of most managers, which is to have about 50% of their assets in stocks, perhaps 35% to 40% in bonds, and the balance in short-term investments. Let us suppose that stock prices have been slowly gaining, due to the buying by foreigners and the dwindling supply of sellers which we described earlier. This means that as the results of the various money managers are announced each week, those managers who have more of their assets in the stock market are going to be doing better than those who have a larger proportion in cash and bonds.

Remember that the interest on a short-term investment with no downside risk may seem great when the stock market is going down, but the stock market can go up 5% in one month, as it did, for example, in August 1979. This means that in one month the stock market almost equaled what those other investments did in six months or more, and that is in capital gains alone, ignoring the dividend yield of the stocks! So it isn't very difficult to see that as the stock market begins to go up, those money managers who have large proportions of their funds in stocks are going to look good. And as the market goes up, there will be pressure on the others to begin to commit more of their money to stocks also.

The worst thing that could happen to a money manager is to be left owning cash and bonds when a major bull market gets underway; once that has happened, there is no way on earth that he can catch up with his competitors, and he knows it. Furthermore, professional managers are very well informed, and they know that stocks are very cheap right now on their fundamentals. They also know that there is plenty of cash around. In other words, the professionals realize that if a stock market rally ever began, it could just keep on going. The institutions have over $30 billion on the sidelines just waiting to invest when they believe that the market is about to start its rise. And with that much money around, it will be very easy for stock prices to rocket up.

Of course, as always in the past, there will be many professional money managers who will watch stocks move up and will sit back and decry what they see as a "bear trap." They will say that the rise is only temporary and that people who buy stocks then at the new higher prices will regret it in the future. They will sit on their cash and perhaps take advantage of the higher prices to sell out some stocks. But these sellers will be in the minority for the simple reason that almost all institutions now have as low a proportion of their money in stock as they wish to. They are definitely not interested in selling more stock. The result is that there will be few sellers. And as the prices of stocks start inching up, those holdouts who are not buying stocks are going to look worse and worse.

In addition to the constant measurement and intense competition which professional money managers undergo, there are periodic reviews in which the manager is called in by the institutions and asked to explain his recent performance. If the stock market has been going up and a money manager has an unusually heavy proportion of his money in bonds and cash, he is going to look bad. The institutions will start asking about the fact that the market is going up and he seems to be missing out on it. Of course, he *could* continue to say that he believes the market will go down, but that takes some courage, as well as making the manager very vulnerable at the next review if the market has continued up. ("Remember that last time, George, we pointed out to you very clearly the risk you were taking by being overly committed to bonds and cash. Now your performance has suffered.")

With the old saying "three strikes and you're out" applying here, it isn't difficult to see that if George is wrong one more time, he may not be around to defend his views again. In other words, as the market goes up, it will be much easier for a money manager to pick up a few thousand shares of stock before the review meeting and be able to say, "I didn't want to rush in and buy stock when the market was still trying to find its way, because we've been burned before and I didn't want to take any needless risks with your money. But now that there is some confirmation that a better market is here to stay, it seemed appropriate to commit some more of our money already earmarked for stocks." Good talking, George. Those guys don't get to be professional money managers unless they are very good at explaining things. And so George and hundreds of people like him are going to start buying stocks.

And what they are going to find is that as they and their colleagues go into the market to buy sizeable chunks of stock for the first time in many years, there just isn't going to be so much stock for sale. Therefore they are going to have to pay more for the stock. And as prices of stocks go up, those portfolios which already are loaded with stock are going to look better and better, while those which have shunned stock in favor of bonds will be looking worse and worse. Hence, there will be ever more pressure on those who have not bought stocks to get in and buy them fast.

The only way they will be able to catch up with those who bought stocks earlier will be to buy a larger amount. And so the self-fulfilling prophecy will begin to work. As more and more big money comes into the market from institutions which have been sitting on cash for years, the prices of stock are going to move up smartly. And as the prices of stocks move up, they are going to look like a better and better investment, and there will be more and more pressure to buy even more.

Just how far can this cycle go before it begins to run out of steam? We don't even have to ask that question right now, because it will be years before anyone has to concern himself with the answer. In the first place, the new money flowing into institutions is about $30 billion a year. Therefore, if the institutions want to increase the amount of equities in their portfolios, they can commit any or all of that money to equities. To simply maintain the ratio of 50% equities which they now have, they will be net purchasers of $15 billion worth of common stock each year. Just what does this mean in terms of the stock market as a whole?

One way to measure the effect this money would have is to look at the average daily trading volume and see how much that is in dollars. Let's assume an average day of 30 million shares. In that day the total dollar amount of all the shares bought would be about $900 million. Thus, the excess purchasing power of the institutions each year, if they don't try to increase their present percentage of equities, is equal to about seventeen days' purchases, and that is almost one entire month of trading days. While one month out of a year may not seem like a major factor, remember that these are additional net purchases, on top of the regular purchases which occur every day. This is buying without any counterbalancing selling. This is the kind of buying which can only pull the prices of stocks up. If you take a year's volume of purchases and sales, and then add on to it seventeen full days' purchases, that is going to have a profound effect upon prices, because only an increase in prices is going to lure from out of the vaults the equivalent of an additional seventeen days' worth of sales!

But this is only part of the story. If institutions decide that they want to increase the percentage of their holdings which are in equities, then obviously they will spend more than 50% of their yearly net additional funds on common stocks. In order to get them more into line with historical patterns, the institutions could easily decide to devote 75% of their new money each year to stocks, which would mean $22.5 billion a year in new net purchases. This is equal to an additional 25 days or five weeks. That represents a lot of buying.

There is even more, however. For the past two or three years the institutions have not even been spending the money on stocks which has been earmarked for stock purchases. When short-term interest rates were up to over 15%, it was easy to park the money in a safe place and pick up the interest while waiting for the stock market to settle down. What all this means is that there is now a cash pool sitting in the institutional coffers just waiting to come into the market as soon as stock prices begin to move up. How much money is there sitting in these temporary quarters? The latest estimates place this amount at $30 billion. While some of this money will undoubtedly always be in short-term investments, most of the money is clearly destined for a permanent home as soon as the money managers decide that the time is right. Perhaps

$20 billion of that will be committed to permanent investments, and all of that could go into the stock market.

The significance of this upon the stock market surpasses even the $15 to $25 billion of annual contributions which we discussed above. That money comes in through the year and will be invested more or less as it comes in, as part of a regular pattern which would have a slow but continuing effect upon the market. The $30 billion which is now in short-term cash is ready to go tomorrow. Almost the entire amount could be committed to the stock market in a matter of a few months. It is like an airborne division at the ready: In just a few hours the entire division can be in the air and ready to attack the very next day on some foreign shores. So is this money prepared to jump into the stock market at a moment's notice. And it is only a matter of time before it does.

So, on top of the $15 to $25 billion which will now be flowing into the stock market each year, we have a one-time shock wave of perhaps $20 billion which could be committed almost all at once. The effect upon stock prices could be astounding. We are now talking about a total of up to 45 trading days additional net purchasing power. That's equal to all the buying done in two entire months! And remember, this is net additional purchases thrown on top of the regular buying which goes on every day. That is going to produce a lot of big increases in stock prices. And when it is over, the institutions at the end of the year will still not be very far from having the lowest percent of their assets in equities that they have ever had.

In other words, all this buying will not have put them in an overbought situation by a long shot. It would merely put them in an ordinary situation where they are still very lean on equities and still have plenty of room for more purchases should they decide to go back to a more normal mix of equities and fixed income assets. But even as the highly competitive institutions are jumping over each other to start buying stocks so that their own portfolios will not be left behind, the third wave of buyers will begin to come into the picture.

The third wave of buyers, and the ones who I believe will really make this market move, are the members of the public. I have listed them last because they are now not in the market in any meaningful way. As noted earlier, the number of individual shareholders has gone down from 25 million to 20 million, and the equities which individuals own have become far less important to them. In 1965, 43% of people's financial assets were comprised of common stocks, and in 1979 that had dropped to an estimated 20%. That enormous drop indicates that for most people the stock market just isn't very important. They have been burned badly by the stock market, and it is going to take more than a little rally to get them to come back in.

Furthermore, individuals have been putting their money into other investments, primarily real estate, which is not very liquid. Therefore, even if they wanted to take their money out of real estate and put it into the stock market, it would be difficult and time consuming to do so. In fact, so deep is the distrust of much of the public for the stock market that in just the brief period of four years, from 1976 to 1980, they have managed to squirrel away in money market funds over $75 billion. Considering all this, what makes me think that the public can be counted on to be the third wave of buyers who will push stock prices to new all-time records?

Very simple, and very basic. On Wall Street they say that there are only two factors which motivate people to invest or not to invest, fear and greed. When the market is falling, it is fear which makes people get out, even if it means selling stocks or bonds at far less than most people think they are really worth. And when the market is going up, it is greed which impels people to buy stock, even when it is priced far higher than most rational people believe is fair. Right now, we have a public which is still basically motivated by fear of the market, and so they are investing in other things. As they say on Broadway, if your show is a bust, nothing in the world can keep the crowds from staying away in droves. That is the present situation on Wall Street.

Now let us assume that the foreigners have come in and done enough buying to send the market up about 100 points. Then the institutions got interested and they came in in force and sent the market up another 200 or 300 points. All this time, there have been some individual investors who never gave up hope and who have been buying stocks and options on stocks for years, but since their speculations and investments didn't usually work out very well, they never talked about them. Success has a thousand fathers, but failure is always an orphan. So, all the little investments which didn't work out were forgotten and buried in a secret compartment of our mind where we each keep our little failures, safe from the scrutiny of our relatives, friends, and neighbors.

But now, things will begin to change. A 300 or more point rally in the market is going to bring some stocks up 25% to 50%, and a great many options are going to double, triple, quadruple, and increase even tenfold. Suddenly this little band of true believers will have something to cheer about. Suddenly they don't have to hide their failures in the closet. Suddenly that speculative option which they bought for half a point is worth 5 points, and their $500 speculation is now worth $5,000. Now, that's something to tell your neighbor about.

At the end of the year when the investors are going over their tax records, they will realize that the money they put into stocks really did pretty well, and they will decide that next year they should put more of their money into the stock market. The profits which they have realized on the sales of stocks and options will be reinvested into more stocks and options, and this fact alone will create more buying power which will in itself pull up the market. But in addition, these investors will begin to commit a greater part of their assets to the stock market.

The point is that they have a great deal of money available which they can use to put into the market. There is that $75 billion just sitting in the money market funds, much of it clearly waiting for the right opportunity to come into the stock market. Then there is the fact that now only 20% of individuals' wealth is in common stock compared to over 40% for the entire period from 1955 to 1972. This means that individuals could literally double the amount of stock they own, and they would just be back to what was normal a few years ago!

You think that individuals will never come back into the market? Sure, some will never come back. But remember, there is an entire half a generation which has come into its investing years since the last big boom of 1968. These are millions of young, affluent Americans who have simply avoided the market because no one ever seemed to make any money there; their parents had lost money in it, and besides it was exciting and fun to buy real estate. But they have no deep-seated aversion to the stock market as such. Let them hear, from friends, relatives, or neighbors whom they trust, some good, concrete examples of investments in the stock market which have really paid off, and they will start coming into the market by the thousands.

After all, what could have been a worse time to start a bull market than 1950? Most people still had memories of the great crash of 1929, and if not that, then certainly of the great despair which the stock market created in the 1930's. No wonder that the New York Stock Exchange estimated that only 6 million Americans owned common stock in 1950. That number then increased almost geometrically. By 1960 there were about 11 million, and by 1970 there were 25 million shareholders, an increase of 300%. Furthermore, that represented 15% of the population. With today's much larger population of 230 million, we have only 20 million shareholders, representing less than 9% of the population. In other words, not only do those who own stock own less than they used to, there is a far smaller percentage of Americans now who own any stock at all. The number of shareholders would have to go from the present 20 million up to 34.5 million to equal the percentage of Americans who were shareholders in 1970.

What this means is that there is literally enormous, untapped buying power resting with the American people. History repeats itself. Stock prices will start to go up through buying by foreigners and institutions. Some individuals will be in there making a lot of money for themselves. And they will tell their friends. Their friends are not now in the stock market, and they have plenty of money available for investing. America today is far more affluent than it was in the early 1950's when the last bull market got underway. According to the Conference Board, in the last fifteen years per capita income adjusted for inflation has increased by 50%. That's a lot of extra money that could be invested. There is an entire class of professionals, for example, doctors, lawyers, MBA's, and accountants, who never had as much discretionary money as they have today.

A very good friend of mine wanted to start as a lawyer in a Vermont city. In 1955 he was told by the senior partner of one of the city's largest law firms that Vermont was a great place in which to practice law, but you must never expect to make more than $10,000 a year. Today my friend is making well over $100,000 a year and looking forward to increasing his income in the years to come. Yet he invests almost nothing in the stock market because his past investments have never been profitable. Multiply him by millions, and you have a slight concept of the tremendous amount of buying power which will be unleashed by the new wave of stock buying by the public.

Nonbelievers in the stock market became believers in the 1950's and 1960's and they will become believers tomorrow. The basic human motivation is just the same today as it was then. Once stocks have gone up and people have made money from them, they will start to invest more. The total amount of dollars which could be spent on stock purchases in the next few years is almost unfathomable. If you add purchases by foreigners and the annual purchases by institutions to the money which could be unleashed by the public, it would become a tidal wave of buying.

And let's not forget that in previous times, much of this buying was soaked up by new issues. So far, the new issue market has all but disappeared, so initially, at least, the torrent of buying power is going to have to be met from existing stocks. The only way that the existing supply of stocks is going to be able to meet that demand is for the prices to start climbing.

At the beginning of the new bull market everything will be orderly. Even when they have gone up by many points, most of the stocks will still be good values. For example, General Motors could double from its recent price and still pay over 5% yield if it resumes its former dividend. Ford could double and still be selling at less than 8 times 1979 earnings. So everything will be in favor of the buyers.

Let there be a little rally, and all the technicians or chart readers who have been bearish for so long will suddenly realize that their charts are looking super. The fundamentalists will feel vindicated at last and will continue to point out what tremendous values are represented by common stocks. Last but not least, the investors who actually risked their money to buy the stocks will feel good for a change. They will have beaten the return on bonds and, what's better, they will have actually beaten the rate of inflation. And so the market will begin its ascent, like a giant jet with every engine purring smoothly, delivering maximum thrust as it climbs into the sky.

How high will the market go? Right now we don't even have to begin to ask that question. As the founder of the modern labor movement, Samuel Gompers, said when he was asked what labor really wanted: "More." So my opinion as to how high the market will go at this point is simply: "Higher," and much higher.

In order to project where the DJIA will be in the future it is necessary to make two assumptions. The first is what the earnings of the stocks comprising the average will be in future years, and the second is what the appropriate P/E to apply to those earnings will be. By taking conservative assumptions for both of these, we can see just how much higher it will go on an almost worst case basis.

First, let us assume that earnings of the stocks comprising the DJIA increase by 8% a year. Given the fact that we now have inflation of 8% or more a year, a growth rate assumption of 8% merely means that the companies are going to be able to maintain their actual earnings. It does not even allow for any real growth in profits. Nor does it take into account the possibility that inflation will be at a rate greater than 8%, and therefore just keeping real profits even would mean a growth of more than 8%. In any event, it would seem that 8% is a very conservative figure to project for earnings growth.

The total earnings of the companies comprising the DJIA are compiled quarterly, and the earnings for the twelve months ending March 31, 1980, were $121. Increasing these earnings by 8% a year gives $130.68 for the quarter ending March 1981, $141.13 for 1982, $152.43 for 1983, $164.62 for 1984, $177.79 for 1985, and $192.01 for 1986.

The more difficult part of the projection is selecting a likely P/E ratio to apply to these earnings. Here we can look to history for help. During the period 1958 through 1972, the P/E reached 15 times earnings at some point in each of these years. So we would have ample justification to use a P/E of 15 if we were trying to find out how high the Dow Jones Industrial Average could go. Unfortunately, we have not seen a P/E that high since 1972, and to be more conservative we could use a P/E of 12. The DJIA was at a P/E of 12 as recently as the quarter ending March 31, 1976, and there is every reason to believe that in only a few years it will be back at that level.

But to be really conservative in our projection, so that we cannot be accused of being a raving bull, we will take a P/E 33% lower than that, specifically 8. A P/E of 8 is clearly within reason since the DJIA has been there just very recently. For no quarter from the beginning of 1975 through September 29, 1978, was the P/E lower than that. Clearly, it is not asking very much to imagine that the P/E will return to that depressed level.

Using a P/E of 8 on our projected earnings gives us a DJIA of 1,045 for March 1981, 1,129 for 1982, 1,219 for 1983, 1,317 for 1984, 1,422 for 1985, and 1,536 for 1986. Let me state the obvious here. This is not a prediction of things to come, and if anything is certain it is that these projections are not going to be correct. Either they will be far too low or they will be much too high. But it is reasonable to believe that at some time between now and 1985 the DJIA will be selling at a P/E of at least 8, and that the DJIA will be at these levels or higher. But we don't know when, because we don't know when or if our assumptions will be correct.

For example, we have no way of knowing what will happen to earnings. At the writing of this book there was talk of a cut in the corporate tax rate. If it is enacted, that one fact alone would make our earnings projection understated. Predicting P/E's is even more haphazard. If interest rates return to record-breaking highs, the market might not give the DJIA a P/E of 8. But all the weight of history and reasonableness says that we will see a P/E of 8 or more. And with a P/E of 8 and a mere 8% a year increase in earnings, we will be seeing the DJIA at over 1500 by March 1986.

Let's not forget that for the entire nineteen-year period of March 31, 1954, through March 31, 1973, there was not a single quarter which ended with the P/E at less than 12. At the present time it may seem like wishful thinking to believe that the DJIA will ever again have a P/E that high, but again the weight of history is saying that it will. Are the present times so different from those of that nineteen-year period? People still invest out of fear and greed. The market still goes up and down, the economy expands and contracts, stock prices rise and fall. But basically things are just the same. Once the stock market starts to pick up, a P/E of 12 for a high-quality stock is going to seem like a very good buy.

Using a P/E of 12 on our earnings projections gives us the following prices for the DJIA: for March 1981, 1,568; for 1982, 1,694; for 1983, 1,829; for 1984, 1,975; for 1985, 2,133; and for 1986, 2,304. Again, these are not predictions, but they are definitely statements of where the DJIA could reasonably be expected to be, using only conservative projections.

That figure of 2,304 would represent almost a tripling of the DJIA from its June 1980 level. Is that conservative? Yes. It is not a guarantee and it is not a prediction in the sense that a chemist can predict what will happen when two elements are combined under set conditions. But it is definitely a statement of what is very likely to occur in the future. But how can one say that a tripling of the DJIA is conservative?

Very simply by looking at what happened in the past. For the entire period of 1958 through 1972 there wasn't a single year when for at least one quarter the DJIA P/E didn't reach 15. Therefore, a nonconservative projection of future prices for the DJIA would use a P/E of 15 and would come up with figures 25% higher than the highest ones I have used. And what would a really generous projection be? Once again we will go back into history, not to find the all-time high P/E, but to find what the P/E had been on a consistent basis when the DJIA was doing really well. During the period September 30, 1958, through December 31, 1965, there were 24 quarters which ended with the DJIA at a P/E of 18 or more. If we were to use a P/E of 18 on our projected earnings, they would be 50% higher than the ones using a P/E of 12. That would be a liberal projection, but even that would not be outside the realm of probability.

The point here is that it really isn't too important right now to come up with a precise figure. No matter what type of projection one makes, the result is the same: The prices of stocks in the future seem virtually certain to be higher, and they are probably going to be much higher. Later, when stocks appreciate by a large amount, will be time enough to decide just how high they are going to go. To try to predict what the market will do then would be not only absurd, but totally impossible.

The important point to grasp is that fortunes are undoubtedly going to be made in the stock market in the next few years. For those who can see through the fears of the doomsayers, through the gloom and despair of the skeptics and the cynicism of the sophists, common stocks today represent an unparalleled value. The market is open to anyone who wants to enter. It will sell you a stock regardless of your age, sex, religion, national origin, or race. All it takes is a little objective reasoning, a little courage, and faith in your own common sense.

There are many ways in which people are going to make money from the stock market in the next few years. Buying stocks is just one of those ways. In the next chapters we will discuss buying stocks, including the all-important question of which stocks to buy, and point out some other ways of investing in the market which have important advantages over simply buying stocks. These include buying convertible bonds, buying call options on stocks, and getting into a covered option writing program. There is a world of profit waiting, and the next few chapters will show you exactly what technique is the best for you.

# 9

# WHICH STOCKS TO BUY NOW

The first part of this book was devoted to demonstrating that the stock market is going to go up in the near future. The obvious method of making money from this would would be to buy shares in the stock market and watch them go up. Unfortunately, there is no such thing as "the Stock Market"; there is only a market made up of different stocks. The stock market as described so precisely every day on television and in the financial papers is only an imaginary statistical figure, derived from the prices of various stocks which comprise the averages.

While this book has made liberal use of the Dow Jones Industrial Average, that is only an indication of the price of 30 blue chip industrial companies. It often happens that more stocks go up than down on the New York Stock Exchange and yet the Dow Jones Industrial Average for that day will go down, and vice versa. If you happen to own the stocks that went up, you really don't care if the Dow Jones average went down.

In fact, there is even a disparity between the different stock market averages. The American Stock Exchange Index can go up and the Dow Jones Industrial go down while the broader based Standard & Poor's 500 Index remains almost unchanged. When you go out to buy stocks, you want to pick individual stocks which are going to go up rather than simply having faith that the stock market as a whole will go up. If that were the case, you could just throw darts at the stock market tables and choose whichever stocks they happened to hit.

Before we discuss how you should choose stocks, let's take a look at how other people actually go about making the thousands of decisions a day which lead to their purchases of stocks. Typically the decision begins with the input of information about the company. It could be through a call from the investor's broker, it could be from an article in *Forbes Magazine*, it could be from talking with a business associate who tells him that a company he deals with is about to embark on a new program, it could be from a tip he got from a neighbor, or it could be from a research report put out by an investment service or a brokerage firm.

It makes little difference for our purpose here where the news comes from. Whether he has learned a single fact, such as "I hear that their new Canadian oil field looks as if it is going to strike oil in a big way" or he has studied a 25-page report which analyzes every aspect of the company thoroughly and makes a projection of its next five years' earnings, doesn't matter. The important point is that the potential stock purchaser has learned something about the company.

Whether the decision is being made by an individual who is making his first purchase in the market, a seasoned investor who is making his umpteenth trade this year, or a professional portfolio manager who has given weeks and months of thought to his decision before setting out on a purchasing program which will involve 200,000 shares—the decision process is remarkably similar. Usually, the decision maker has assimilated some information which leads him to believe that the earnings of the company are about to move up in the relatively near-term future. He therefore buys the stock.

Simple, straightforward, and, you might say, obvious. But actually we have only begun to examine the process. There are a number of assumptions hidden in this "simple" reasoning process. The obvious question, and the only one to which the stock purchaser has probably given any consideration, is whether or not the conclusion he reached was true. That is, is the company really about to strike a big oil find on its Canadian exploration fields, or are the company's earnings in the coming year really going to outperform the economy as a whole? This is the obvious risk, and the one which the stock purchaser is fully aware of. But there are two assumptions which the stock buyers are making, without consciously considering them, which will determine ultimately whether or not they make money on the stock.

The first assumption that is made is that the price of the stock more or less represents the value of the company at the present time without the new information the investor has just received. In other words, the buyer of the oil company may know that the company earned $1 a share last year and that the stock is now selling for $10 a share. It is his unconscious assumption that the stock should be selling for 10 times earnings. His second assumption is that when the new oil discovery is announced, investors will project earnings next year of perhaps $2 a share, and that then investors will value the stock at a price of approximately 10 times the projected $2 earnings, which means that the stock will move up to $20.

Note that the two basic assumptions here involve the appropriate price earnings ratios for the stock, and if either of these assumptions is wrong, then the hoped for result will not be achieved. To take the second one first, it is assumed that if the earnings go from $1 to $2 a share, the P/E ratio will continue to be at 10 times projected earnings and therefore the stock price will double. This reasoning assumes that the entire reason the stock is $10 today is that the stock earned $1 in the last twelve months. But is this really true? If it is, then of course a doubling of earnings will mean a doubling of the price stock.

Thus, the question comes down to one of "Does the present price of the stock reflect solely the fact that the company earned $1 in the last twelve months?" One of the basic concepts we introduced in the earlier chapters of this book was that the price earnings ratio of a stock goes up with investor expectations that future earnings are going up.

We therefore have to ask ourselves whether the P/E ratio of our stock, here 10, is based upon the fact that it earned $1 in the past twelve months or upon investor expectations that it will earn substantially more in the future? This question is crucial, because if the current P/E of 10 is due to the fact that investors expect the company to double its earnings and earn $2 next year, and if they believe that a risky venture like an oil exploration company should be selling at only 5 times its actual earnings, then even if the tip which the investor heard is true and the new oil field does prove to be a bonanza and the stock earns $2 next year, the investment community could decide that the stock was adequately priced at 5 times earnings. Result: Earnings double, price of the stock stays exactly the same. For once a tip turned out to be true, but once again the speculator failed to make any money.

This example has been exaggerated to simplify it, and undoubtedly a company that doubled its earnings would see an increase in its stock price. But not necessarily. The point of this example is that the current price of the stock may already reflect anticipated earnings improvements. That is to say, just because the company earned only $1 this year and is priced at $10, does not mean that the stock will double to $20 next year on a doubling of earnings, if the investment community today has reason to believe that the earnings of the stock are going to double.

In fact, when the oil discovery is announced and the increased earnings become a certainty, they may have been so completely anticipated that the price of the stock will actually fall on disappointment. Thus was born the famous saying of Wall Street, "Buy on rumors, sell on news." When everyone heard the rumors that the earnings could double, they bought the stock. This in turn caused its price to rise to $10. But all the people who owned the stock at $10 fully expected that the earnings would be $2 a share. Therefore, they were not surprised or even pleased by the announcement. They wanted that news to cause other people to buy the stock, and they then wanted to be able to sell.

What often happens is that when the news comes out, there are so few people who hadn't anticipated it that few people rush in to buy. But all the people who had bought on the rumors are ready to sell. On the day of the big news, they are in close touch with their brokers, and when the price of the stock doesn't go up, they decide to sell anyway. And when they begin to sell, the stock starts to go down. Other people watching the price of the stock were also expecting the stock to go up, and when it goes down instead, they panic and decide to sell also. Therefore, this news, which any member of the uninformed public would have expected to send the price of the stock skyrocketing, actually pulls the price down.

Thus, the current price of a stock reflects not only its present earnings, but also its anticipated earnings. Therefore, whether the actual earnings are up or down is not the fact which will determine the changes in the price of the stock. That is determined by whether the earnings are higher or lower than the investment community expects them to be. Once again the public is befuddled by this phenomenon. But there is nothing surprising about it, when one considers that the current price of a stock reflects all the thinking about future earnings.

If analysts have been predicting that a company's earnings for the year will be down from $5 a share to $2.50, the price of the shares will be consistent with that forecast. If the earnings actually come out at $3.50, that will still be a major decrease from a year ago, but not as much of a decrease as was forecast. Yet the public will wonder why such a large drop in earnings produced an increase in the price of the stock. The answer is that the stock was priced not at its last year's earnings of $5 a share, but at the predicted earnings of $2.50 a share. When the earnings actually came in substantially above the forecasts, the price of the stock shot up to incorporate this new "good" news.

Since the price of a stock reflects all the current opinion about the future, where does that leave us in terms of which stocks to buy? Let's assume you have received some interesting favorable information on a stock. If you were the only person to have that information, then you might be in a position to evaluate the future prospects of that stock better than other people. But this is almost never the case. How did you get your information? Unless you got it directly from an officer of the company or a comparable source, the only way you could have gotten the information is through a source which is also in touch with many other investors.

This point is worth ruminating upon. Let's say you have a very good broker who is tuned in to what is happening on Wall Street. He calls you up and says that he has heard a very strong rumor that XYZ company is about to be acquired by one of the giant German chemical firms and that they are going to pay about 75% above the current price. He urges you to buy 1,000 shares. Two things are possible.

The first is that what he is telling you is true, and the stock will go up by 75%. But if he *knew* that what he was telling you was going to happen, he wouldn't be talking to you now. He would be out trying to refinance the mortgage on his house so that he could buy all the call options for himself that he could lay his hands on. He would also be telling his brother, his father, and his brother-in-law that they should do the same. In other words, if your broker *knew* that this acquisition were about to happen, he would be banking on it. But obviously he doesn't *know* that it will happen. It is just that he heard from someone else, probably another broker, that the acquisition is going to go through.

He probably hasn't even assigned any precise probability factor to its happening. In fact, just to let you in on a little secret, there is a very good chance that he isn't even buying any of the stock for his own account. Remember that most professional arbitrageurs never buy a single share of stock on rumors, and these professionals are among the very few groups on Wall Street who consistently make money year after year.

So your broker is not letting you in on the bargain of the year. He is not telling you about a stock which is going to go up by

75%. He is telling you about a stock which has a chance of going up by 75%. Just how much chance is difficult to say, but we do know a few facts about the situation. The fact nearest at hand is that your broker is telephoning a number of people about this hoped for acquisition. The second fact is that your broker is not alone. After all, he told you that he had heard a rumor. Therefore, at least the person who told him knows also, and the chances are that a great number of brokers know. And if they didn't, they will shortly, because some of your broker's clients have other brokers, and as soon as they get a call from your broker, they call their other broker for confirmation of the tip.

What then happens is that as people hear the rumor and buy the stock, the price starts moving up very rapidly and on big volume. This volume attracts other traders, and they make inquiries and hear the same rumor. Within a very short period of time the stock will move up to the point where its new higher current price reflects exactly the probability that the rumor is true. Thus, even though there is a possibility that the price of the stock will move up by 75%, the current price of the stock already compensates for that fact. It has moved up to the price where the potential profit on the takeover is offset by the risk of the stock falling if the rumor is wrong. In short, when you hear a tip like this, you are not buying a bargain; you are getting exactly what the investment community believes the stock is worth, and if you want to gamble on the correctness of an unconfirmed rumor, that is your business.

Since all the current news about a company is already factored into the price of its stock, how can one predict the price of a stock by the use of news about the future of the company? Is there any point in learning more about the company? The logical conclusion from this is that the future price of a share is determined by future events which cannot be predicted at the present time. That is to say, there is no way that you can know what the price of a stock is going to be in the future, because you cannot know about the many unexpected events which will control the price of that stock. And if you can know about those events now, then they will not be unexpected and they are already included in the price of the stock.

This theory has gained wide following and is known as the Random Walk theory. According to the Random Walk theory, the future price of any stock cannot be predicted and is apt to change at random depending upon future events. Furthermore, the only price which can be used as a guide is the current price, and the price of the stock is more likely to be at the present price than at any other place.

The Random Walk theory is described in *A Random Walk Down Wall Street* by Burton G. Malkiel, the Chairman of the Princeton University Economics Department. He states that all that is known concerning the expected growth of the company's earnings and dividends, and all of the possible favorable and unfavorable developments affecting the company that might be studied by the analysts, are already reflected in the price of the company's stock. Thus, throwing darts at the financial page will produce a portfolio that can be expected to do as well as any managed by professional security analysts, or as well as carefully studying every stock and picking those which are the recipients of bullish reports.

Although the Wall Street community spends many, many millions of dollars every year doing research on stocks and issuing and distributing reports, and while many of the investing public spend millions on various chart services and investment advisory services, and while many investors, including nearly every institutional investor, pay large fees annually to money managers whose sole function is to select stocks which will outperform the market, there is not one shred of hard statistical evidence that any of these people or services are able to do any better than the market over a substantial period of time. Thus, there is absolutely no evidence that information about a stock enables one to outperform a person who has not acquired the same information.

At first blush that would seem to indicate that one should throw up his hands and forget about stock selection. Why not just pick stocks on any random basis and hope for the best? The answer is that even if we cannot pick stocks which will outperform the market, we can choose stocks which will have many other characteristics we are looking for. By deciding on which of these characteristics we want, we can predict a lot about the stock we select.

One point we should make right now is that all the comments made in this book are for long-term investors. We are trying to buy stocks which represent outstanding value at a time when the investing public as a whole is not willing to pay what we consider to be the fair value of the stock. The reasons the investing public is not willing to pay the fair value have been outlined in this book. We are expecting that these psychological and economic factors will change and that investors will once again be willing to pay the more normal, higher P/E ratios for stocks.

Obviously time is required, because these types of fundamental changes in attitude can only come about over a period of many years. Thus, this book is intended only for investors who are willing to buy a stock and hold it for a number of years until they believe that it has appreciated to what is a fair value. This clearly has nothing to do with analyzing short-term trends of stock prices, the so-called "technical analysis," in an effort to determine which way the prices are going to move in the very near future. This latter type of analysis appeals to speculators who want to make their money quickly from short-term trends in prices or current events. While in theory there is nothing wrong with wanting to make money quickly, the sad lesson to be learned is that there is no proof that any of the technical predictions have validity.

This may be discouraging and even unacceptable to those who subscribe to various advisory services or chart services which believe that through various quite complicated formulas they can predict which way particular stocks will move. But unfortunately, the entire evidence is that over an extended period of time, no method or person has been able to outguess the market. You wouldn't know that from reading the advertisements for these services, and of course anyone is entitled to a lucky period. But you might ask yourself a question. If the editors of these chart services and advisories are so smart, why don't they get into something where they could really prove themselves? That is, why don't they take some real money under management, and then make their records public?

A few years ago the most famous market adviser of that time did start a mutual fund, and the results were very disappointing to all. As long as he only had to issue forecasts like, "The odds favor a strong market in the near future but keep a sharp watch out for a near-term correction," he could impress his readers. But when he actually had to make decisions of which stocks to buy and sell and when, the task became much too difficult.

So, what can we really hope to accomplish? As long as we are concerned with a long-term appreciation in stocks, there are a number of items we can look for, and even though we accept the basic tenet of the Random Walk approach that we cannot predict which stocks will outperform the market, we can hope to make a substantial profit.

Some of the traits of a stock which we can learn and which are extremely valuable to us are: riskiness of the company, P/E ratio, dividend, book value, and past price action of the stock.

First is riskiness of the company. Just because any stock has the same chance of making money as any other doesn't mean that the degree of safety is the same. A group of brand new high-technology companies may have the same chance of going up as American Telephone & Telegraph, but the new companies also have a very good chance of going bankrupt, which is hardly the case with AT&T. So, by studying the history of a company, the trend of its profits, the position it has in its industry, and the health of its balance sheet, we can come to a pretty good conclusion about the chances of a company's surviving.

Second we note the earnings of a company. How much are we paying for each dollar of earnings, or what is the P/E of the stock? Clearly, if we are paying a very high P/E there is a larger possibility that the stock can fall down. If we are paying a low P/E and the earnings' projection for the next few years is not sharply downward, then the downward action of the stock is somewhat limited. Although P/E ratios can get very low in a bear market, there is a limit. Better to own a stock with a low P/E ratio that has gone down than to own one with a high P/E that can still go down even further.

Third is the dividend. Here again, there is no guarantee that a stock paying a good dividend cannot go down. But at least if its earnings are enough to cover a good dividend and leave enough money for reinvesting in plant and equipment for future growth, then once again you have some downside protection. It may be limited, as was shown in 1974 when there were utility stocks paying dividends of almost 15%, but let us note that that was only temporary. They were only paying that at the very bottom of the market, and they came back fairly soon.

But even if the stock doesn't come back right away, if you buy a stock which is paying a 7% dividend and a real shock hits the stock market which cuts your stock in half, you are then earning 14% on the current value of your stock. Thus, although you will have suffered a terrible loss on the stock, at least you can stay in the position knowing that you are getting a very rich return on your investment. Far better than worrying whether it will go down even further.

Fourth, we can ask how much we are getting for our dollar in the way of assets. This is another way of asking what the book value is per share of stock. Again, the answer to this question does not guarantee that you will not lose money on the stock, but if times get tough, it will be reassuring to know that the stock has become a bigger bargain than ever. For instance, if the book value per share is $25 and you buy the stock for $20, this means that you are getting assets at a cost of 80 cents on the dollar. The replacement cost of these assets is probably sharply higher, and the true appraised value of the firm's assets may be higher still. Therefore, if the stock starts to go down, again you don't have to panic. You will know that there is true value behind your investment.

Finally, we can study the price action of the stock itself to see what its likely future action will be. We cannot predict whether it will go up or not, but we can find out whether it has been volatile in the past. The volatility of various stocks has been computed, and it is easy to subscribe to a service which will give you the volatility figures. A stock which has been highly volatile in the past is likely to be very volatile in the future, and one which has not been volatile is likely to remain relatively constant.

Similarly, the Beta of a stock tells how likely and by how much the stock is likely to move when the market as a whole moves. A stock with a high Beta coefficient will move up more rapidly than the market when it moves up, and will move down more rapidly than the market as a whole when it moves down. Therefore, you pays your money and you takes your choice. The important point here is that studying the stock before you buy it will give you important information about its likely future price behavior.

If you look into these five factors before you buy a stock, even accepting the Random Walk theory, you will obtain valuable insights into the stock you are considering. Furthermore, there are a number of problems with the Random Walk theory which even its proponents admit. The first problem is that it is contrary to human nature. Even if all its implications were true, who among us would not want to know as much as possible about something as important as the company into which we are investing large amounts of our money. It just seems to make sense that by studying the company carefully we will be better able to judge what its stock performance will be in the years ahead. Second, as we pointed out above, there are many useful aspects of a stock's probable future behavior which we can learn from studying the stock and the company. Finally, there is the fact that there are times when the stock market as a whole is cheap; there is nothing in the Random Walk theory which denies that it may be possible to predict when stocks as a whole are cheap and therefore good buys. If you were able to pick out those times when the entire market was cheap and buy stocks then, it would not matter if the stocks you chose did not outperform the market. Even if they did only as well as the market as a whole, you would have made a very successful investment.

So let's examine some of the indications of stocks to see whether we can learn something which, if it does not enable us to beat the market, will at least enable us to buy stocks which we believe have great value. The theory which promises to work best for an investor is to buy stocks which one believes offer greater value than other stocks, anticipating that at some future time other investors will realize the greater worth of the stocks and will come forward to buy the stock, pushing the price up.

How do we get the most value in a stock? Even with all the latest theories on the stock market, the basic ideas on choosing the best values in stocks were set down by Benjamin Graham and David L. Dodd in their book *Security Analysis,* first published in 1934 and now in its fourth edition (McGraw-Hill). These theories are further described in a book for laymen, *The Intelligent Investor* by Benjamin Graham (Harper & Row).

In the fourth revised edition, published in 1973, of the latter book, Graham sets out seven rules for stock selection. In order of importance they are:

1. Adequate size of enterprise. Graham was very concerned that small companies are more vulnerable to economic strains than the larger companies.

2. A sufficiently strong financial condition. Specifically he suggested that current assets should be at least twice current liabilities, a two-to-one current ratio, and long-term debt should not exceed the net current assets.

3. Earnings stability. This means some earnings for each of the past ten years.

4. Dividend record of uninterrupted dividends for the past twenty years.

5. Earnings growth of at least 33% over the past ten years.

6. Moderate price/earnings ratio. In 1973 he defined this as not more than 15 times average earnings for the past three years.

7. Moderate ratio of price to assets. This he defined as being a price for the stock of no more than one and a half times the assets of the company.

Note that there are a large number of criteria here based upon the assets of the company. A moderate price earnings ratio is relegated to rule number 6. It was natural in 1949 when the book was first published to concentrate on stability and financial condition.

When you bought a share of a steel company, it was as though you were buying a small part of all those blast furnaces, and you wanted to make sure that your steel company was large enough to compete with the others, that there were not too many mortgages on the steel mills, and that it had a good record of making a profit for many years in the past. Those are still sound ideas, but today, when so many industries are more service oriented, and when the actual manufacturing process of an industrial company accounts for only a portion of the firm's assets and management talents, there is much less emphasis placed upon financial stability, size, and assets.

Today there are many industries in which the assets are quite unimportant, and one recognizes that in a severe recession there could easily be a year or two with losses. An excellent example of companies which don't need much in the way of assets are advertising agencies. While they do have office machines, working capital, and so on, their real assets are the people whom they employ who can create and sell advertising that will move their clients' products.

For firms such as this the emphasis has switched from the balance sheet approach to the profit and loss approach. When one buys a share in an advertising company, he is buying not so much a part of the office furniture as a portion of the earnings of that agency. It is therefore the earnings which we must focus on. Today the paramount factor in selecting a stock is the earnings of the company and what we pay for those earnings.

If two firms with equal growth rates each earn $1 per share, does it matter to the shareholders that one company requires massive heavy equipment and large factories valued at $30 a share, while the other company makes its product in a small assembly plant worth only $2 a share? As long as the earnings of the two companies are equally secure, we really don't care very much about the amount of capital it takes to produce those earnings. Therefore, the current approach to share evaluation places more emphasis on the earnings of the company and less on the assets.

We are now ready for the rules which I recommend in selecting stocks for long-term investing. I call these The Five

Commandments of Stock Selection. When Moses descended from the mountain with his tablet containing the Commandments, it took Ten Commandments to outline the basis for an ethical and religious life. It takes only five to explain how to select stocks. Whether this is because it is twice as hard to select stocks that are going to appreciate as it is to lead an upright life, or whether it is because it is twice as easy, I will leave for others to decide.

In order of importance the Five Commandments of Stock Selection are:

*Commandment 1. Buy Stocks with a Low P/E Ratio.* Throughout this book we have emphasized that the purchase of a stock is really buying the earnings of a company. Therefore, the most important question is: What am I paying for these earnings? An easy way to see the importance of this question is to imagine that you are considering buying a small local business, such as the local drugstore. You know the owner, and he is willing to sell you a third of the business. What's the first thing you ask? Simply, how much am I going to earn from my one-third investment? Whether the drugstore owns the building or just rents it, whether it owns the inventory or owes its suppliers for just about everything in the store are both important questions, but the most important question is how much you are going to earn. Once you know that, you can decide how much you want to pay for the one-third interest in the company.

It's similar for a stock. Stock represents earnings of the company, and even though you cannot touch these earnings unless they are paid out in dividends, the earnings are just as real. Either they are paid out in dividends or they are reinvested in the company to make it grow.

The big question is how much should you be willing to pay for one dollar's worth of earnings. You will remember that Graham, in the 1973 edition of his book *The Intelligent Investor*, said that you should not pay more than 15 times the average earnings of the past three years. Today that figure is much too high. There are many good stocks for 7 or 8 times earnings, and a lot of stocks at substantially less—another indication of how cheap the stock market is. A quick look at the P/E column of the stock market page will show you the wide variety of P/E's which are available. It seems obvious that one should try to get the highest earnings for each dollar one pays for a stock, but things are not this simple.

The first reason is that this figure is based upon the earnings for the latest twelve-month period. If a company had good earnings during the last twelve months, but because of changed economic conditions is currently expecting much lower earnings, then you are looking at a P/E figure which is not meaningful. People buy stocks for the future, not the past. Therefore, the P/E you should be looking at is price divided by this year's expected earnings.

But the main reason for the wide divergence in P/E's is that earnings of companies are not static but are constantly changing. If investors believe that the earnings of a company are unstable and that the company could experience sharp earning declines in the future, they will not be willing to pay as much for those earnings as if there were an assurance that they would remain constant. Therefore, cyclical companies typically have low P/E's.

Even more important is the concept of growth. When a company has a consistent growth pattern of 20% a year, it is easy to project that in just four years its earnings will double. If a person is willing to hold the stock for four years, he might well be willing to pay twice as much for those earnings as he would for a company which has earnings without any growth trend.

In general, the companies with the high P/E's are the ones which are considered likely to grow in the future. It is the import of this rule that at the present time when there are so many very good solid companies at rock bottom P/E's of 4, 5, or 6 times earnings, there is no need to pay a lot more to get "growth." And that word is in quotation marks because it is a concept resting in the future.

Remember that we do not know at the present time whether there will be any growth in the future or not. Many growth companies over the years have gone into bankruptcy. Paying more money for present earnings means that unless the company continues to grow in the future, the stock will go down. In fact, almost all of the big losses in the stock market have come from the so-called "growth" stocks which suddenly no longer were growth stocks, with a resultant drastic drop in P/E. The big advantage of buying stocks with a low P/E is that it is very hard for them to go down very far but there is the good possibility that when the market heads up, those stocks you bought for a P/E of 4 or 5 will be selling at 8 to 10 times earnings, and that the earnings will have gone up appreciably, meaning that your stocks will be selling for far more than double what you paid for them.

When you pay a high P/E for a stock, you are buying a stock which has already been discovered by others. Its P/E is high specifically because a lot of investors have reason to believe that its earnings are going to go up in the future. You are a Johnny-come-lately who has probably already missed much of the price rise. What will happen to the stock now? If the earnings improve as the optimistic backers hope they will, the stock may not move up in price, because the market might decide that the company no longer deserves such a high multiple. Or the earnings could be disappointing, in which case the price will certainly come down fast.

On the other hand, when you buy a stock with a low P/E, you are buying a stock which is out of favor with investors. They believe that things are going to get worse for this company, or at least not improve, and therefore have sold their shares and forced the price of the stock down. Where will this stock go? If the dire predictions of the average investors turn out to be correct, the stock may not go down at all, because the present price already reflects all the anticipated bad news. If, however, the company does better than expected, you will certainly get a double leveraged gain. First, because the earnings are better than expected, the price of the stock will go up just by maintaining its present P/E, and second, if the earnings do go up, there is every likelihood that the P/E will go up on what has suddenly become a "turnaround situation."

Statistical studies confirm that purchasing stocks with P/E's among the lowest 20% of all stocks and then annually reviewing your stocks so that you stay with those that have P/E's in the lowest 20% will provide a superior return. In his book *Contrarian Investment Strategy*, David Dreman (Random House, 1979) cites a number of studies showing that while the average return on stock purchases for various periods was 9.3%, the profit from investing in only the lowest P/E stocks was 14.7% for a substantial 51% greater profit.

To sum up the reasons for buying stocks with a low P/E, when you buy a stock, you are buying earnings of a company, and the lower a P/E, the bigger a bargain you are getting in your purchase. While there are other factors which might argue for a higher P/E, the fact is that we do not know what is going to happen in the future, and guessing that any company will continue to experience future growth is a dangerous game. Companies which have a high P/E are companies which have already been pegged by other investors as growth companies, and the chances are that even if they are right, the stock might not go up in price, but if they are wrong it will certainly tumble. By buying stocks with a low P/E you are getting exactly the opposite opportunity to make money; namely, if future earnings are nothing special, the stock will probably not go down, but if they go up, the stock should be a real winner.

*Commandment 2. Consider the Earnings Growth of the Company.* Note the difference between the wording of this rule and that of the first rule. The first commandment said simply buy stocks with a low P/E. The second commandment is not nearly so empirical in tone. It is not a command to buy growth stocks, simply a suggestion that you carefully consider the growth of the company and think about where the company's earnings are going to be in five or ten years.

The big difference between buying a bond and buying common stock is that when you buy stock, you are getting a share in the future earnings of the company. If the current dividend based upon the current earnings is less than the rate of interest which the company is paying on its bonds, and this is usually the case, then you would be better off buying bonds in the company unless you were quite certain that the stock market were going to go up or that the earnings of this company were going to increase. While the entire thesis of this book is that the stock market is going to move up, it would also be a help if you believed that the earnings of the company were going to grow.

Growth is essential to the price of a stock because the P/E ratio is almost directly tied in to the company's growth rate. The higher the growth rate of the company, the higher the P/E of the stock is going to be. Here comes the dilemma. Being long-term investors, we want to buy stocks which are going to appreciate because the earnings of the company are going up, but as purchasers of the stock, we want stocks with low P/E ratios. Since the two are almost mutually exclusive, how does one resolve this quandary? As we clearly stated in the first commandment, the paramount rule is to get the low P/E. But, even within low P/E's (which we could define as 10 or under), there are various growth rates. It is the relationship between growth and P/E which requires judgment and skill for stock selection.

The key to picking any stock is therefore the relationship of earnings to future growth. It is easy to find stocks selling at low P/E ratios which have no growth. Their P/E's are low because, if current projections hold, they will still be earning the same amount of money per share five or ten years from now. If this proves to be the case, you might just as well buy a bond.

It is also easy to find companies which are growing at rates of up to 30% a year and which seem able to maintain that rate of growth for many years to come. Companies that come to mind are in the computer industry, telecommunications, and cable television. But these industries and the fast-growing companies within them have already attracted the attention of the investment community. Investors are willing to pay much more for a dollar of this year's earnings if they have good reason to believe that the company will be earning much more than this in five years. And so the P/E ratio of the fast-growing companies can be as much as 20, 25, 30 or more times the past twelve months' earnings. But does this mean that the P/E is too high and that therefore the stock is not worth the money being charged for it? Not necessarily.

Clearly what is needed is a method for synthesizing the current P/E ratio of the stock with the projected earnings growth rate to come up with an appropriate P/E ratio for today's earnings. Analysts have argued for years about the proper weight to give future earnings projections, and about how to mesh future growth with the current P/E accorded stocks which did not have any growth.

Now this book presents the P/E Evaluator Chart, which contains a clear, precise, and easy-to-use method for determining exactly what the appropriate P/E ratio should be for any stock, with any projected growth rate from 0% to 40%, at any time in the stock market when the P/E ratios of stocks with no growth are valued from a P/E of 3 to a P/E of 7. Furthermore, the chart enables the investor to decide whether he wants to project the earnings growth out to five years or all the way out to ten years.

Let's take a look at how this P/E Evaluator Chart works. First you have to determine the projected earnings growth rate of the stock you are considering buying. To do this you will rely upon the earnings estimates made by analysts, stock advisory services, or your own opinions based upon past history and your views of the future of the company. This figure is obviously crucial to the accuracy of the entire process. Therefore, it is worth remembering that high growth rates can generally not be sustained, and so if you are going to calculate the stock price of a company with a very high

THE P/E EVALUATOR CHART

*Projecting Five Years Out*

| Annual Growth Rate 0% | Current P/E of No-Growth Companies | | | | |
|---|---|---|---|---|---|
| | 3 | 4 | 5 | 6 | 7 |
| 5% | 3.84 | 5.12 | 6.40 | 7.68 | 8.96 |
| 10% | 4.83 | 6.44 | 8.05 | 9.66 | 11.27 |
| 15% | 6.03 | 8.04 | 10.05 | 12.06 | 14.07 |
| 20% | 7.47 | 9.96 | 12.45 | 14.94 | 17.43 |
| 25% | 9.15 | 12.20 | 15.25 | 18.30 | 21.35 |
| 30% | 11.13 | 14.84 | 18.55 | 22.26 | 25.97 |
| 35% | 13.44 | 17.92 | 22.40 | 26.88 | 31.36 |
| 40% | 16.14 | 21.52 | 26.90 | 32.28 | 37.66 |

THE P/E EVALUATOR CHART

*Projecting Ten Years Out*

| Annual Growth Rate 0% | Current P/E of No-Growth Companies | | | | |
|---|---|---|---|---|---|
| | 3 | 4 | 5 | 6 | 7 |
| 5% | 4.90 | 6.53 | 8.17 | 9.80 | 11.44 |
| 10% | 7.78 | 10.37 | 12.96 | 15.56 | 18.15 |
| 15% | 12.13 | 16.17 | 20.21 | 24.26 | 28.30 |
| 20% | 18.59 | 24.78 | 30.98 | 37.18 | 43.37 |
| 25% | 27.92 | 37.23 | 46.54 | 55.85 | 65.16 |
| 30% | 41.32 | 55.10 | 68.87 | 82.65 | 96.42 |
| 35% | 60.26 | 80.35 | 100.44 | 120.53 | 140.62 |
| 40% | 86.80 | 115.74 | 144.67 | 173.60 | 202.54 |

These charts indicate precisely the relationship between annual growth in earnings and the current P/E ratio of the stock. By simply looking at these charts the investor can quickly determine whether he is overpaying for future earnings or whether a stock is actually a bargain based upon projected growth rates of the company.

growth rate, you should either be sure to use only the five-year set of figures, or else reduce the growth rate to an amount which would be sustainable over a period of time. To cite an example, if a company's earnings were growing at a rate of 40% a year, in just ten years they would be earning 28.93 times what they are earning now. How many companies can you realistically expect to increase by that much?

It is also well to keep in mind that forecasts of earnings are not particularly accurate and that this low level of accuracy deteriorates even further when the time span for the projection is increased. Therefore, the five-year projection is recommended rather than the ten-year one.

The second step is to determine what the going rate for a P/E is in the stock market for stocks which are essentially not growing. This gives us a base upon which to project the additional P/E we should be willing to pay for future growth. The way to determine the P/E of a no-growth company is to jot down from your newspaper the current P/E ratios of those types of companies which are generally considered to be stagnant. Examples of this are meat packing, life insurance, utilities, supermarket chains, tire companies, some consumer product companies, and certain rail-roads which are not serving growing parts of the country. As you go through the P/E column of the stock tables, write down the low figures that you find. There may be a few oddballs caused by the fact that the price of the stock has collapsed because earnings next year are expected to be substantially lower, but basically, if you simply note what the lowest P/E ratios are and then take the average of them, you will have the P/E for stocks with little or no growth.

The next step is to look on the chart at the top horizontal column, which is the P/E for stocks with zero growth. Go across to the column heading which you have found to be the current P/E of no-growth companies. Then go down until you come to the figure for the annual percentage growth rate which you have determined is correct for the stock you want to buy. The figure you find will be the appropriate figure for the P/E that the stock should be selling at if you are willing to evaluate the stock on the basis of what it will be earning in either five years or ten years, depending on which table you have picked.

As a specific example, let's say that you find a company which you believe will be growing at a rate of 15% a year for the next five years. Your first step is to determine what the going P/E ratio is for companies which do not have a growth rate; in other words, what is the going P/E rate for static earnings? By looking at the P/E tables of your newspaper's stock market page, you find that the average of the low P/E ratios is 4.5. If you want to use the five-year projection table, you look down the left-hand column headed "Annual Growth Rate" to 15%, then read over to the column headed 4, which is 8.04, and 5, which is 10.05. Since 4.5 is just in the middle of 4 and 5, you would take the average of the two numbers, coming up with a figure of 9.05.

This means that at the current P/E being paid for static earnings, you could now pay 9.05 times the current earnings of this company, and if your 15% projection holds true, the stock will be selling at 9.05 times its present earnings in five years, *even if in five years it is believed that its earnings growth has stopped and it is then valued as a no-growth company.*

Thus, the big riddle of how much one should be willing to pay today for future earnings can be solved by use of this chart. A couple of notes are pertinent. First, the academic scholars who devote themselves to preparing mathematical models of what stock prices should be would point out that there is a deficiency in this chart, because it gives the P/E ratio that you would be willing to pay today for a company which had earnings today equal to what you expect them to be in five years. The fallacy is that you are going to have to wait five years for these earnings to come due, and you are putting up your money now. Therefore, to be correct, one should take the expected price of the stock five years from now and discount it by the current rate of interest to determine the present value of earnings which will materialize in five years.

While this is correct, it is not practical because we do not know what the rate of interest is going to be over the next five years. This discounting would tend to reduce the price of the stock, but there is another equally important factor which tends to increase the value of the stock. This is that we are projecting a growth rate out for five years, but we do not know what is going to happen after those five years. The odds certainly are that if the company is successful in maintaining its growth for that period of time, it will not suddenly stop growing when it gets into the fifth year. On the contrary, it will almost certainly continue to grow, even if perhaps at a reduced rate.

The fact that the company is growing at that time means that its stock will not be selling at the P/E of a no-growth stock, but will be selling at a higher multiple based upon future growth expectations. This will have a far greater impact upon increasing the value of the stock than eliminating the discount will have upon pulling the price down. Therefore, we can safely remove the discount factor and still have a reasonable estimate of what the P/E ought to be.

Let's go back to our example in which we came up with a five-year projection of 9.05 for our P/E. This means that if the company were to stop growing in five years, and if the P/E ratio at that time for no-growth companies were still 4.5, then the stock would be selling at 9.05 times its earnings today. In other words, with a $1 per share earning today the stock would be selling at $9.05, if investors were evaluating it on the basis of its earnings five years from now.

But, five years from now the company will probably still be growing. Therefore, even if the P/E ratio then being applied to no-growth companies is 4.5 times earnings, there is no reason to believe that your company will be a no-growth company. The assumption of this chart is that it will be computed as a no-growth company, and in that respect this chart is very conservative. But let us make the quite reasonable assumption that since the company had an earnings growth of 15% for the last five years, it will very likely do so in the future. Therefore, it might well be that the stock would be valued at that time as a growth stock growing at the rate of 15% a year.

In that case, using the same logic which we used to determine that its P/E today should be 9.05 times earnings, the stock market then might value the stock at 9.05 times its then earnings. We are projecting its earnings at that time at $2.01 a share, which means that the stock could be selling for 9.05 times that, or $18.19, rather than the $9.05 which we are ascribing to it today.

Thus, it is possible that this chart actually understates the present value of stocks, or put another way, allows you to make a large profit even if you pay the P/E ratios indicated on the five-year portions of the chart.

Now we know how to combine the first two commandments. The first two commandments together are worth about 70% of the weight in deciding which stocks to select. The remaining three rules are given a weight of about 10% each.

*Commandment 3. Favor Stocks With High Book Values.* This rule is subservient to the others but still, when you have a choice of two different stocks and one has highly valued assets while the other doesn't, there are large advantages in the former. First, if a company has a high book value, it means that it would be hard for any new competitors to enter the field, for the following reason. The company in the past invested large amounts of money and the stock does not adequately reflect this value. It would be foolish for any other company to purchase the same assets, undoubtedly at today's much higher costs, and see the value of its stock decline. The second reason you should choose the stock with the higher book value is that if the company ever gets into real trouble, the pure liquidation value of its assets will help to keep the value of the stock up. Companies selling at greatly less than book value have been known to sell off part of their assets and distribute the cash, to the glee of their stockholders.

*Commandment 4. Get Dividends.* In theory it doesn't really matter whether a stock pays dividends or not. To go back to our analogy of buying a small business, if you didn't need the money for living expenses, it wouldn't matter very much to you whether you kept the profits of the company as added working capital or paid them out to yourself and put them in your own savings account. The same is true with a corporation. The important fact is what the company earns; whether it reinvests those earnings in its own business or pays them out to shareholders in the form of dividends shouldn't really affect the value of the stock.

However, in today's world there is so much skepticism that a bird in the hand is worth more than two in the bush. When you get that dividend check, you know that you have received money, but when the annual report tells you what the earnings are, you are entitled to wonder whether all those reinvested earnings really went to increase the value of the company, or whether a portion went into making up for overstated profits.

Because dividends are a cash payout, they will give the stock a floor if they are well protected by earnings so that they are not likely to be cut in times of economic adversity. The floor can be quite low, but one of the hallmarks of the successful long-term investor is to be able to sit out the bad times and wait for the good. A regular dividend coming in makes it a lot easier to wait for the good times.

Perhaps the real value of a dividend is that it shows that a company has reached a mature stage. As we said in Commandment 1, you are buying earnings when you buy a share. And when the Board of Directors of a company believes that it has reached the stage where it can share some of its earnings with its shareholders, then you know that they believe the company is adequately financed and has enough working capital to meet its future needs.

Furthermore, studies made in the past twenty years show that the amount of dividends returned to stockholders plays a definite role in increasing the total return to them over a period of time. The studies found that stocks which did not pay dividends did not outperform those which did pay dividends. Thus, if the price action of the stocks was similar, the shareholders of those stocks which paid dividends ended up richer by the amounts of the dividends. Admittedly this occurred during a bad market, and in a good market those stocks which do not pay dividends should increase faster than those which do not. But in a good market we will all be happy. It is in a bad market that we need all the help we can get, and that is when the dividends appear to do the most good.

*Commandment 5. Look for Sex Appeal.* Sex appeal in a stock? Well, not the kind you find between the covers of *Playboy*. What I mean here is that extra something which can excite the fancy, emotions, and imagination of investors to make them lose their cold analytical approach and decide that this is a stock which can really take off. It doesn't have to be very important in terms of the overall business of the company, but it must be something highly visible and very much in demand on Wall Street.

One of the maxims in salesmanship is "Sell the sizzle, not the steak." What this means is that while most restauranteurs are telling customers how wonderful their steaks are—tender, thick, tasty, properly aged—the really successful one doesn't bother bragging about the steaks themselves; he tells the customers that they are so hot and fresh from the grill that you can still hear them sizzle. That's salesmanship. Nowhere was it ever said that a steak with a sizzle is tenderer, tastier, or bigger than one without the sizzle, but it certainly can impress customers.

A similar phenomenon can occur in the stock market. Tell a potential investor about a good company with a nice growth record, low P/E ratio, and book value higher than the price of the stock, and he is likely to yawn. But tell him that one of the company's divisions is working on solar energy, and suddenly if you have touched the right person his entire view of the stock will change. It doesn't matter if solar energy is never going to amount to 1% of the company's earnings; that is this company's "sex appeal" for that investor.

So we will define sex appeal as that somewhat emotional additional factor which can excite an investor and make a fine, but perhaps dull, company seem like a sexy young person.

In the next chapter we will analyze eight stocks using these Five Commandments, and you will see how they are applied to actual cases. But selection of a stock is only a part of making money in the market. You must select a number of stocks, and you must know when to buy them and when to sell them. That process is called "portfolio management." Fortunately, as with stock selection, the basic principles of portfolio management have been well known for years. Applying them successfully is another matter, but basically there are Four Keys to Profitable Portfolio Management.

1. *Diversify*. There is no more important guide in the entire world of investment than the single word "diversification." It applies to anyone who wants to be a survivor in relatively risky situations. Buying stocks is a fairly risky business, and therefore anyone who seriously wants to see his capital grow and survive must diversify. As soon as one grasps the basic principle that no one can foretell which stocks are going to go up and which are going to go down, it is axiomatic that you must not put all your eggs in one basket.

If you wish corroboration of this rule, just look at how other successful financial institutions operate. Banks make loans and never know which particular loan is going to go bad. They are under very strict laws which prohibit them from having more than a small percentage of their assets in any one loan. Casualty and life insurance companies take risks with the lives and liabilities of their insureds, but because they are insuring such a large number of people, the actual risk at any one time to the company is quite small.

So when buying stocks, it must be a cardinal rule to diversify. Just how many different issues you should have one cannot say, but it certainly is more important to have at least ten different stocks than to be sure that you have a round lot of each. It is important to diversify not only into different stocks, but into different industries and also different types of industries. There should be a balance of industrial companies, banks, and service companies.

The argument against diversification is that you can't get rich unless you are willing to have faith in one stock, invest all you have in it, and then wait to see it go up. That, claim the adherents to this way of thinking, is the way to get rich. And they will back up their claim with stories, undoubtedly true, of people who put all their money into a certain stock just before it went up and made an absolute killing. What they will not tell you is the large number of people who put all their money into other stocks just before they started going down.

The history of Wall Street is filled with stories of men who risked everything on one stock. Many of these people got very rich. But most of them died broke. If the principle of diversification has worked throughout the ages for every major investment institution, it will work for you. The profits may never be as spectacular as those of the person who invests in one big winner, but your savings are too important to play Russian roulette with them.

2. *Take your time about investing.* There is never any rush to get fully invested. Since no one can know whether the market is going to go up or down in the short run, the great value in investing over a period of time is that no matter what happens you are not going to invest all of your money at the top. If you invest all at once, the odds are better than you might think that just this could happen. The reason is that the market always looks good when it is moving up, so one is naturally inclined to buy when stocks are at the highest. Once prices fall down, you will feel like kicking yourself, but aside from that, there is not too much you can do. As an example of what can go wrong, I am reminded of a man who invested one million dollars in an option writing program. This was supposed to be a hedged program, so that his losses could not be too great. He started out in October 1978, and within one month had lost $170,000 simply because the man he had trusted with the investing committed all the money in the first few days of the month. Imagine what would have happened if this had not been a hedged program!

Therefore, it is my suggestion that any investment program start slowly. There is certainly no harm in thinking of taking an entire year in which to invest a large sum of money. Remember that this book is talking about a market rise which could take a decade to accomplish, and that during that decade there will be major bear markets as well as bull markets, so there can be no assurance that the stocks you buy will go up in the few months after you acquire them. When it comes to investing in the stock market, one can truly say that it pays to make haste slowly.

3. *Don't be afraid to take profits.* At the time of writing this book there were a great many stocks which were selling at very low prices and represented outstanding buying opportunities. There were relatively few stocks which appeared to be fully priced and therefore worthy of being sold. I anticipate this will change. I believe that the top-grade blue chip stocks will soon begin to move

up dramatically. If those are the stocks which you have bought, then you should be watching for the time when you have a good profit in them. After all, the purpose of buying stocks is to make money, and you haven't really made any money as long as your money is tied up in the stock. Only when you sell it have you actually made a profit. So when the stocks which you own have risen to what appears to be a reasonable level, then don't be afraid to sell them and get into something else. If you don't see any other stock that you like, then don't be afraid to park your money in a money market fund for a while until you see something that you do like.

4. *Reassess your entire portfolio regularly.* Presumably you have purchased each stock in your portfolio because each one fulfilled the Five Commandments; it had a low P/E ratio, reasonable growth rate, and good book value, it paid a dividend, and it had sex appeal. As time goes on, some of your stocks are going to change for various reasons, and they will no longer fulfill all of these requirements. For example, if the earnings of the company go down, the P/E ratio may go up. If the price of the stock goes up, the P/E ratio may also go up and the dividend yield may become ludicrously low. Or changes in the economy can make it unlikely that the company will be able to continue its growth rate.

Whatever the reason, you should periodically, let's say every month, go over every stock in your portfolio and ask yourself this question: "If I did not already own this stock, would I now go out and buy it?" If your answer is no, then you must ask yourself why you still own the stock. If you would not be a buyer of the stock, and you actually were a buyer of it earlier, then some conditions must have changed. Perhaps now you should consider being a seller of the stock.

In addition to evaluating the stocks which you own, you must also constantly evaluate the stocks which you do not own. You could own them if you wanted to by simply swapping out of some of the stocks you now own. Thus, managing a portfolio consists of reviewing the stocks you already own and comparing them to what you don't. If the ones you don't own come out looking better, then perhaps it is time for a change.

There you have the Four Keys to Profitable Portfolio Management. They probably seem like just plain common sense, and that's what they are. But it's very easy to ignore them, and the prudent investor will take pains to follow them conscientiously.

Now that we've discussed the way to select your stock and manage your portfolio, let's move on to some actual stocks which you might select by using these rules.

# 10

# EIGHT STOCKS FOR THE EIGHTIES

This chapter lists eight stocks which I believe are outstanding long-term investments. The real value of this chapter, though, is not the list of names it presents, but rather the fact that it demonstrates the type of analytical reasoning which goes into selecting a stock, according to the process described in the previous chapter. By the time you read this chapter, the eight stocks listed may have changed so much, either in price or some other vital statistics, that these recommendations will be completely out of date, but the reasoning utilized here can be applied by you from any time between now and infinity.

Let me say at the outset that this list contains no real surprises. There is no little company which is projected to grow at 50% a year for the next ten years and which is now selling for six times its current earnings. There is no unknown emerging company which is going to be the next Xerox or is definitely going to be the stock of the decade and is therefore going to make you rich. Consistent with my philosophy concerning the Random Walk theory, I do not believe that it is possible to predict such an outcome about any stock. Even if it were, then others would already have come to similar conclusions and the price of the stock would be so high compared to its current earnings that it would not be a stock with a low P/E, which is the most important characteristic I seek.

In fact, the selections here are almost the very opposite extreme from the hot little stock which may have been the subject of the latest tip you heard. These companies are all large, they are all well known to the investment community, and in many cases there are reasons why investors deliberately are avoiding them. In our analysis we will look not only at the reasons why I believe that they represent good investments, but also at why many other investors are shunning them. Perhaps the reasons others are avoiding these stocks are not as significant or as valid as is generally believed, and if this is the case, then the fact that others are not buying them simply creates a greater bargain for us.

But if these stocks are not the hot little companies which are going to make you rich in twelve months, they all do have a great many other attractions to offer you. They are all financially sound, well-established companies which are leaders in their fields. They have weathered recessions, depressions, and inflations in the past, and they are very likely to do so in the future. They are not dependent upon a single patent or trademark, they are not going to rise (or fall) with the success of a new and untried technology, they are not dependent for their future growth upon their ability to obtain new financing, nor are they completely beholden to one marketing or technical "genius" to continue their progress.

Instead they have years and years of solid growth behind them, they have developed layers of good management, they are well financed, and with one exception they are marketing a range of products or services which have been in demand for decades and which will continue to be in demand for decades to come. It can reasonably be stated that these companies will be around to supply these demands.

What each of these companies offers, therefore, is a large, well-run and financed business which is flourishing and will likely continue to grow. What the stocks offer is outstanding value. We will apply the Five Commandments of Stock Selection to each of these stocks to determine just how good a value it is. What they all have in common is that in each case the P/E ratio is low, which means that you are buying a dollar's earnings for a low cost, and, perhaps even more important, you are buying a dollar of quality earnings in a high-quality company. Furthermore, each of these companies is growing, although at varying rates, with some of them admittedly cyclical. Nevertheless, all the companies show dramatic earnings growth over a complete economic cycle. The most important aspect of each company here is that it is a solid company, with a low cost of earnings and solid growth.

You will also see that each company has impressive assets behind its stock, that each pays dividends, and that in almost every case there is that little extra bit of "sex appeal" which can excite the fancy of stock buyers when the right time comes.

In summary, these stocks may not turn out to be the biggest price gainers of the eighties. That doesn't bother me a bit, because I don't believe that anyone can predict which will be the biggest gainers of the coming years. What I do strongly believe is that these stocks are definitely not going to be the big losers of the eighties; they are all such well-established companies that they are unlikely to go out of business or suffer serious reversals, and it is therefore very unlikely that their earnings will shrink drastically. Second, since you are buying the current earnings at a very low cost, there is little chance that the price of the stocks will decline drastically.

What these stocks offer is solid investment opportunities with low downside risks and extremely low risk that the stocks will substantially decline. That is important, because the reason people got so burned in the market in the past was that they either were buying little "growth" stocks which turned out to earn much less than had been expected, or they purchased good companies but paid so much for the earnings that even though the company continued to do well, the price of the stock just kept falling. With these stocks that possibility is greatly reduced.

Finally, the fact that there is no little "wonder stock" here which no one ever heard of is completely consistent with my basic view of the stock market today: In a time of general market depression, when almost every stock is underpriced, there is no need to stretch for grade B or C stocks when you can purchase top-quality grade A stocks for minimal prices. At times like this you can afford the best.

Let's make an analogy. Suppose you are traveling in one of the relatively few countries left where the U.S. dollar is worth a great deal. You are deciding which hotel to stay at, and you find that prices are so cheap that you can stay at the greatest luxury hotel in the country for $20 a night, or at a more typical modest hotel for $10 a night. Which of us would not say that if prices are this cheap we might just as well have the best? Sure you could save another $10 a night by taking a chance at that slightly shabby place off the highway, but if the legendary Grand Ritz is so affordable, why not take the opportunity to live well?

The same type of reasoning applies to stocks. If all stocks are now priced so cheaply, why not take advantage of the stiuation to buy the best? Remember, these very stocks were some of the "one-decision" stocks which were so highly thought of in the sixties that they were selling at P/E's of 20, 30, 40, or even higher. With the present depressed stock prices, there is no need to reach for the untried, unproven, high-risk company.

The time to buy the little emerging companies is when the blue chips are once again selling at such high P/E ratios that it is questionable whether they are good values, for instance at 20 times earnings or more. Then, if the smaller companies are selling at substantially lower P/E's, that might be the time to switch out of some of the blue chips into the more speculative companies. But now is not such a time. Ironically, right now many of the really first-class companies are selling for significantly lower P/E's than many of the smaller, more risky companies.

So, here are my recommended stocks. As I mentioned, the names are not nearly as important as the process of selecting them. You are encouraged to use the same process to find companies of your own. Also, it must be emphasized that these are not the only stocks I recommend. It would be possible to come up with another good list of eight outstanding stocks which did not include a single one of the stocks named here. This just shows once more that today is simply a good time to buy high-quality stocks.

### GULF + WESTERN

Gulf + Western is one of those companies which is not as well known as some of its subsidiaries and their brand names. These include Paramount Pictures Corp; Simon & Schuster; Pocket Books; Kayser-Roth Corporation, which manufactures Excello, Interwoven, Bostonian Shoes, Supp-Hose, and No Nonsense Stockings; Simmons Co., maker of Beautyrest; Consolidated Cigar Corp., which makes Dutch Masters and El Producto, among others; Nibroc Paper Products; and New Jersey Zinc. It is also big in automotive parts manufacturing and owns large sugar plantations in the Dominican Republic.

It is a large company with sales for fiscal year 1979 of $5.3 billion, making it the 52nd largest manufacturing company in the United States. With such widespread interests in so many areas, it is, yes, a conglomerate. As we know, that is now a dirty word on Wall Street, and one reason Gulf + Western stock is selling at its current low price is because of this fact.

In analyzing the stock, let us first follow the first commandment and see what its P/E ratio is. Recently, G + W stock was $16.25, and for the twelve months ending January 31, 1980, the company earned $4.13 a share, which gives it a P/E ratio of just 3.93. At the same time the Dow Jones Industrial Average was selling at a P/E of 7.2. Why should there be such a discrepancy? Is Gulf + Western so shaky and risky that its earnings deserve to be selling at 55% the price of the other industrial companies? For such a reduction you might think that G + W was trying to sell leftover "U.S. Olympic Team— Moscow 1980" uniforms or perhaps they got the license to operate nuclear generators at Three Mile Island or the exclusive rights to reissue the Pet Rock. None of the above.

On the contrary, since the company is made up of eight operating groups, each in a completely different area, it gains some resistance to economic trends. For example, when times are bad, people go to the movies more often rather than do more expensive things like take vacations or eat out, so Paramount Pictures should do well. In a recession people keep their cars longer and need more replacement parts, and since G + W is a major factor in automobile replacement parts, this area also does well in a recession. On the other hand, G + W is one of the largest zinc producers, and in times of inflation the profits from this division soar. It also has an important interest in financial services, such as insurance and small loans, which is fairly consistent. In summary, the diversification of G + W's interests gives it a degree of solidity.

Thus, we can conclude that its low P/E, at roughly one-half the other industrial companies, makes G + W a real find. Why should it be so cheap? One of the reasons is of course that it is a conglomerate. Another is that a few years ago the S.E.C. began a major investigation into the company and issued a report with some criticisms which are now being litigated in the courts. Although this created a blemish upon the reputation of G + W, the significant part of the S.E.C.'s conclusion from our point of view is that nothing was found which would cost the company a large amount of money even if it is finally resolved that the company is guilty.

Second, we want to know what the growth of earnings has been. Earnings for the past ten years have been growing rather consistently except for a dramatic dip in 1977, when a number of negative factors came together. Nevertheless, because of the businesses that G + W is in, one cannot say that this is a growth company. Cigar consumption is going down, there is not an ever-increasing demand for mattresses, world sugar consumption is increasing slowly, and the automotive area is also not one of rapid growth. The real growth in G + W in the past has come from acquisitions, and there is every reason to believe that this will continue. To what extent this will show up in per share increases in the future is open to question. Nevertheless, the record shows that for the past ten years earnings per share have gone up at a 9.5% rate, and over the past five years at an 11.5% rate.

Thus, while not a "growth" stock, G + W is a company which is slowly but consistently growing over time. It is fair to project that it will be able to maintain a 10% growth rate over the next five years. Looking at the P/E Evaluator Chart we see that for a company growing 10% a year, with the current P/E for a no-growth company at a low 3, we would be willing to pay a P/E of 4.83, times earnings $4.13 gives $19.95. Notice that even this price is based upon using a P/E for a no-growth company of 3, which I believe is highly unlikely to be the P/E applied to a no-growth company in five years. The figure is far too low. If the figure at that time is 4, then the chart shows that we would be willing to pay 6.44 times earnings for the stock, which would give it a current value of $26.60.

Moving on to the lesser commandments, we look at the assets behind the stock. At the end of its 1979 fiscal year G + W had a book value of $23.72, which means that at a price of $16.25 it was selling at just 68% of its book value. This means that in terms of book value G + W was a real bargain. Even tangible book value was $16.34. While G + W does have a heavy debt burden, as a percentage of equity it has been declining for many years, and management continues to have an objective of increasing equity faster than debt, so that this ratio should improve.

Dividends are now 75 cents a year, which gives a return of 4.5%. This is not particularly high by today's standards, but the dividends have been growing consistently. In fact, when the rate was raised to 75 cents in 1979, that marked the fourteenth consecutive year of higher regular cash dividends. There is no reason to believe that this trend will not continue.

Finally we come to the intangible factor which could give investors a feeling of excitement about G + W stock. That area is in the research they are now doing in a zinc chloride battery. The company has a substantial commitment to develop a new battery which could provide the power source for the electric car of the next decade. With the price of gasoline increasing out of sight, and the supply limited, there will be increasing demand for a commuter car which will not use gasoline and can be used for short trips. G + W management states that their new battery could power a car for 125 to 200 miles before recharging at speeds of 60 miles per hour. It is currently under development and testing under grants from the Department of Energy.

Thus, Gulf + Western is a large, diversified company whose stock is now selling at a rock bottom P/E and at a very large discount from book value. Its variety of activities gives it a resistance to economic downturns, and its past growth indicates that it will continue to flourish in the future. With its low price relative to earnings and book value, and its rising dividends, it is an outstanding candidate to increase sharply in price while offering relatively little downside risk.

## CITICORP

One of the basic principles of this book is that when stock prices are cheap, you can afford to buy the best. And when it comes to top-quality firms, what could be more blue chip than a major bank? Inherent in the capitalist system is the function of a bank, acting as a savings depository for people with funds to invest and lending money out to worthy borrowers.

Ever since it was discovered that one could make a good living by charging a bit more for the money that was being lent out than for the money that was coming in, banking has been a wonderful business. And for various reasons the U.S. banking industry has become extremely prosperous while at the same time the prices of the stocks of many of the banks have been falling. Sounds like a natural opportunity for the value-minded investor.

Although there are many banks which would make good long-term investments, I have selected New York's Citicorp for various reasons. First, it is the biggest bank in terms of international operations, and I believe that the international area will continue to outgrow the domestic in the years to come. Second, it is the largest bank in terms of retail business in New York City. Finally, it is the second largest bank in the country, being second to California's BankAmerica. Citicorp has 2,000 offices in nearly 100 countries, 51,000 employees, and a net worth of $3.9 billion. Now let's look at how Citicorp stacks up in terms of our Five Commandments.

First, what is it costing us to purchase the earnings of this bank? In 1979 the bank earned $4.36 a share (excluding profits or losses from securities transactions which fluctuate from year to year), and the stock was recently selling for $22. This means that the stock had a P/E of 5, which is amazingly cheap for a stock of such quality. Let's remember that as recently as 1976 the average annual P/E for the stock was 10.2 and that in 1973 the P/E actually got over 20. So we now have a company which is bigger and stronger than ever and selling at one-quarter of the previous price per dollar of earnings. Another way of looking at the P/E of 5 is that at the time Citicorp was at 5, the Dow Jones Industrial Average was selling at a P/E of 7. So the second largest bank in America was selling at a substantial discount from the average large industrial firm.

Second, we look at the quality of the earnings and see whether it is likely that they will grow in the future. First let's take a look at the industry. Is banking likely to grow in the future? One thing we know about banking is that, unlike the buggy industry, the banking industry is here to stay. Wherever and whenever there is any other type of business, there will be banking. And banking has recently been growing faster than business in general. Will Citicorp continue to grow with the industry? In New York City, Citicorp pioneered in having within its banks 24-hour mini-banks which were operated by electronic tellers. The result is that they can service customers at less cost to the bank, and customers can get service whenever they want it. Within the banking industry it is generally believed that Citicorp has the best management of any full-service commercial bank. If past is prologue to the future, they should be growing at a rapid clip. For the nine years from 1970 through 1979 the bank more than tripled income per share from $1.33 to $4.36, achieving an average annual growth rate of 10.5%.

What the future holds on the short-term horizon depends upon the spread which Citicorp is able to obtain on its loans, that is, how much more it is able to charge its borrowers than it must pay for the money which it borrows itself. But on a longer term basis, the company is poised to continue its growth into the future. There is reason to believe that it will earn about $6.25 by 1983, which would mean a continuation of a growth rate of about 10%.

Coming now to the Third Commandment, we look at the assets behind the company. The one figure which tells it all is that the tangible book value per share of Citicorp is $31. This means that at a price of $22, the stock is selling at a discount of 26% from its book value! And in the case of a bank, we don't have to ask just what that book value represents, because most of it is simply hard cash. There are no large manufacturing facilities with a high book value, but perhaps a negligible liquidation value. This is a real book value, made up for the most part of cash or loans to some of America's most credit-worthy borrowers.

Fourth is the dividends. Citicorp is paying at this writing $1.42 per share a year, which gives it a yield of 6.4%. That is not the highest yield on the big board, but it is not bad, especially when you consider the growth rate of the dividend. Since 1970, cash dividends have increased every year except 1972, when federal law prohibited it. In every year since 1973 the percentage increase has exceeded the rate of inflation. There is no reason to believe that Citicorp will not continue this policy of increasing its dividends, especially since the current dividend represents only 30% of earnings.

Finally we come to the mysterious "X" factor which could cause the stock to ignite the imaginations of future stock buyers. Two factors were already mentioned: that Citicorp is the leader in international banking which could resume its rapid growth at any time in the future, and that it is the leader in New York's retail banking. But even more potentially powerful is the possibility that the United States may be changing the basic way in which it conducts banking. For almost two centuries American banking has been strictly limited, in that each bank was able to conduct business only in that state in which it was organized. Each state banking commission jealously guarded the profits of its own local banks by keeping out all banks from other states. But as the needs of America's great multinational corporations have grown, this concept has become anachronistic.

In 1978 Congress passed the International Banking Act, and under it there is a proposal that Edge Act subsidiaries of banks formed to finance international transactions be allowed to branch nationwide and conduct all international transactions and full domestic banking business with qualified international customers. This could lead to a major penetration in local banking business by major U.S. banks such as Citicorp. Some states are also considering reciprocal banking arrangements, whereby a bank in one state can operate in the other. Citicorp is now issuing Master Cards to people in many parts of the country, which means it is already in a part of consumer banking across state lines. These innovations could lead to a greatly enlarged role for Citicorp. If Citicorp could change from a very large New York City bank into a very large bank doing business in most of the states of the country, it would be an explosive growth.

## GENERAL MOTORS CORPORATION

If you believe in America, you almost have to believe in General Motors. Nothing is as pervasive in influence upon the U.S. way of life as its largest manufacturing corporation which in 1979 produced 60.5% of all domestic cars. There has been a lot of moaning and complaining recently that the domestic auto manufacturers were making the wrong cars at the wrong time and that they were unresponsive to consumer needs. The argument is that when Americans were craving small cars which got high mileage, the U.S. manufacturers continued to try to push their large gas guzzlers upon the public, and the result was that Americans bought imported cars in unprecedented numbers, until today VW's, Datsuns, and Toyotas are as popular as some domestic brands.

In defense of American manufacturers, it should be pointed out that for decades Americans had been buying and preferring the large, comfortable, and peppy domestic cars. When the price of gas suddenly shot up in the late seventies and early eighties, consumers' needs changed. Foreign car manufacturers for years had been designing cars for countries where gasoline cost $2 or more a gallon, so they had the kinds of cars Americans wanted, and they had them instantly. It takes many years for a car company to bring out a completely new car, and it will take the American manufacturers a few years to convert completely to fuel-efficient cars. During that period they will suffer, but they will and already are changing.

The fact that foreign makers already were producing these cars does not make them inherently better car manufacturers or designers. They just happened to be in the right place at the right time. What if the price of gasoline suddenly fell back down to 60 cents a gallon? How long would it take Toyota to come out with a full line of large, comfortable, powerful V-8 cars?

If fact, GM has already responded to higher gas prices with its X-Body series, which is so popular that GM sells all of them it can make. And to keep things in perspective, let's remember that even when imported car sales were at their height in the early 1980's, GM sold more cars in the United States than all the imports combined, and by a two-to-one margin!.

So GM is a large, successful company. It has its problems converting to the new demands of car buyers, but there is every reason to believe that it will successfully meet this challenge, and once it does, its sales will go up significantly as it competes head on with the imports.

The recession posed another problem for the auto industry. Since automobiles can last anywhere from two years up to ten or more, it is easy for the consumer to defer purchase of a new car when times get hard. Thus, the automotive industry is by its very nature cyclical, and it always has suffered hard during a recession. However, by the same token, it will always bounce right back once the recession is over, because Americans don't stop driving during a recession, they just stop buying new cars. What happens is that their cars get more and more worn out, and finally, when prosperity returns to the economy, there are a lot of drivers who all discover that it is time to trade in the old jalopy for a new car. In other words, total demand for cars does not really decline during a recession, it is just deferred.

When the recession ends, GM will be there, building cars for every taste and every pocketbook in the country. Therefore, when we look at the numbers of GM, it is more realistic to ignore the recent quarters during the recession and look at what it was like in 1979, with the expectation that it will certainly return to at least that healthy a position once the recession ends.

In 1979 GM earned $10.04 a share, which at its recent price of $49 means that it is selling at just under 5 times earnings, which is cheap in the extreme for a company of such outstanding caliber. It is estimated that earnings per share for the period 1982–84 will be $16. This represents an annual increase of 15% a year. Looking at the P/E Evaluator Chart, we find that if we use a P/E of 4 for a company with no earnings increase, then we would be willing to pay a P/E of 8 today to get a P/E in five years that was growing at a rate of 15%.

The third of the Five Commandments is to look at its financial soundness. Here it is difficult to find a better company than GM. The tangible book value per share is $65. In other words, the stock at $49 was selling at 24% below book value. Its long-term debt was only $4.8 billion against a net worth of $24.5 billion. Thus, the company is very sound financially.

Dividends were set at $4.60 a year plus special dividends when profits warranted, but in May 1980 the regular dividend was cut to $2.40 a year. At this rate it was only a 4.9% dividend. But I believe it is more realistic from the long-range point of view to look at the dividend before the recession year of 1980, which represented a return of 9.4%. This rate of dividends will probably be resumed as soon as the economy returns to normal and would represent an excellent return on investment.

Finally, we come to the special "X" factor. GM is in the transportation manufacturing business. It is not wedded to the internal combustion gasoline engine. It is a pioneer among domestic manufacturers of the diesel engine for passenger cars, and looking toward the future there is the possibility of GM's introducing special purpose electric vehicles by the mid-eighties. When and if they announce cars which will run without gasoline, the stock could become a real glamour stock.

In summary, GM is the workhorse of American manufacturers. It will be around for a long, long time. While it is in a highly cyclical industry, GM has proven itself able to ride the troughs better than its competition and to come out ahead. As long as there is a U.S.A., people are going to drive cars, and as long as they do, GM will continue to build them.

### INTERNATIONAL BUSINESS MACHINES

For many years International Business Machines was known among stockbrokers as "The World's Best Stock." For many years it acted exactly that way, going ever higher and higher in price. Adjusting the old prices for recent stock splits, the price went from a low of $26.30 in 1965 to a high of $91.30 in 1973. Since then, it has done nothing except go down to its mid-1980 price of $60, along with so many other blue chip stocks. But let's take a closer look at this company, and see how it got its nickname.

Can you think of a better way to choose a good stock than to find the fastest growing major industry in the world and then find the most successful company in that industry? If you had to pick the fastest growing major industry in the world over the past 25 years, there are a lot of names that would come to mind, such as airplanes, telecommunications, and medical apparatus; however, in my opinion, the winner in that category has to be computers. Here is an industry that barely existed at the end of World War II, and today there isn't a company in the world of any size which doesn't use a computer.

Once one has found the industry, it is easy to pick the most successful company in it. IBM has about 40% to 60% of the computer systems market, and it operates on a worldwide basis. When you consider the dozens of companies which are manufacturing computers, you will understand why people analyzing the computer market say that there are basically two factors in it: IBM and all the others. Gross income of IBM in 1979 was $22.8 billion, making it the eighth largest industrial company in the nation. What's more, this is a large company which is a true "growth" company; its earnings have increased at an average of 14.5% over the last ten years. In terms of financial stability, it cannot be beat, and until 1979 it didn't even have any long-term debt.

If the company is so great, you may be wondering why the stock has done so badly. After all, $60 is a long way from its high of

$91, and many other stocks are now back close to their previous highs. There has been a conflux of two influences. First, the company was regarded so highly in the late sixties and early seventies that the stock was clearly overvalued. In 1971 and 1972 it sold at an average annual P/E of 35! Given the current stock market climate, there is no large company which could possibly justify a stock selling at this rarified P/E.

The second factor was that in 1979 many analysts began to wonder whether IBM really was a growth stock at all. The reason was that earnings appeared to be tapering off. In 1978 the company earned $5.32 a share, and in 1979 only $5.16. Not exactly a growth company—until you look below the surface. A quick review of the facts shows that in 1979 shipments of data processing equipment were substantially ahead of 1978. So why the decline in earnings? It simply has to do with the way in which IBM customers decided to acquire the computers.

IBM has always given customers the choice of purchasing the machines outright or of leasing them. Normally, the larger customers always purchased the machines because it was cheaper. But in 1979, when interest rates began to approach 20%, it made sense for many more users to lease their computers. When IBM sells a computer, the entire profit is recorded that year; but when it leases a computer, it can record only that portion of the profit which was actually received in that year. Therefore, if it leased a computer at the beginning of the year on a five-year basis, then only one-fifth of the profit from that computer could be recorded that year. If it leased on the last month of the year, it could record only one-twelfth of that 20%, or just 1.6% of the total profit. On the other hand, it could sell a computer on December 31 and record 100% of the profit. Thus, every computer which is leased for five years instead of bought has the effect of reducing profits by at least 80% in the year of lease.

This is the immediate short-term effect. But what happens in the next year? On the computers which were sold, there is no more income. But on the computers which were leased, let's assume on a five-year basis, another 20% of the profit will come in the second year. Therefore, the more computers that are leased, the greater the profits will be in successive years. Thus leasing reduces profits in the short run but actually helps them in the intermediate run. That is why it is so important to note that profits did not fall because fewer computers were acquired by customers, but that, on the contrary, more computers were shipped in 1979 than ever before. We can conclude, then, that IBM is still a growth company, and now with a bigger lease base, that it has more financial security than before.

Let's look into the statistics. With IBM selling at $60 and earning $5.16 in 1979, it was selling at 11.6 times earnings. This is higher than many of the companies described in this chapter, but this is a real growth company. What does future growth look like? Computer demand continues to be strong, and as the industry brings down the cost of memory, the users for computers increase each year. IBM has invested heavily in new manufacturing facilities and spends an enormous amount each year on research and development, estimated at 6% of revenues, which would mean over $1 billion a year. No wonder it is able to keep the lead in its industry. Another big advantage IBM has in its continued growth is that, being as large as it is, it has the support people around the world to sell and service its computers, an extremely important factor in a complex business like computers.

Summing it all up, the company should earn about $9 a share in 1984, which would mean that it will continue to grow at about 12% a year.

Thus, this is one of the rarities, a quality growth stock. And you can get it now for just over 10 times earnings. Is this a bargain? If you consider that in 1973 the stock earned 47% less than it did in 1979, and that then the stock was selling for up to 65% more than it is now, I think you might agree that it is indeed an enormous bargain by historical standards. Now, let's look at the P/E Evaluator Chart. We find that if the going P/E for a nongrowth company is 4, then the P/E that we would have to pay today for a company growing at 12% a year is 7.2 times earnings. That would give us a company in five years with a P/E of 4.

In this case, however, where we are talking about the largest company in the fastest growing major industry in the world, it seems more than reasonable to assume that the company will still be growing in five years. Therefore, one would not expect that the company would be selling then at only 4 times earnings. If instead it were then selling at only 6 times earnings, it would be selling at 10.86 times current earnings, or just below current market prices; and if it were selling at 8 times earnings, it would be selling at 14.5 times the current earnings; and if it were still selling at its present P/E of 11.6, it would be selling at 21 times its current earnings, which is simply another way of saying that if the earnings growth we have projected of 12% a year for the next five years is correct and the P/E ratio of the stock stays at 11.6, then the stock will be selling for 76% more than what it is selling for now, or $104 a share.

## INDIANAPOLIS POWER & LIGHT COMPANY

How would you like to own a part of a business whose profits are regulated by the government? Thinking back upon what the Internal Revenue Service does to you each April 15, you may decide that you definitely do not want to be in a business where the government tells you how much you can make. But what if the role of the government regulators was also to make almost certain that you did make a reasonable and fair profit, and what if it were in their power to see to it that you did make such a profit because you actually had no direct competition, and what if the regulators let you raise your prices whenever your profits went below that reasonable and fair profit? Maybe then it wouldn't sound so bad.

In that case you ought to like the idea of owning some stock in a utility company. Each utility is regulated by a state regulatory body which makes sure that the public is not over-charged for electricity and that the utility makes a fair profit for its stockholders. Unless there is some catastrophe, as there was at the Three Mile Island nuclear reactor, the stockholders of a utility have very little to worry about.

The history of earnings and dividends of utilities is not one of the most exciting subjects in the world. It competes for attention with watching grass grow and paint dry. The reason is that when you have Big Brother watching to make sure that you make a reasonable profit, and your customers have to buy from you, it's pretty easy to make a steady profit year after year. Because their costs and income are so steady, utilities traditionally can pay out a large proportion of their earnings as dividends to stockholders.

The big negative in utilities is that since everyone is already a customer and will probably not buy much more elec-tricity next year than they did this year, the opportunities for growth are limited. In assessing which particular utility company to invest in, there are three main factors to be considered: future growth prospects, future cost of production, and regulator attitudes.

Future growth is determined primarily by the geographical location of the utility. If it is in an old stagnating part of the country, say in the Middle Atlantic states, with declining urban centers, then clearly its prospects for growth are poor; but just as clearly, if it is in the booming sun belt area, then it ought to keep on growing rapidly.

The second factor is future costs of production. If a utility is producing electricity by a method which is cheap and will continue to be cheap in the future, then it will be easier for them to make a good profit. Basically the question of whether they will have low-cost electricity is tied in to the type of fuel which the utility uses to generate electricity. If it burns oil, as do many of the utilities in the north and especially the northeast, then as the price of petroleum goes up, their cost of producing electricity will go up. If they burn coal, there is less likelihood that its price will go up because there is so much coal available in the United States. If the utility is using nuclear reactors, that is all right, but if it has plans to construct many more in the future, then with the new post-Three Mile Island attitudes in this country, it could be very difficult for them. In short, when rating utilities, coal is generally preferred, followed by existing nuclear, then proposed nuclear, and worst oil.

The final consideration is the attitude of the particular public utility commission which has the power to set the rates. There is a large difference among the attitudes of the different states. While they are all trying to accomplish the same objective of giving both the customers and the utility a fair break, in some states the commissions are much more in favor of the consumers and in other states they are more in favor of the utility. If you are considering buying stock in a utility, guess which states you are going to be more likely to buy stock in?

Now let's take a look at a specific utility. First I must say that this one was picked out of many; there are dozens of others which are just as good as Indianapolis Power & Light. Also there are many others which may not be as "good" but which pay a higher dividend and therefore may be preferable for someone who is concentrating on dividends and doesn't care as much about other considerations.

Indianapolis P & L was recently selling at $22 and earning $3.46 for the year 1979, giving it a P/E of 6.3. While that is reasonable, it is the quality of the earnings which give it appeal. Except for one year, it has earned over $2 a share for every year since 1965. Given the nature of the utility industry there seems to be every indication that it will continue to earn a handsome amount per share into the future.

What about growth? Admittedly the utility industry is not a growth industry in any normal sense of the word. But the prospects for Indianapolis look good. First, Indiana's state utility regulatory climate is among the best of any state, meaning that the company will be able to get reasonable rate increases when they need them. Second, they use coal for 99% of their generating, so they don't have to worry about skyrocketing prices for oil, or the need to build more nuclear reactors. Since they serve a mature industrial and residential area, there will not be any surge in demand, but it is safe to assume that they will continue to grow at a slightly faster pace, perhaps 6% a year, giving earnings per share in the $4 range by 1983. Since this is such a slow rate of growth, there is no point in looking at the P/E Evaluator Chart.

Third, we find that Indianapolis has a book value of over $30 a share. The Fourth Commandment is unusually important in evaluating utilities, because they are definitely companies which exist for the present rather than the future. Their dividends are among the main reasons for buying the stocks. The company paid $2.12 a share in dividends in 1979, which comes out to a yield of almost 10%. This is a beautiful return, because due to the certainty of the continuation of its dividend, this return can be compared to the return you would get on a bond or from money in the bank. Of course, there is a risk of principal here, and there is no assurance that the dividend will be continued, so it is not the same as a bond or money in the bank.

The favorable factor is that, unlike the interest on a bond which is fixed, the dividend on a utility stock can be increased. The dividends on Indianapolis have been increasing every year since 1976. If the dividend continues to increase at a rate of 6% a year, which seems reasonable at the present time, it will be paying 13.3% in five years and 17.8% in ten years. Either interest rates will have to be very high in ten years, or else the price of the stock is going to rise to a point where the dividends at that time represent the normal return on capital. In other words, it seems likely that in addition to getting a 10% return on your capital, you will also be getting an increase in the capital itself due to increased earnings and dividends.

Finally we come to the Fifth Commandment. Is there any sex appeal in an Indiana utility company? I've tried hard to find it but just couldn't seem to get there. Any readers who want to supply me with the missing ingredient are invited to send in their suggestions for the next edition of this book.

In summary, we have here an excellent way to earn a good rate of interest on your money, with a small risk of capital and the potential of a modest but steady increase in dividends and principal for many years to come.

## EXXON

The most dramatic economic development in the past decade has been the sixfold increase in the worldwide price of petroleum. Whereas the sixties were the decade of constant gasoline discount price wars, the seventies became the decade of doubling and quadrupling prices at the gas pump with occasionally not enough gas to go around at any price. The result of this change has been that money has poured into the hands of the oil companies at an unprecedented rate. With demand for petroleum constantly going up and the supply now partially controlled by OPEC, investors cannot ignore this increasingly important area.

There are basically two types of oil companies, domestic and international. The international companies get their crude oil from various overseas locations, including the Middle East, the North Sea, and South America, and make their money by drilling and operating the oil wells on leased land, or by purchasing it in bulk, transporting the crude, refining it, and marketing it. Domestic companies have their oil fields right here in the United States where they usually have complete rights of ownership. It doesn't take too much thought to realize that in a time of constantly rising crude oil prices, the domestic companies are in a stronger position. Furthermore, a lot of other investors have already thought of that, with the result that stocks of domestic companies are usually priced appreciably higher than the stocks of the international companies on a cost per dollar of earnings basis. Is it really worth paying twice as much for one dollar of earnings in a domestic oil company than in an international company?

If there were some danger that the earnings of the international companies might collapse suddenly because of a shortage of crude available overseas, or that their functions would be taken over by some Middle Eastern governments, there would be ample justification for this. But in fact, there is little likelihood of the supplies of the international oil companies drying up; the hard facts of life are that the oil-exporting countries need our dollars as much or more than we need their oil.

Almost every one of these countries has ambitious industrial, housing, and cultural developments in progress which take huge amounts of Western currencies to bring into being. Without the flow of money that comes from the export of oil, these countries are dead. Therefore it is in their own self-interest to continue to export all the oil they can. And now with the high price of oil and a slowing increase in demand, there will even be more competition among the supplying countries.

Furthermore, the large international companies do much more than produce crude oil. They transport it, refine it, and market it, and each of these activities can be profit producing in and of itself; more important, these are functions which the oil-producing countries cannot do themselves. Therefore the international oil companies do have power, and they do have an important and continuing role to play in the years to come.

The question is, then, which international oil company does one choose? One company is repeatedly mentioned as the best-managed company in the world. It also happens to be the company which is rated as the largest industrial company in the United States according to the Fortune 500 list. That company is Exxon, and while biggest is not necessarily best, in this case it has a lot going for it. Exxon is not just an oil company, because it is also a large factor in natural gas, exploration and mining of coal and uranium, and petrochemicals. Sales in 1979 were a massive $79 billion and its profits were $4.2 billion. It is so big that when it bought the large Reliance Electric Company for $1.2 billion, that amount was just about a quarter of Exxon's "cash flow" for 1979.

First, let's take a look at its earnings. In 1979 the company earned $9.74 a share, and at a recent price of $68, that means that it was selling for about 7 times earnings. As with so many other stocks, this is near its all-time low. Certainly a P/E of 7 is reasonable for a company with just about the strongest financial position of any company in the world.

Second, we look at growth. As we said at the beginning, the past decade has not been typical of what has happened in the oil industry, but Exxon's earnings have been increasing 8% a year compounded over the last ten years. The future looks good, because Exxon is taking a broad view of its role in the world. No longer just an oil company, it sees itself as a broad-based energy company. That is why it is also involved in coal mining and uranium mining, and why it purchased the Reliance Electric

Company. Whether future energy needs are met by oil, coal, nuclear, or any other type of energy which is transported via electricity, Exxon will be there. Because of these factors, some analysts estimate that Exxon's earnings will grow by about 11% a year for the next five years.

Next we look at the assets behind the stock. Book value per share is $51.39, but this includes a lot of proven reserves of oil and natural gas. When this figure is restated to take into account inflation, the shareholders' equity per share comes out to $79.02. Thus, even though you are buying a company which is rich in one of the most prized commodities in the world, you are still buying it for less than its actual replacement cost. The entire organization of management and the ability to make a profit from it are thrown in for free. You are getting the actual assets at less than even their inflation-adjusted value.

Dividends were $4.40 a year, which comes out to a yield of 6.5%, which is very generous. Furthermore, the company has a policy of constantly increasing dividends, as witness the fact that as recently as 1977 they were paying only $3 a share.

Finally, what kind of sex appeal can there be to the largest company in the world? It's not easy, but believe it or not, there is one. Exxon has taken the step of diversifying into a number of unrelated fields, and one of them is office equipment, particularly communications equipment associated with the office of tomorrow. They manufacture Qwip Systems, which enable messages to be sent over a phone, and their Vydec brand includes a series of computer and information processing machines. This is still a tiny area for Exxon, with revenues of only $149 million in 1979, but the important point is that revenues were double that of the previous year. They might keep on doubling for many years to come.

So put it all together, and you have a well-managed company sitting on about $33 billion of proven reserves, with an impregnable position in the world energy system. At 7 times earnings the stock is a bargain, and with indicated growth in the future, plus a 6½% dividend, this is a stock which even widows and orphans can buy and sleep well, knowing that they have much more to win than to lose.

## UNION CARBIDE

If General Motors and Exxon are typical of the well-known companies which provide products and services to the people of this country, then Union Carbide is just as typical of the giant companies which are almost completely unknown to the public because they sell their products to other businesses. With the exception of its relatively few consumer brands, such as Eveready batteries, Prestone II antifreeze, and Simoniz car wax, the company's products are completely unnoticed by the average American. What can you say about low-density polyethylene, ethylene oxide/glycol, ethyleneamines, cellosize thickener, or organo-functional silanes?

While we can't understand what all these and many more products like them do, we can understand the important role they play in the American economy. In the metal-making industries the gasses and metals made by Union Carbide are extremely important; in the packaging industries their plastics are crucial; in the welding industry their gasses are what make it all possible; and in agriculture they make sprays which are invaluable for farmers. In short, Union Carbide makes a wide variety of industrial products essential for the manufacture of the other products which we can understand.

The fact that Union Carbide does not generally deal with direct consumer products has certain advantages. By selling to a wide variety of industries, it is relatively well hedged against a slowdown in one sector of the economy. If retailing slows down, capital goods manufacturing may increase, and vice versa. Because it sells to so many industries and it is selling items which are used up every day, rather than capital goods which can be stored up or saved for years, it is a relatively stable industry. Earnings per share for the six years between 1974 through 1979 have never gone above $8.69 or sunk below $6.05, which is pretty good considering that this period included the worst postwar recession yet as well as some big boom years. Because Union Carbide is big, with sales of $9 billion a year, and stable, it makes an ideal candidate to consider for the prudent long-term investor.

Recently the stock was selling at $44 a share. In 1979 the company earned $8.47 a share, which gave the stock a P/E of 5.2, very low for such a stable high-quality company. Thus, the company passes the test of the First Commandment with flying colors.

As for the Second Commandment of growth, it is difficult to compute for a chemical company such as Union Carbide because growth does not come evenly, year by year. In some years there are increases in earnings, and in other years earnings are flat.

Perhaps the best way to come up with a figure is to go back to 1969 when the company earned $3.08. This means earnings have been advancing at an annual rate of 10%. The company recently projected net income of about $12 a share in 1983, which would be an increase of about 10% a year. Combining these growth rates gives an average growth of about 10%. If we use a P/E of 4 for a no-growth company, then the P/E Evaluator Chart indicates that we should be willing to pay 6.44 times earnings now for this company, which would give a price for the stock of $54.

As for financial solidity, the company is excellent with a net worth of $3.9 billion and long-term debt of $1.7 billion. Dividends have been increased almost yearly, until they are now at $2.90 a share for a yield of 6.6%.

As for sex appeal in this company, it's pretty hard to find. But there is a perverse type of sex appeal in a company that has no sex appeal. No wonder product on the horizon, no rapidly expanding market, no dramatically increasing profit margins, no genius at the helm. Just a company making a thousand mundane products which are needed by almost every other company almost every day. It may not be glamorous, but it rings up the cash register.

## GATES LEARJET

In many of our previous recommended companies we looked at increases in earnings over the past few years and projected, with a fair degree of certainty, that earnings would continue to grow at that rate. But sometimes there is a special reason why one can anticipate that earnings will suddenly grow at a greatly expanded rate within a few years. For example, if a company has devoted a number of years and a great deal of expense to creating a new profit center, one which will be coming onstream in the foreseeable future, it is reasonable to expect that earnings could take a quantitative leap forward when that happens.

For a particularly good example of this, one could take an industry which has been growing at about 14% annually over the past twenty years. Then take one of the industry's leading companies, whose earnings have been growing at a 10% annual rate for the past five years, and add it to the fact that it has been spending substantial amounts of money developing a new model which it is scheduled to start selling in 1981 and which will have a price approximately twice the price of its present model. The really good news is that the new model will not replace the existing model, as is the case with cars, but will be an additional model, so that unit sales should be 57% higher in 1983 than in 1980. But because of the price of the new model, the impact on revenue will be an increase of approximately 120%.

The industry is the general aviation industry, which manufactures planes for everything except the scheduled airlines, and the company is Gates Learjet, which makes only jet planes for the business plane market (as distinguished from the sports planes or single-engine propeller planes purchased by individuals). First let's take a look at the industry. There is every indication that the industry will continue or even exceed its 14% growth rate. This estimate is based upon the following factors: (1) The deregulation of the scheduled airlines has encouraged them to drop service to many small airports, which now can be served only by general aviation planes. Most airline passengers are unaware that only 3% of all U.S. airports receive scheduled service. (2) American industry is becoming increasingly decentralized as companies seek low-rent areas and nonurban areas which can attract employees with the good quality of life. (3) Technological advances have sharply increased the range, speed, and fuel mileage of most aircraft, thereby making them more useful and economical to industry. All these factors indicate that the general aviation market, and the business jet market in particular, will continue to grow at a rapid pace.

Now let's look at Gates Learjet within this industry. It is by no means the largest company in the industry, but if you look at its area of specialization, which is jets for business, it is the largest factor. Gates has sold 26% of the business jets, with Cessna the next biggest at 17%.

Gates Learjet has done this with one model, the Century model, sold in a number of different types. For 1977 through 1980 they have spent four times their normal level of expenditures on research and development in order to develop the new wide-body Longhorn 50 Series. This has temporarily depressed profits because these expenditures were not offset by any revenues. Once the new series 50's come off the production line, the R and D expenses will drop and the revenue will begin to come in.

For this reason it is estimated that earnings, which were $2.54 for the fiscal year ended April 30, 1980, and were predicted to be just slightly lower for 1981, could almost triple to $7 a share in

1982. Furthermore, it is anticipated that production of the 50 series will be increased in 1982, which will mean more planes for sale in 1983 and thus another sizeable earnings increase.

Let's take a look at how this special growth situation fits into the Five Commandments. First the $2.54 earnings which we are buying for a recent price of $32 a share (on the American Stock Exchange) gives us a P/E of 12.6. This is high in comparison to the other stocks we have mentioned here, but it is still reasonable, and the current P/E is not the main reason we are buying a stock.

The main reason for acquiring Gates Learjet is the growth which may be possible. If the company earns $7 a share in 1982 and substantially more in 1983, that means in three years the earnings would increase by over 176%, or at an annual rate of approximately 40%. Since this is a one-time improvement, we cannot call this a growth company growing at 40% a year and look up the appropriate figure in the P/E Evaluator Chart. But it is clear that such a growth would mean that at the present time the stock is selling at just 4.5 times its possible earnings, and that it is in a growing industry, has a growing segment of that industry, and is the major factor in that segment. Surely such a stock should be worth far more than 4.5 times earnings. Just how much more we will leave to the reader's own estimate.

Third, we note that the book value of Gates Learjet is about $20 a share, meaning that you are paying 60% over book for this stock.

Fourth, the company pays dividends of 40 cents a year, which is practically no dividend at all, for a yield of just 1.2%. What this means is that this is the most speculative of all the stocks mentioned here. It is not a sensational value under Commandments 1, 3, or 4.

But what about the Fifth Commandment? The sex appeal factor is the new model plane which they are producing. It is going to happen, it is exciting, and if the large number of initial deliveries prove satisfactory, then there is the likelihood of continuing earnings at a greatly increased level.

I've left this stock to the last because it is an exception to the Five Commandments and it shows that occasionally an outstanding rating on some of the Commandments may make a stock worth considering even if it is not a smashing success in all of the categories.

# 11

## CONVERTIBLE BONDS: THE ADVANTAGES OF STOCKS WITHOUT ALL THE RISKS

So far we've talked about the many advantages of buying common stocks. There is no denying that there are also a great many risks, however. Common stocks are by their very nature volatile in price, and even in a bull market there are times when stocks go down. For the person who is wary of risking his money in even high-quality, low-priced common stocks, there is another technique which could just fill the bill. That is to purchase convertible bonds instead of the stock.

First let me ask a question. Assume that you are the type of person described above who is reluctant to take the plunge into common stocks. If you could find a security which offered the following, would you be interested: (1) a yield which is usually substantially higher than on the common stock and is not subject to change at the whim of the board of directors but must legally be paid every six months as long as the company is solvent, (2) a guarantee that the security will be redeemed by the company at a specified date in the future for a specified price, usually substantially more than the present price, and (3) a rise in value whenever the common stock of the company went up in value by any appreciable amount?

If these characteristics would be of interest to you, then convertible bonds are worth investigating. Convertible bonds can provide all of these three characteristics, and they are as easily bought and sold as common stocks. There are now 611 outstanding convertible bond issues, and one of them is certain to be right for you. First, just what is a convertible bond?

A convertible bond is a bond which can be converted by the owner of the bond into common stock of the issuing company at any time that the owner of the bond wishes. Each convertible bond states on it the number of shares of common stock into which the bond can be converted. It is this ability to convert the bond into stock which gives the bond its property of rising in price with the stock once the stock gets above a certain value.

For example, if a convertible bond were convertible into 48.8 shares of stock, and if the stock of the company were selling for $25, then the bond would have to be worth at least 48.8 times $25 or $1,220 each. For every one dollar increase in the price of the stock, the price of the bond would have to increase by $48.80. This is why convertibles must go up with the price of the stock, unless the stock is selling at too low a price; we will discuss this point later. If the bond did not go up in price, then anyone who wanted to sell the bond would simply convert it into the 48.8 shares of stock, sell the shares for $25 each, and realize $1,220. Since he has this right, there will always be a purchaser for the bond at this price.

Of course if the price of the stock goes down, the price of the bond will decrease also, but we shall see that there are various reasons why it might not go down quite as much as the stock itself.

Now let's look a bit more closely at just what a bond is. In brief a bond is a way of lending money to corporations; the bond is the I.O.U. which the corporation gives out in which it promises to repay the loan and sets forth the conditions of repayment. Thus the bond contains all the information which is contained in any loan agreement.

The first and most important item is the amount of your bond. This is the *face amount*, the amount that the corporation will repay on the maturity date. In almost every case the face amount is $1,000. In those very rare instances where the bond is not for that amount, the bond will prominently so state. But $1,000 is so universal that we will just assume here that every bond we discuss is for $1,000.

The second most important item is when the loan is going to be repaid, and this will be prominently featured on the bond. The exact date is given, such as "July 7, 2001."

Next is the amount of interest the company is going to pay on this loan. Currently corporations are paying about 10% to 16% for regular bonds, but the rate on convertible bonds is usually less than that. Furthermore, when many of the bonds now being traded were issued, the going rate of interest was much lower, so there are many convertibles around with interest rates of 3½% or even less.

The interest is paid twice a year. The date on which it is paid is the same as the maturity date of the bond, and then six months after that. So if you buy a bond maturing in November 1998, you will be paid interest every November and May. The total amount of annual interest you receive for each bond is equal to the rate of the bond times $1,000. So if you buy a 9% bond, you will receive $45 on one payment date and $45 six months later.

As interest rates change after a bond is issued, and as the price of the stock changes, the price of a convertible bond changes to reflect these conditions. The price of a regular bond will fall if interest rates go up, and it will go up if interest rates decline. A convertible bond acts the same way, but its price is also influenced by the price of the common stock, especially if the price of the stock goes up, when the bond must also go up.

There are a number of terms which are useful in discussing bonds. The first is that a bond is said to be selling at a discount when it is selling below $1,000. This means that if you purchase a 4% bond at a discount, you are really getting more than 4% on your investment. For example, if you pay $800 for a 4% bond, then you are receiving $40 a year for an $800 investment, which divides out to a return on your investment of 5%. That is called your *current yield*, because it is the rate of return which you are receiving now in the form of interest payments.

In addition to this current yield, when you buy a discount bond you are guaranteed another form of gain by the fact that the corporation is going to redeem the bond at maturity for $1,000. This gives you a profit of $200 over your purchase price. Bond traders calculate what this additional $200 profit will mean to you each year, and the current yield plus the annual portion of that ultimate $200 are combined to provide the *yield to maturity*. It is the yield to maturity, rather than the current yield, which is the most important factor in determining the current price of a bond.

Bonds are also strongly influenced by the financial condition of the company issuing the bond. Because there are so many companies issuing bonds, and because it is so important to bond dealers to know what the financial condition of the issuing companies is, the job of assessing the financial condition of companies has been largely delegated to independent rating agencies. The two best known are Standard & Poor's (S & P) and Moody's. Here is a table explaining the ratings so you can understand at a glance just what the financial condition of each company is. Incidentally, your dealer can tell you the rating of any company, or perhaps even give you a bond guide which contains the listings.

On the S & P ratings the ratings from AA to BB may be modified by the addition of a plus or minus. For Moody's a number 1 after a rating indicates that it is the highest within that category.

| Standard & Poor's | Moody's | Description |
|---|---|---|
| AAA | Aaa | *Highest rating. Capacity to pay interest and repay principal is extremely strong.* |
| AA | Aa | *Very strong capacity to pay interest and repay principal. Differ from AAA only in small degree.* |
| A | A | *Strong capacity to pay interest and repay principal, although they are somewhat more susceptible to adverse effects of changes in circumstances and economic conditions than AAA or AA companies.* |
| BBB | Baa | *Adequate capacity to pay interest and repay principal. While they normally have adequate protection parameters, adverse economic conditions or changing circumstances are more likely to lead to a weakened capacity than higher rated bonds.* |
| BB, B, CCC, CC | Ba, B Caa, Ca | *Regarded as predominantly speculative. While they have some quality and protective characteristics, these are outweighed by large uncertainties or major risk exposure to adverse conditions.* |
| C | C | *No interest is being paid on bonds.* |
| D | | *In default on payment of interest and/or repayment of principal is in arrears.* |

While all these descriptions may seem quite vague and devoid of any specific meanings, they are nevertheless very useful in judging the value of one bond over another. There is one practical watermark, and that is that BBB bonds are the lowest grade which are considered "investment grade" under present regulations. That is, they are the lowest grade which are eligible for investments by bank trust departments.

Now let's take a look at a specific bond and see how the system would work. Since one of the companies I mentioned in Chapter 10 has a convertible, we might as well use that one. Gulf + Western has issued a 5½% convertible bond due in July 1993 which is convertible into 48.8 shares of common stock. Incidentally, this bond carries only a B rating by S & P so it would not be legal for banks to put into a trust account; inasmuch as Gulf + Western is a very large, profitable company, you can see how strict the rating companies can be.

Gulf + Western stock was recently selling for 16¾ and the bond was selling at $850. If you looked up the price of the bond in the newspaper, you would find its price given as 85 because the newspapers always leave off the last digit, and so will your broker when you discuss bond prices with him. Since this is a 5½% bond, we know that it is paying $55 a year in interest.

You are paying only $850 to get this $55 a year, so to find your current yield, divide $55 by $850 and you get 6.47%. The yield to maturity is a bit more complicated to determine, but it works out to 7.24%.

Nothing in life is ever perfect, and that is particularly true in the investment world. If there ever were a perfect investment, then everyone would flock to buy it and the price would rise to such a point that it would no longer be the perfect investment. So far convertible bonds may seem like the perfect investment. Now we'll consider one disadvantage of these bonds: the fact that they usually do not sell at their exact conversion price (number of shares into which the bond is convertible times price of shares), but instead are priced to be at a premium over conversion value.

Here the actual conversion price of the bond is found by multiplying the current price of the stock, 16¾, by the number of shares which you are entitled to as a bondholder, 48.8. The result is $817.40, whereas the price of the bond was actually $850. What is the reason for this additional $32.60 which you are being forced to pay? The answer is that since convertible bonds are such a good investment, this additional charge, the premium, is the price which purchasers are willing to pay in order to receive all the advantages convertible bonds have over the common stock. It would appear to be a small price to pay, amounting to just 67 cents a share.

What you are getting for this additional 67 cents a share that you wouldn't get with the common? The most important benefit is some protection of the price of your investment. While the price of the common stock can decline drastically due to the psychology of the marketplace and the prospects for future earnings by the company, the lowest price for the bond is constrained by the fact that this is a bond. We know that in 1993 it will be redeemed by Gulf + Western for $1,000 provided only that the company is solvent. Since this date is not that far off, there is a limit to how far the bond can fall. For every $1 that the bond falls, the current rate of interest is going up by just over 0.1% and the yield to maturity is going up by even more. Thus in addition to the future redemption is the fact that the interest rate increases as the bond falls in price, so that when the price gets so low that the yield to maturity is equal to what other B-rated nonconvertible bonds are paying, the price will not fall any further.

At that point it will be selling solely on the basis of being a bond without consideration of the fact that it is convertible. This then is your price protection. In other words, the price of a convertible bond can fall only to that point where its yield to maturity makes it competitive with other nonconvertible bonds with a similar rating and maturity. This price itself may change— for example, when interest rates rise, the price of a regular bond will also fall—but at least it is a price which can be determined in advance with a simple calculator. There is no way to determine in advance what the lowest price of a stock is going to be.

To verify what has been said one need only check the record books. The lowest price that Gulf + Western stock reached during the period of 1968 to 1980 was ¾ whereas the lowest price the bond reached was 43. Quite a difference. So our theory has actually worked in practice. And it must work. If the price of the common stock falls through the floor, this bond is left with its price held up by its bond characteristics.

When you buy a convertible bond, it is an easy matter to estimate how far the price of the bond would fall if something went drastically wrong with the stock. Here one would simply look for a nonconvertible bond with a maturity close to 1993 and a single B rating to see what its yield to maturity would be. At the time of writing this book, Texas Industries was a B-rated company, and its 7¾% bonds, due 1992, were selling with a yield to maturity of 13.76%. This means that if worse comes to worst and the price of Gulf + Western stock were to fall through the floor, your bonds should still be selling at a yield to maturity of 13.76%. This would give a price of approximately $51 in 1980.

Although this might seem like a pretty low price, and not much downside protection, just remember that anyone who owns the Gulf + Western convertible can simply hold on to it and it will be redeemed for $1,000 in 1993. Therefore, for the long-term investor who is willing to hold on to his investment until maturity, the only risk in owning a convertible bond which has been purchased for less than $1,000 is that the company will become insolvent. I submit that this is a far more pleasant alternative than the risk of owning the common stock itself.

Our discussion of convertible bonds wouldn't be complete without a discussion of how the price of the bonds moves in relation to the price of the common stock. In brief, they do not move up quite as fast as the stock itself, but they do not move down nearly as fast either. This is because as the price of the stock goes up, the premium on the bond is priced more and more solely on the conversion feature and less and less on its value as a bond. This means that as the stock rises in price the premium which you originally paid over the conversion price is shrinking. Finally, when the stock gets to a point where the bond is selling considerably over $1,000, the premium is merely a reflection of what the current yield on the bond is in comparison to the current yield on the stock. Incidentally, if you do buy a bond for over $1,000, don't worry that it will be redeemed for $1,000 and give you a substantial loss. You will always have the right to convert the bond before it is redeemed. Thus, when you buy a bond for less than $1,000, you can be sure that it will go up to $1,000. However, when you pay over $1,000, it does not have to go down to less than $1,000, provided, of course, that the price of the stock stays high enough.

On the way down the premium factor starts working to your advantage, because as the price of the stock declines, the bond begins to trade more and more as if it were just a regular bond and the price of the stock becomes less relevant. This means that the premium over conversion price is constantly increasing, and it provides that floor which you want.

Thus one can summarize the price action of convertible bonds by saying that as the price of the stock falls, the convertible is priced like a regular bond, and if the price of the stock rises high enough, the convertible is priced just like the stock. This has obvious lessons for anyone contemplating the purchase of a convertible. First, if the price of the stock is too high you are not really getting much protection when you buy the convertible bond, because every time the stock falls in price the bond will also fall. Therefore, while you have bought a convertible bond in name, in fact the price of the bond acts just like the price of the stock itself, and you really haven't gotten any of the advantages of a bond, except perhaps for getting a bit more interest on your money.

On the other hand, if you buy a convertible bond when the stock is too low, you will have the downside protection of a bond all right, but the stock can go up for quite a bit while the price of the bond doesn't move.

Therefore, buying a convertible bond for your purposes involves a careful weighing of all the factors. Buy one where the stock is too high and you get little downside protection; buy one where the stock is too low and you lose out on the upside potential.

There are two ways to tell that you are getting the right bond when the stock is at the right price. The first is to compute the premium for the bond. As we noted above, simply multiply the current price of the common stock by the number of shares convertible per bond and compare this with the price of the bond. The excess should be about 20% to 30%. This means that you are getting some of the benefit of the bond plus the potential price appreciation of the stock. If the premium is too low, then when the stock goes down the bond will go down also. If the premium is too high, it may not move up when the stock goes up.

A second point to look for is that in general it is better to buy a bond selling below $1,000. That way you know that the bond is eventually going to be redeemed for more than you paid for it. If you are a long-term investor and something goes wrong with the price of the stock, you can just hold on to your bond and wait for the bond to be redeemed. Since everyone interested in the bond knows that it will be redeemed at $1,000 eventually, it isn't even necessary that you personally hold the bond until it matures, because its market price will reflect the fact that it will eventually be redeemed at $1,000. Its price should appreciate each year as it gets nearer to its maturity date, so you could sell it at any time and realize the benefit of having bought it at a discount.

An easy way to get an idea of how the price of the bond trades is to look in the newspaper for the high and low prices for the last year of the stock, and then note the high and the low on the bond. By comparing prices at these levels with the current prices for both, you will get a very rough idea of how they move together.

There is one possible surprise in convertible bonds which you should be aware of. In many cases the corporation has the right to call in the bonds before maturity. This is especially likely to happen when the bonds are selling at more than $1,000. Since these premature redemptions require that the bonds be redeemed at $1,000, there is no incentive for the corporation to buy in its bonds early when they are selling at less than $1,000. If a bond is redeemed early and it is selling at more than $1,000, all you have to do is convert it into the common stock, and then if you want to get out of the position, sell the stock. Thus you do not lose any money, but it is the end of your convertible bond position and you will lose any premium that the bond commanded.

Incidentally, if you use a taxable corporation to do any investing, you might be particularly interested in convertible preferred stock. These are like convertible bonds in that there is payment of a fixed amount of interest each year, although it is called a dividend since this is stock, but it is similar to convertible bonds in that it can be converted into shares of the common stock if the common goes up. There is no maturity date, so it is like a convertible bond which is issued in perpetuity. The big advantage is that if a corporation owns convertible preferred stock, 85% of the dividend is exempt from taxation by any corporation receiving it. Therefore the net after tax yield to corporations is unusually high.

To summarize this chapter on convertible bonds, they offer what can be a highly attractive mixture of potential for large gain if the price of the stock goes up, with a floor on the price of the convertible if the price of the stock declines. In addition, all the time that you hold this security, you will be collecting interest payments which can be substantially higher than the holders of the common stock are collecting.

Here's a tip for sophisticated investors. Professional managers often take advantage of the swings in the amount of premium in convertible bonds to enhance their performance. This can be done because as the price of the common goes up, the amount of premium in the bond goes down. In other words, when the stock is high, you can get out of the stock and into the convertible bond for very little extra cost, and this small extra cost can be made up in the extra yield in perhaps a very few years. On the other hand, if the price of the stock goes down, the premium goes up and you can sell the bond and get back into the stock, pocketing the profit from the much larger premium.

Here's an example. Let's say a stock is $50 and the bond which is convertible into 20 shares is selling for $1,050, for a $50 premium. The investor switches from the common into the convertible. Now the price of the stock falls down to $30. The bond falls only down to $800. The investor now sells the bond and buys the stock, picking up the premium of $200 on the bond (20 × $30 = $600. The difference between the $600 conversion value of the bond, and its $800 price is the premium.) Of course when he does this it is also because he believes that the stock is not likely to go down much further. Hopefully for this investor the stock will move back up again. If it goes back up to $50, he will very likely decide to get back into the bond. In other words, when the bond is selling at a price close to its conversion price, the sophisticated investor elects to be in the bond and get the higher yield plus the downside protection of the bond, but when the bond becomes too expensive in terms of the stock, he elects to take his profit in the bond and get the greater upside potential of the stock.

One other detail on the interest payments needs to be mentioned, and that is that the interest on a bond is computed in a more sophisticated fashion than the dividends are on a stock. Those of you who have bought stock know that if you buy stock before the ex-dividend date, you are entitled to the dividend, and if you buy it the day after you are not. As a result the price of stock usually drops by the amount of the dividend on the day that it goes ex-dividend. This is not the case with convertible bonds. The purchaser of the convertible bond pays the seller the amount of interest which has accrued since the last interest payment. Thus, if a bond pays $40 interest in December and in June, and if you buy the bond three months after the interest payment date, you will be charged $20 of accrued interest which is added on to the price you pay for the bond. This is fair, because you will be receiving the full six months interest in three months, even though you owned the bond for only half that time. The result of this system is that the prices of bonds do not change with the interest payment dates.

# 12

# *THE POTENTIAL BIG PROFITS FROM LIMITED CAPITAL WITH CALL OPTIONS*

Throughout the ages people have dreamed of a way of investing without any risk and with the possibility of giant profits. If anyone could devise such an investment, it would be relatively easy to raise untold billions of dollars in a very short period of time and become unbelievably rich. I am sorry to say that I have not discovered that elusive utopia. However, I can offer something approaching that. It has the potential of very large profits at the risk of a relatively small amount of money. This is appealing, because many investors who would not want to risk a large portion of their assets buying common stocks might be willing to take a much larger risk with a small amount of their capital, if they believed that the possibility existed of making a meaningful amount of money.

There is indeed such a security and it is called the *call option*. I would not term it an investment but rather a speculation. Yet when used by the intelligent investor as part of an overall strategy, it can have a very important role in a conservative investment strategy. They are now available on almost 300 stocks. Before we define a call, let us state what it does. A call intensifies the risk and price volatility of a stock and compresses it into a very low-priced security. The result is that you may be able to get most of the upside potential of an $80 stock for a security which costs you only $4. Obviously, if you can do this, you have just reduced the theoretical amount of your risk exposure by $76. Thus this strategy can appeal to very conservative investors, although taken by itself it is very speculative indeed, as we shall see.

As an illustration, if that $80 stock should move up to $90, for an increase of 12.5%, the price of the option could rise from $4 to $10, for an increase of 150%! That's what we call leverage, and it contains the key to the incredible power which options have to make money for investors while risking only a small amount.

If the stock should move further, then the increase in the option would be even greater. Some examples from the past are that when Boeing went from 29⅞ to 72⅛, the 35 option went from ¹¹⁄₁₆ to 37. And when Bally Manufacturing Co. in the course of a few months went from 16 to 65¼, the 20 option went from ⅞ to 48. Both of these options, as it happened, increased by about 5,300%. This means that if you had speculated with $1,000 in either of these options it would have been worth $54,000 in just a few months.

That is spectacular. The only word of caution I should insert is that such gains are very unusual, are the exception rather than the rule, and even in these examples would have occurred only if you had bought the option near its low and sold it near its high, and had been willing to keep it for the entire intervening time period. In reality, it is rarely possible either to buy an option at its low or to sell it at its high, and since most option buyers hold them for only a few weeks, it is extremely unlikely that anyone actually made the profits mentioned above. But this is not to say that handsome profits are not possible. They can often be made very quickly.

To understand how the price of options can go up so fast one must understand what an option is. An option is defined as the right to purchase 100 shares of a named stock for a specified price within a given period of time. For example, you might acquire the Ford June 30 call option. The 30 means you have the right to buy Ford stock for $30 a share. If the price of the option were stated as $3, you would pay $300 for your one option since it entitled you to buy 100 shares. Once you own this option you have the right to purchase 100 shares of Ford stock for $30 a share at any time you wish between the time you bought the option and its expiration date, which is the business day, generally Friday, preceding the third Saturday of June. If Ford stock goes to $35 in the middle of April, and you now have the right to buy it for just $30 a share, you will be saving $5 on each share. In other words, your option would entitle you to buy the stock at a discount of $5.

Since the world of Wall Street is a very efficient one when it comes to the value of money, your right to buy Ford at $5 below the current market price of the stock is in itself worth $5. Therefore you could sell your option for $5, thus saving yourself the commissions and capital outlay which would be required actually to buy 100 shares of Ford at $30 and then to sell it at the market price of $35. Thus most option owners do not exercise their options, but sell them out before they expire.

In fact it is not necessary to hold an option for very long if the stock moves up soon. The option exchanges provide a liquid market for every option they list. You can buy the option in the morning, and if the stock goes up enough, you can sell it in the afternoon and make a nice profit. Another stock selling for $50 may have gone up by $1, just a 2% increase in the price of the stock and not even enough to cover the cost of the commissions, buying and selling the stock, but your profit on the option could be 50%, more than enough to cover the commissions on the option and to give you a terrific profit.

The price of the option is fixed in the marketplace by the forces of supply and demand in exactly the same way that the price of a stock is determined on the New York Stock Exchange or any other stock exchange. The only difference is that the price of the option is tied in directly with the price of the stocks and will tend to move with it.

Various options are issued with the right to purchase the underlying stock at different prices. There may be options on Ford giving the owner the right to buy the stock at $35 a share, at $40 a share, and at $45 a share. This price is called the *exercise price* or *strike price* of the option, and the directors of the option exchanges select exercise prices which are close to the current price of the stock. Exercise prices are usually available every $5 from $10 up to $50, at $10 intervals from $50 to $100, and at $20 intervals from there on up.

Options mature every three months, and at any one time there are always three different months available, those being the closest three expirations. For example, one stock may have options on the January, April, July, and October cycle. If it were now August, the options available on this stock would be the October, January, and April expirations. As soon as the October series expired, the July series would begin to trade. The other cycles are the February, May, August, and November cycle, and finally the March, June, September, and December cycle.

Options can perform two valuable services to the investor or speculator. The first is the one which most people are familiar with, namely that they provide great profit potential at the cost of great risk. But the second service they can provide is that as part of a well thought out investment program they can actually serve to reduce the risk taken, by serving as a substitute for owning common stock.

Let's discuss the first point. We have seen how the price of an option can go up 150% from a relatively small move in the price of the stock. This is the fun of the option game. But what if the stock does not go up? Suppose that when you bought your option with the $30 exercise price in our first example, the stock just stayed right where it was at $30 instead of moving up to $35. What would your option be worth at its expiration date with the stock at $30?

The answer is readily determinable. Your option gives you the right to purchase 100 shares of the stock for $30 a share. But, since the stock is now selling for that on the open market, anyone without your option can buy the stock for $30 a share. Since they can do the same thing without your option that you can do with it, your option has a value of exactly zero. Obviously, if the stock were selling for less than $30, your option would also be worth zero.

Therefore the option game can be a winner-take-all type of speculation with the loser losing all if he is not careful or lucky. But even among options there are varying degrees of riskiness. In general the degree of riskiness is determined by the exercise price and the length of time remaining in the option.

The exercise price of any option can be above the current price of the stock, near its price, or below its price. If the stock is selling at $80, there may be an option which gives you the right to buy the stock for $90. Even though that option has no intrinsic value if it were to be exercised today, it still has some value in the marketplace because there is always the possibility that the stock will go up above $90 in the future before the option expires. This is called an *out-of-the-money option*. It is the most speculative and risky of the options, because unless the stock actually moves up by more than $10, this option is going to be worthless at its expiration. On the other hand, since it is so risky, it probably is selling for a very low price. For example, if it had two months to go, it might be selling for $1. This means that if the stock goes up to $95 before the expiration of the option, that option will be worth $5, for an increase of 500%.

Next in riskiness and profit potential is the *on-the-money option*, where the stock is near the exercise price. In this example the 80 strike price option would be the on-the-money option, and it might be selling for $3. This means that if the stock moves up to $83, at the option's expiration you would be breaking even; if it moved up to $86, you would double your money; and at $90 your option would be worth $10 for a profit of 233%. Of course if the stock does not go up but stays at $80, the option also becomes worthless, as it does if the stock moves down.

The 70 strike price option is called the *in-the-money option* and in many ways this is the least speculative of the options. It would probably be selling for about $11, which is a lot of money to pay for an option. But the advantage is that if the stock moves up by just $1 you are breaking even, and for every $1 above that you are making a $1 profit. Even if the stock stays still and remains at $80 when the option expires, this option will be worth $10, which means that you will incur only the minor loss of $1. Remember that in the cases of the other two options, if the stock stayed still you would lose all of your money.

The disadvantages of the in-the-money option are twofold, both arising from the fact that the option is so expensive. The first is that you are risking a great deal of money, and while the loss will be very slight if the stock stays where it is, you could lose your entire investment of $1,100 if the stock price falls below $70 at the expiration date of the option. Thus your risk per share is extremely large in comparison to the on-the-money or out-of-the-money option. Second, the high initial cost of the option means that if the stock does go up, your percentage gain is going to be much smaller than with the other types of options.

So there you have the different risk and profit comparisons for the different strike price options. The greatest speculation is the out-of-the-money option, but with all the options you risk the entire amount you paid for them. The only difference is that with the in-the-money option you will not lose all your money unless the stock goes down sharply. Therefore one can say that it is less risky than the others because the probability of losing all your money is less likely than with the others. The other advantage is that you start making money with a much smaller move up in the price of the stock.

The duration of the option also plays an important role in determining its cost to you and how it reacts to changes in the price of the stock. The most volatile options are those which are on the money with just a very short time to run, such as one week or less. It is not at all unusual for options in this category to double or lose half their value in one day. For example, if a stock is 39 and the 40 option just has two days to go before expiration, the option may be selling for ½. If the stock goes up 1½ points that day, the option could easily be selling for $1 at the close. If the stock declines by just as little as $1, down to $38, the option could decline to ¼. So if you really like fast action and are willing to take the attendant risks, nothing can beat the low priced on-the-money options with just a few days to go.

Longer duration options, on the other hand, are much less volatile. They are more expensive to start with and react less sharply to changes in the price of the stock. The stock mentioned

above would also have an option available with just over six
months left to run. This option at the 40 strike price could be
selling for $4. An increase in the price of the stock from $39 to
$40.50 would not have the effect of doubling the price of this
option. Instead it might move up from $4 to $4.75. So while the
short-term option was increasing by 100%, the long-term option
was only adding on 19% in value. The good news is that when the
stock declines it will have a similarly mild impact on the option's
price. Let the stock decline by $1, down to $38, and the option
might decline by 50 cents, down to $3.50. This is a percentage loss
of just 12.5% compared to that 50% beating which the short-term
option took under similar circumstances.

To summarize our discussion, if you want to buy an option
which has some resilience to short-term swings in the price of the
underlying stock, then you would be better off with a longer
duration option. Another advantage is that you can be wrong for
the near term on your opinion as to whether the stock will go up
and still make money if you prove to be correct later. Only very
rarely does one buy a stock and have it go up the next day; but with
a six-month option, you can buy the option, have the stock go
down for two or three months, and then still make money in the
end if it goes up enough in the following three months. Thus you
can be right in your general direction of the stock without being
tied down to an extremely short time schedule.

The price you will have to pay for an option is set by the
forces of supply and demand on the floor of the options exchange.
We have already discussed some of the factors which determine
that price. First is the strike price of the option in relation to the
current price of the stock. Obviously the higher the price of the
stock in relation to the option's strike price, the higher the price of
the option will be. The second main factor is the length of time left
in the option's life. The longer the remaining life, the more
expensive the option will be. But there are other more subtle
factors which have a large function in determining the price of the
option. The most important of these is the volatility of the
underlying stock. If a stock has a history of hardly moving at all, as
is the case for some utility stocks, no one is going to be very
interested in buying options on the stock. After all, what chance is
there that the stock will suddenly take off if it hasn't done so for
over half a century? But if a stock has been running up and down
like a volcano for the last year, there will be many people who
believe that it is going to go up again, or if it is still up, that it will
go even higher. Therefore, an option on that stock will be much

more expensive than the same strike price option on a quiet stock at the same price.

Other factors which determine the price of options are whether or not a stock pays any dividend, and if it does how large the dividend is. Even the going rate of interest on money plays a role, since buying options can be a substitute for laying out large amounts of money to own stocks. Therefore when interest rates are high, investors can save a large amount of money by buying options instead of stocks and so the price of the options goes up.

Options can be bought and sold as easily as stocks and this can be done through the same broker whom you use for stocks. The commission rate schedule on options is generally the same as it is for stocks. Unfortunately, this schedule is derived in such a way that the commission on very cheap stocks is a higher percentage than on expensive stocks. Since most options are much less expensive than stocks, the result tends to be that the commission on options is a higher percentage of the money spent, typically ranging from 8% down to 3% of the money involved, depending upon the price of the option and the number of options being bought or sold.

Now that we've described the basics of options we can concentrate on how they can be used by the careful investor. There is one big way in which they cannot be used, and that is as a means of speculating with a large amount of money. No matter what you believe about a certain stock going up, and no matter how safe you believe your long-term in-the-money option to be, remember that whenever you buy options your entire commitment is completely at risk, and most of the time if you hold an option until its expiration it will become totally worthless. So you must always keep in mind that any money you are using to speculate with in options is very likely to be drastically reduced or completely lost. Whenever you buy options, your mental set should be that you kiss the money good-bye. If you can't afford to lose the money painlessly, then for goodness sake don't buy options with it.

If you want a bit of elaboration on the above, just remember that an option is unlikely to remain at the same price it is because it magnifies moves in the price of the underlying stock so much. A small move in the stock and the option can double, but a small move down can cut the option price down to nothing in just a short period of time. Therefore, the option you buy is apt to become worth a great deal or worth nothing.

It is very easy to have the option become worth nothing. For the most popular type of option, that is slightly out of the money, all that need happen is that the stock stay right where it is, go down, or even go up a bit but not quite enough to get to your option's strike price. The option will then become worthless on its expiration date.

The practical application of this rule is as follows. Let us assume that the stock market has been going up and you have quadrupled the money which you originally devoted to options. Convinced that the market is destined to go up higher, you reinvest all that money and add some more so that you will really strike it big. This time the market does not go up but stays just where it is. Or the market goes up, but the five stocks which you have picked do not go up. Or the market is in the midst of a strong bull market, but just the week before the expiration date some bad news comes out about interest rates, unemployment, international affairs, or any of a hundred other facts, and the market takes a temporary dip just as you are about to sell out all your options.

In any case, the result is that you have lost all your money. If you think about it, you will come to the conclusion that buying options is very much like betting double or nothing. It can work out for a long time in a strong bull market, and you will be able to make incredible profits. But sooner or later, even in every bull market, there comes a period of time when the market pauses to digest its gains. It doesn't have to be a very long time period either. If your options are maturing during that period, you could lose every penny that you had put into options. When you are betting double or nothing again and again, you may be lucky for a while, but eventually you are going to lose, and then you will lose all your money. It is virtually inevitable. Don't say that you weren't warned.

Therefore the intelligent investor will look for a method of using options which can make money for him but which will not have the Draconian consequence of losing all his money.

The clear answer is to use some variation of placing most of your money in something which is relatively secure, and then using only the balance of your money to speculate with in options.

Furthermore, there should be some means of bringing profits from the options back into the safe investment. If this is not done, and if the profits from the options are allowed to accumulate and be reinvested into options, you are committing the same mistake that you are trying to avoid, namely just postponing the day when you are destined to lose a great deal of money.

One method was subject to a careful computer study as to what its results were. This method was to invest 90% of one's money in a completely safe security such as a Treasury bill, and than speculate with the remaining 10%. Every six months the two amounts of money were added up and the money was once again divided so that 90% went into Treasury bills and the remaining 10% was employed in buying options. For example if you started out with $100,000, then you would use $10,000 to buy options and have $90,000 sitting in Treasury bills earning interest. If you were fortunate and the stock market took a nice turn up, that $10,000 in options might grow to $20,000 in six months. You would then add up the two components of your investment, get $110,000, and now designate 10% of that, or $11,000, for options. This means that you would sell $9,000 worth of options and return that money to Treasury bills. Now if in the second six-month period you lost all the money which you were using to speculate with in options, your investment would still be worth $99,000 plus whatever interest you had earned on your Treasury bills, which could be a quite substantial sum. If you had lost all of your original $10,000 in options, then the total amount of your investment would be $90,000 plus interest you earned on the Treasury bills. You would then compute 10% of this and take $9,000 out of Treasury bills to use for options in the second six-month period. With the current rates of interest, and considering the fact that you are actually quite unlikely to lose *all* the money you have committed to options, you could go along for many years without any rise in the market and still lose only a small amount of money. If the market really began to take off, you would be making a large amount of money from the 10% that was in options, plus interest on the growing amount that was securely in Treasury bills. Of course, the big advantage is that no matter what happened to the stock market, you could be sure that at least 90% of your money was safe.

A simulation of this investment method was conducted by Robert C. Merton of MIT, Myron S. Scholes of the University of Chicago, and Mathew L. Gladstein of Donaldson, Lufkin & Jenrette, Inc. for the period from July 1963 to December 1975. Their conclusion was that over this period this investment method outperformed all other methods they studied. The other methods, which did not do as well, included straight purchases of stock, option writing, which we will discuss in the next chapter, and various other methods of purchasing options. So if you are looking for a good method of investing which combines a rock solid conservative approach along with something that can increase your profit dramatically, and has a computer-proven record, then you ought to give consideration to this 90%–10% approach to options.

Once you have decided whether you want to speculate in options and have determined the amount of money you wish to risk on them, the next step is to decide exactly which options to buy on exactly which stocks; then you must decide when to sell. None of these questions is easy to answer, and in fact answers are impossible. Nevertheless, it has always been my contention that a guiding philosophy or set of strategy rules can at least prevent a person from getting whipsawed. You may not be right all the time, but at least you are guaranteed not to be wrong all the time. So here are my rules of strategy for trading options, adapted from my book *The New Options Market* (New York: Walker & Co., revised edition, 1979).

*Rule 1.* Never buy a call when the underlying stock is more than slightly below the option's strike price. This means that if a stock is selling for $44 you should normally try to buy the option with a $45 exercise price rather than with the $50 or $60 exercise prices. The obvious reason why people might want to buy the higher strike price options is that they will be substantially cheaper. For instance, while the 45 strike price option might be $4, the 50 strike price option could be just $1.75 and the 60 strike price option might be as low as 50 cents. It is easy to see that some traders would rather risk just $50 on an option than a full $400. After all, if the stock goes down, you would lose all your money if you hold the option until expiration, so why not lose just $50 instead of $400? On the other hand, if the stock goes up, once it gets past $60.50 you will be making an additional 100% profit on the 60 strike price option every time that the stock goes up another 50 cents, whereas when you invest $4 a share with the 45 strike option, the stock has to go up a full $4 past the break-even point in order to gain an additional 100% profit.

These are all the easy reasons for buying the furthest out-of-the-money option you can find. And once in a blue moon you will be lucky and make a small fortune from your out-of-the-money option. Unfortunately, purchasing this type of option ignores a fundamental fact about the movement of stock prices: Most of the time most stocks don't move very much from where they started out. This is especially true in the relatively short time spans which are involved in purchasing options. The longest possible time duration is nine months, and most options are purchased when most of the life is already gone from them, so that we are usually talking about three months or less. In three months, most of the stocks are even less likely to move. You are lucky if the stock moves in the right direction, to say nothing about whether it moves far enough!

Therefore, the purpose of this rule is to get you to buy options which will make money if the stock moves up by even a relatively small amount. For instance, if you bought the 45 strike price option we just mentioned for $4, you would be assured of making some profit if the stock were at $50 when the option expired. That is because with the stock at $50, the option givng you the right to buy the stock for $45 must be worth at least $5. If you sell the option when it still has some time to run, it will undoubtedly be worth more than $5 because of the additional time available. In any event, once the stock goes above $49, you will begin to make a profit, and the amount of your profit will be $1 per share for every dollar that the stock is above your break-even point of $49. Thus, at $54 you will have a profit of $5 on your option for each share. Since one call option is for 100 shares, your profit will actually be $500. That means that you have made a profit of 125% on your original outlay of $400. This is just the kind of profit you are hoping to make and it required a rise in the stock of $10 or 23%, which isn't completely implausible.

Suppose that instead of buying the 45 option you had bought the 50 option for $1.75. With the stock at $54, it would be worth $4 and you would have a profit of $2.25, which turns out to be a profit of 128%. This, coincidentally, is almost exactly the same percentage profit as with the 45 option. But in this situation we are supposing that the stock goes up by 23%.

What if, instead of going up $10, the stock had gone up by $6 to $50? In that case the 45 option would be worth $5, and since it cost you $4, you would have a profit of $1, which is a 25% profit and nothing to sneeze at.

How much would the 50 option be worth if the stock were just at 50 when the option expired? The answer is that since the 50 option gives you the right to purchase the stock for $50, and anyone can purchase the stock for $50 by going to the floor of the stock exchange, your option has no value and would be worth nothing. So here we see the reason for buying the option with the lower strike price. If the stock moves up but doesn't move up very much, you can make a profit on the option with the strike price close to the price of the stock, but you could lose all your money with the out-of-the-money option.

The option with the $60 strike price is an even more extreme example of the type of option I would suggest that the new investor avoid. What if the stock were to perform amazingly well and get all the way up to $60? This would be a gain of $16 from its original price of $44, an increase of 36%. If you had bought the 45 option for $4, it would then be worth at least $15, for a profit of 275%. If you had purchased the 50 option for $1.75, it would be worth $10, for a profit of 471%. But how much is your $60 option worth? You should be making a lot of money because you not only picked a stock that did remarkably well, but you even speculated in it in a way that should produce enormous profits when it really goes up.

You should be rich, all right. You should be able to splurge on the luxury you always wanted, take that vacation you really couldn't afford, or buy your wife that fur coat she wanted. The only trouble is that by picking the wrong option you won't be able to do any of these things. In fact, you may have to give up some of the things that you figured you had the money to do. Because in spite of being so right, the option you purchased will be worth exactly zero. Sorry, Charlie.

Hence Rule 1. Don't buy an option with a strike price that is too far above the current price of the stock. You will be sorry when the stock moves up but not quite far enough to save your option from becoming worthless. If your option becomes worthless, then the stock might as well have gone down. When you are actually right in having picked a stock that is going to go up, and you pick the time period in which it is going to happen, don't take the chance of cheating yourself out of the rewards of your prescience by being greedy.

*Rule 2.* Never buy a call when the underlying stock is substantially above the option's strike price. Let's illustrate this by using the same example we did in Rule 1. The stock was $44 and had a 45 strike price option for $4. In addition, let's say this same stock had options with lower strike prices, as low as 40 and 35. Of course, these options would cost a lot more money, because when you owned them you would be able to purchase the stock for so much less, that is, you would be able to buy the stock at a bigger discount and therefore the options would have to be worth more.

The price for the 40 strike price option would likely be about $7 and the price for the 35 strike price option would probably be about $10. The advantage of both these options over the 45 option we discussed above is that you are paying less money for what is called the *future time value* of the option. The future time value of an option is the additional amount you are paying above the actual *current value* of the option (if any). When a stock is $44, there is no current actual value to the right to be able to buy the stock at $45 and therefore there is no current value to the option. Hence the entire cost of $4 in our example is for future time value. The 40 strike price option has a current value when the stock is $44, and that current value is $4. Therefore, if you are paying $7 for the option, you are getting $4 worth of current cash value and paying $3 for the future time value of the option. The future time value which you pay for represents the additional amount you are paying for the privileges of owning the option, which are primarily high leverage and limited risk.

The advantage of buying the 40 strike price option instead of the 45 option is that you are paying only $3 for this privilege, whereas with the 45 strike price option the entire $4 you paid went for future time value. The advantage of the 35 strike price option is that with the stock at 44, that option was actually worth $9 at the present time, and since your cost for the option was just $10, you are paying only $1 for future time value. Obviously, a savings of money spent for future time value is an important advantage. What it means is that if the stock stays still, you will be losing less money, because unless a stock moves, every penny which you pay for future time value will be lost. Therefore, there is something to recommend options which have a strike price well below the current price of the stock. We call those options *deep-in-the-money* options.

There is, however, a major disadvantage to these options. That is simply that they cost too much. Sometimes it pays to buy the best and the cost be damned, but we will see that in this case paying a lot of money for an option is not the best course, for two reasons. First, you can lose a lot more money per share if the stock goes down. Second, if the stock goes up, you will not make nearly as large a percentage return on your cost as you would have with a lower cost option.

Let's look at the risk side first. Remember that no matter how solid a stock may seem or how sure you are that it is going to go up, no one can predict with any degree of certainty what will actually happen to the price of that stock, and certainly no one can guarantee that the stock is not going to go down below the strike price of even the lowest level option. In 1979, for example, Itel went from 37 to 5. The deeper in the money that the option you bought was, the more money you would have lost. The point here is always to remember that every penny you put into buying options is at total risk; you must assume that it can be completely lost. It is true that a deep-in-the-money option is less likely to go down to zero than an on-the-money option or an out-of-the-money option, but nevertheless the risk is still there. And on those occasions, hopefully rare, when a stock or the entire market takes a nose dive, the in-the-money option buyer is going to take heavy losses. So the first reason to avoid options which are too deep in the money is that you are risking too much money on each share of stock.

The second reason is equally compelling, and that is that when the stock does go your way and begin to go up, the return on your original outlay is going to be relatively modest. After a certain point, every option goes up about $1 for every $1 increase in the price of the stock. If you paid $1 for your option, that represents a 100% increase, if you paid $4 it is only a 25% increase, and if you paid $10 then it is only a 10% increase. Thus when you buy an expensive option, you are necessarily limiting the percentage increase you are going to be able to get.

In our example, if the stock goes up to $54 for a rise of $10, this means that the 45 strike option will go from $4 to $9 for an increase of 125%. The 40 strike price option would go from $7 to $14, which is an increase of 100%. This is not a major difference, but then the 40 strike price option was not deep in the money; it was merely in the money. Now let's take a look at what happens to the 35 level option. It would go from $10 to $19. This is an increase of 90%.

Thus, summarizing deep-in-the-money options, we find that they have one advantage in that they do tend to move up with small movements upward in stock prices. This may appeal to a person who is buying a call as a substitute for the stock itself. But for most traders who are looking upon options as a means of gaining leverage from a stock's increase, deep-in-the-money options simply don't fit the bill for two reasons: First, there is too much money at risk on each share of stock, and second, if the stock does go up there is not enough leverage to compensate for the big risk one is taking or to give the high rewards which are possible from options. Therefore, Rule 2 is to avoid buying options which are deep in the money.

*Rule 3.* Carefully check all three durations before buying any option. As you recall from our description of options, there are always three different durations of each option available, three months apart. If the nearest option has one month to go, there will also be options available which have four and seven months to go. Most traders and speculators tend to want to get the most action for their dollar that they can, and so they generally buy the shortest duration option since it is always the cheapest. But in options, as in many other areas of life, the cheapest commodity is not always the best value. In fact, when it comes to options, the shortest term, cheapest option is often the most overpriced. The reason is that that is the option the public is buying, and the market makers on the floor are just as happy as clams to be selling them to the public while they hedge their positions by buying other options which are much better values.

Let's take an example. With a stock at 70, the near term option with three weeks to go is selling for 2½, and the option with three months and three weeks is selling for 7, while the longest term option is selling for 10. To most people, paying $7 per share for an option seems like so much more money than $2.50 that they are inclined to buy the short-term option.

Now let's look at these options from another point of view, namely, how much each option is costing you per unit of time. After all, you are paying for future time value, and that is like renting the stock's upward potential for a given period. When you rent anything, don't you want to know what it costs you per unit of time? If someone says you can rent a summer house for $100 a weekend or $1,500 for the season, you would immediately find out how many weekends there were in the season and then divide to find your cost per weekend if you rented for the whole season. This is what you should do for options.

Dividing 2½ by three weeks gives a cost of 83 cents per week. Dividing the intermediate option at $7 by its 16 weeks gives a cost of just 44 cents per week. If we divide the long-term option priced at $10 by its life of 29 weeks we get a cost per week of 34 cents. Before jumping to any conclusions it must be pointed out that there are reasons why a short-term option should be selling for more on a per week basis than a long-term option. First you are simply risking less money, and second, there is obviously a much greater chance that a stock is going to go up by a small amount in just one week than go up by a much larger amount in a longer period of time.

Nevertheless, if you are inclined to believe that a stock is going to move up, then you should really consider purchasing a longer term option and saving money on a per week basis. One big advantage of a longer term option is that if you do decide to get out of the position in a few weeks and the stock has really not done anything, you will still have something to sell. Whereas the three-week option will have gone down to nothing, causing you a loss of $2.50 per share, the intermediate option will still have a full three months of life left and might be selling for $6 or perhaps even more, leaving you with a very manageable loss of just $1. Not a bad price for being able to capture the upside potential of the stock for that period.

For those of you who are mathematically inclined, the proper relationship of various duration options is based upon the relationships of the square roots of the amount of time. For instance, if there are three-month, six-month, and nine-month options available, the prices of the options should be in the ratio of 1.732, 2.449, and 3. If you have a square root key on your pocket calculator, it is quite easy.

Everyone likes to make a sensational profit, and certainly if you buy an option for less than $1 with one week left to go, and the stock goes up $5, you may be able to make a 300% profit in just one week. But remember, you are paying a very high price for that possibility. That $1 or less is going to expire in just one week, and the probability is that you will be left with nothing. On the other hand, if you had purchased an option with three months and a week to go, you might have paid 3 or 4 times as much but you would have gotten an option which would last for 12 times as long. And if the stock went up $5 in the first week, you would still be able to sell it at a good profit—maybe not 300% profit, but a very good profit nevertheless.

If the stock does not go up but just stays right where it is, your one-week option will go to zero, for a 100% loss to you, but the three-month option might not even decline in price at all. That's the difference. So remember that before you buy an option, be a comparison shopper. Get the best value for the time you are buying. Option buying is speculative enough without risking everything on a one- or two-week bet.

*Rule 4.* Annualize the option price in order to appreciate the price you are paying for the call. The sellers of options are some of the most sophisticated investors around. Option sellers tend to be wealthy individuals who understand the market very well, or they are large institutions who are advised by professional money managers who have analyzed option prices down to a tenth of a percentage point. These investors all have complicated computer programs which tell them exactly how much money they are receiving from their sale of options in terms of the percentage profit they will make on the underlying stock they own. Shouldn't you as the option buyer be just as knowledgeable?

One easy method of appreciating how much money you are turning over to the option sellers is to annualize the cost of your option, that is, to figure its cost on an annual basis. Thus, if you buy an option which has one week to run, you would multiply its cost by 52 in order to find out your annualized cost. If the option has three weeks to run, you multiply the cost by 52 and then divide by 3 to get the annualized cost.

Let's take an actual example. A stock is selling for $68 and you buy a 70 option with eight weeks to go for $5. To annualize this cost you multiply $5 by 52, getting $260. You then divide by 8 and get an annualized cost of $32.50. If you want to complete this analysis you can divide $32.50 by the cost of the stock, which is $68, to get an annualized percentage cost of 47.8%. This represents the percent of the price of the stock which you would be paying if you could continually purchase options identical to this one for a one-year period.

The advantage of this figure is that it gives you a standardized measurement which you can use in determining how much you are paying for the option. Thus you can easily compare various options on the same stock and can compare what you are paying for options on different stocks.

Incidentally, this annualization is to be done only with the future time value portion of the option. In other words, if a stock is selling for $53 and you buy the option with the $50 strike price for $7, the option has a current cash value of $4. This amount should not be annualized because it would be the same whether you were buying a one-week or a nine-month option. The only portion you should annualize is that portion which represents the extra money you are paying for your option, which here is the $3.

In making these comparisons, remember that annualized cost is only one factor in determining whether an option is a good buy. There are a number of factors which will affect this figure. First of all, the farther an option is out of the money, the lower the annualized cost will be. Naturally if a stock is selling for $70, the annualized cost of buying the 70 strike price option will be and should be substantially higher than buying the 80 option. Similarly, as we mentioned in the previous rule, the shorter term option will normally cost you more on an annualized basis than the longer term option. Also a deep-in-the-money option will be far cheaper than one on the money, because we are computing the cost of only the future time value of the option, and a large amount of the money paid is to purchase the in-the-money portion of the option.

Then there are the general rules for determining the price of an option. The option on a volatile stock will always be more expensive than on a dull stable stock, and the option on a stock with high dividends will always be less than the option on a stock which pays no or low dividends. Closely related to volatility is the fact that a stock which has made a major move recently and is still continuing in that direction will have more expensive options than a stock which is simply volatile without any major direction at the moment.

*Rule 5.* Sell half your position when the price of your options has doubled. Let me say right at the outset that there is probably no mathematical or theoretical basis for this rule. I am sure that there are numerous professors of finance as well as a lot of astute traders who can easily refute this rule and who never apply it themselves.

It is easy to see why. If you believe that a stock is going to continue to go up, then you hold on to your entire option position, they would say maybe you even add to it. Let your winnings run and cut your losses short. I am prepared to admit that this rule of selling half your position when an option has doubled is short on theoretical justification. My only answer is that sometimes in the real world we do things because they work, and if experience has shown them to be satisfactory guide rules, then we continue to use them.

My reasoning for this rule is that buying options is highly speculative. We must never for a moment lose sight of the fact that all the money placed in buying options is money which is totally at risk and can be lost in an instant. An entire diversified portfolio of options can lose 90% of its value in just one week. If you think that statement is farfetched, just pick out any selection of options which you would be likely to own, then estimate what they would be worth if each of the stocks went down by 10%. There have indeed been a number of instances in the past few years where the market as a whole declined by almost 10% in one week; look up October 1978 and October 1979. So it can happen, and when one is talking about an individual stock, it can happen in not just a week, but literally an instant.

What normally happens in such a case is that there is no way to sell out on the way down because there is no movement down. What happens is that there is an announcement of some sort on the news tape which has a negative effect on the stock. Trading is halted in the stock for perhaps an hour to give everyone a chance to assess the impact of the announcement, and then trading resumes with the price of the stock 5% or more lower. Naturally, the options respond in kind. An option which was selling for $5 may stop trading and the next trade may be for $1.50. That's how mercurial options are. This is the basis for my rule of selling half your options when you have a double.

Once the option has doubled and you sell half your position, you have received back an amount of money approximately equal to the original cost of the entire position. Therefore, you now have no money at all of your own riding on this position. In short, no matter what happens to the option from here on in, you will not lose a nickel.

This means that you can now be as fearless as you want. You can hold on to the options until the very last minute. You can sell a few when they go up higher and hang on to the rest, or you can sell them all out if they go down. The important point is that once you have sold half your position you are now totally free to do whatever you wish without any risk. The proceeds from the sale of half your position can be used to purchase other options, or if you want to maintain your initial risk exposure, you can put the money in the bank and consider it a profit or a reserve for a rainy day.

Obviously the basic reason for this rule is that in many cases an option will double in price and then the stock will stop moving up and begin to move down, and before too long the option will be practically worthless. That's why it's so comforting when you have made a profit to cash in on at least half your position.

*Rule 6.* Know the volatility and the Beta of the underlying stock. This is one of the advanced rules which not everyone has to be concerned with, but for the person who is serious about trading in options it is important. We have pointed out that the price of an option depends heavily upon the volatility of the stock. This is obvious, because if a stock in the past has shown that it is capable of moving up by large amounts in a very short time, then clearly there is a greater probability that it will do so again, and thus the option will be more valuable.

The Beta of a stock is a figure which measures the amount by which a particular stock is likely to move for a given move of the stock market as a whole. For example, if a stock has a Beta of 1.00, that means that it is likely to move up 10% in price when the stock market as a whole moves by 10%. An extremely volatile stock which was likely to move in the same direction as the market might have a Beta of 2. A Beta of, say, .24 is extremely low; such a stock does not move with the market at all, and in fact is very likely to move against the market, so when other stocks are going up this one might be going down. Thus, Beta in itself does not measure the volatility of a stock, but rather how much of a move it is likely to make in the direction of the market. Therefore, if you believe that the stock market as a whole is likely to move up, you want a stock with a high Beta.

Remember, Beta does not measure volatility. Volatility is simply the tendency of a stock price to move up and down. That is a separate measurement and is often expressed in percentage. A typical stock might have a volatility of 35%; an extremely volatile stock could have a volatility of 74%, and a stock which was not likely to move at all could have a volatility of as low as 14%, which happens to be the figure for American Telephone & Telegraph.

If you do not have any particular views of the market but want to buy an option on a stock which has a very good probability of going up without any movement by the stock market, then you would select an option on a stock with a very high volatility percentage.

These figures change constantly, depending upon the recent price of the market and the individual stocks. The Beta and volatility figures are not published in the regular stock market pages of the newspapers, but they are published by many stock market services, including the Value Line Options and Convertibles Service, or the Daily Options Graphs published by William O'Neil & Co.

The importance of Rule 6 cannot be overemphasized to the buyer of options. Most option buyers have at some time been buyers of stocks, and when one buys a stock there are so many other things to look for in addition to the price action of the stock as measured by Beta and volatility. The stock buyer should rightly be interested in the fundamentals of the company, the earnings prospects for the coming years, the balance sheet, the prospects for the industry, and in short the value he is getting for his money. Whether the stock is likely to go up in price over the short term may not be of interest to him at all. In fact, the best money managers are totally unconcerned with short-term price action. If the price of a stock they like goes down, they simply take advantage of the opportunity to buy more at the new bargain price.

But such a waiting game is usually something which the option buyer cannot afford. He is not concerned with the underlying fundamentals of the stock, because he is going to be in and out of his position within nine months at the maximum and usually in far less time. The fundamentals of the company are basically the same now as they will be in a few weeks when most option buyers plan to close out their positions, so the fundamentals are not going to help the option buyer by themselves. He is going to have to make his profit from factors which influence stock prices over the short term. And since these factors are notoriously difficult to predict, one sensible method of selecting an option is to pick a stock which in the past has shown extraordinary powers of moving sharply up. This movement either can be on its own in reaction to factors affecting its own destiny, as is true of some companies in unique positions, or it can be the reaction of an industry, as for example the gold mining companies. In such a case the option buyer needs a stock with a high volatility.

On the other hand if you think that the market as a whole is going to move up, then you need a stock with a high Beta. The stock buyer can afford to buy a solid stock which might move up after everything else has moved, but the option buyer needs something which will move as much as or more than the market as a whole and will move at the same time that the market moves.

*Rule 7.* Be sure to check a chart of the stock before you buy the option. Some people on Wall Street believe that by looking at the chart of a stock's past performance they can predict what it is going to do in the future. The art of doing this is called *technical analysis.* The world of technical analysis is filled with its own special vocabulary. The practitioners of this arcane art can see "heads and shoulders," "inverted Pennants," "triple peaks," and so forth, with the result that they can tell you whether a stock is going to go up or down. There is no doubt that they can tell you, but whether the stock actually does as they have said is quite open to debate. In any event we don't have to evaluate the validity of technical analysis here. Suffice to say that there is a lot about a stock which you can tell from looking at its price performance. At a glance you can tell whether it has been volatile or stable. Has the price moved dramatically in the past few months? If the price of the stock has gone up substantially simply because the market has gone up, there is a good chance that it will go back down again, but if there was a basic change in the company then perhaps the rise will be permanent and could form the base of an even higher rise.

One thing you can easily check on a chart is whether or how often in the last few years it has made the kind of change you are looking for. For example, if a stock is now 67 and you buy the 70 option for a price of $5 with the hope of doubling your money, then at the expiration of the option the value of the option will have to be $10, which means that the stock will have to be selling for $10 over the strike price of 70, or $80.

This means that you are expecting the stock to move from 67 to 80, or a gain of $13, a 19% gain. Now if you have three months to go on your option, it is relatively easy for you to go back over the chart of the stock and calculate how many times in the past the stock has gone up by 19% in three months. You will probably be surprised by how few times there were. Obviously, this does not mean that it won't do it in the next three months. Even if it has never moved up 19% in three months in the last ten years, that does not mean that it won't do it in the next three months. But it does make you think, or at least it *should* make you think, and it should give you some humility. Here laid out for you in black and white is a record which is telling you in no uncertain terms that if you had bought this same option at *any time* in the past ten years, you would not have achieved your objective. How many three-month periods were there in the past ten years? To be technical there were an almost limitless number, but if you are counting only periods starting at the beginning of each month, then there were 120 periods. Imagine, 120 chances to have doubled your money, and perhaps not a single one of those chances succeeded. Now can you come along and really expect that you are going to succeed on the 121st try? If you like those odds, you're going to love Las Vegas! Or how about the Irish Sweepstakes?

*Rule 8.* Never put all your eggs in one basket. As we have stressed over and over again in this chapter, buying options is a very speculative endeavor. There is an excellent chance that you will lose all your money on any option at any time. Therefore, if you invest a large portion of your money in one option, you had better be prepared to lose all that money. The more sophisticated investors are those who want to make money now but have some left over if things don't work out the way they expected. Of course, if you are right, you will make more by buying a large number of options on just one stock. Then you will go on and do the same thing again, and again and again. Eventually you will lose all your money.

Perhaps history can teach us something. One of the greatest traders and speculators ever to operate on Wall Street was Jesse Livermore. During his lifetime he made millions by taking positions in stocks and holding on to them until he was ready to sell at his price. He took great risks and he made great amounts of money. He became famous, and even today his name is synonymous with cool daring and successful speculation. But let us never forget that the great Jesse Livermore died broke.

These eight rules will not necessarily make you rich. Obviously, the only thing which can do that is the underlying stock's going up by a substantial amount. Your major task is therefore to pick a stock which is going to go up within a relatively short time. Unfortunately, this is as difficult to do as predicting which marble in a glass jar filled with marbles will roll the farthest when you empty the jar onto the floor. Whatever system you happen to use and like, or is recommended by your broker, or whatever news item or article you have read which makes you feel positive about a stock, will in all probability work equally well. In short, from the scientific point of view there is little that you can do to really improve your odds for picking a stock which is suddenly going to go up.

However, there is something you can do to improve your odds in making money from stock moves when you speculate on them by using options. By following the rules of this chapter you will avoid options which are overpriced, which do not have enough time to run, which are too far out of the money or too far in the money to give you the most favorable odds, which are based on stocks that have little chance of making the move you need to double your money. By using your head in selecting the right option on the right stock, you will greatly improve your chances of speculating in this very exciting and potentially ultra rewarding leveraged security.

# 13

## HOW TO HEDGE AGAINST STOCK MARKET LOSSES WITH A COVERED CALL WRITING PROGRAM

In the previous chapter we saw how the purchase of options could lead to enormous profits provided one was prepared to take the risk of losing all the money invested. Such a risky course is clearly appropriate for only a small number of investors or for only a very small portion of most investors' money.

There is, however, another facet of options which is appropriate and highly recommended for a much larger segment of investors. This method consists of buying or owning shares of stock and *selling* call options on those shares. Before we analyze this, let us simply state that the result of owning the stock and selling an option on it is to create a conservative investment which has a built-in protection, up to a certain amount, against a decline in the price of the stock. Since the one danger of investing in stock is that the price might go down, obtaining this limited protection against a downturn in stock prices makes owning stock even more attractive for conservative investors.

### COVERED CALL WRITING

Buying stock and selling call options against it is called *covered call writing*. If it sounds like an advantageous form of investment for a conservative investor, it is. The proof is that while *buying* call options is rarely undertaken by professional money managers controlling large amounts of money, *writing* covered calls is becoming increasingly popular with them. It has been approved by the Assistant Comptroller of the Treasury for use by the trust departments of national banks, it has been approved by the insurance commissioners of most states for use by the strictly controlled insurance companies for the investment of their own funds, the Department of Labor has given its blessing for pension plans to use it, and many nonprofit institutions are using covered call writing on their endowments.

The objective of covered call writing is to even out the ups and downs of the market to produce a more uniform result. This is desirable in itself, but even more significant is that in normal, flat, and down stock markets it should outperform a regular portfolio of stocks, and in a moderate bull market it will be able to keep up with most stock portfolios. Only in a steeply rising market or a very volatile market would a portfolio using covered call writing underperform a portfolio of stocks which had not used option writing. In the case of a bull market the performance of the account using covered call writing would be very good also. Depending upon how the program had been structured, the account might be up 20% to 30% (or even higher under circumstances we will discuss later). And if you did this well you should not complain too loudly if the market happened to do even better.

Covered call writing seems almost too good to be true. We'll take a look at its disadvantages shortly. It has, in fact, established an excellent track record of actual performance under a number of market conditions. Even the earliest option writing accounts, however, have not been in existence very long because options started only in April 1973, and it took a few years for people to start using them in a continuous option writing program. One major money manager, whose records start in 1973 and who is now said to have one of the largest amounts of money under management using options, has a record which is outstanding. Through March 31, 1980, the actual results of all their managed accounts are up 70%, versus a 23% increase in the DJIA, including reinvestment of dividends. Furthermore, because of the hedging feature of options, the DJIA has a risk level 48% higher than their accounts.

Another program run by my brokerage firm has a record over a 2½-year period of being up by 30%. During this time the Dow Jones Industrial Average, adjusted to include dividends received, went up by only 7%. An account which I manage for a large investor using covered option writing in 1979 was up 25%, while the DJIA was up by 10%.

So there is ample statistical evidence to support the theoretical claim that option writing should outperform the market in all situations except for a wild bull market or a market which consists of some stocks going up by a large amount while others go down by a large amount. Furthermore, since covered option writing is approved for so many large institutions, you can under-take such a program for yourself secure in the knowledge that you are doing something which has the approval of the best authorities.

As time goes on and more experience is gained in using covered call writing, it seems clear that more and more institu-tions will be using covered options on at least a portion of their stock portfolios. If they are doing it in ever greater numbers after spending a great deal of expertise and time in studying its benefits, isn't it something which you should seriously consider?

If you are going to look into covered option writing, the first step is to have an understanding of the theory. In the previous chapter we pointed out that option *buyers* were speculators in the stock. They had little interest in the stock itself, but wanted only to profit from changes in its price. The covered call writer is just the opposite. He likes the stock itself. He is interested in owning it, perhaps on a long-term basis. He believes that the company is sound and that its stock offers good value, so he is not worried that its price will collapse. He also may like the dividend which the stock offers and he is anxious to keep this. What he does not like is the fact that stock market conditions beyond his control can manipulate the day-to-day price of the stock, often to his disadvan-tage. If there were some way that he could decrease these short-term fluctuations in the value of his stock holding and at the same time gain an equivalent of what he believes is the inherent long-term gain potential in the stock, he would gladly do so. With covered call writing he accomplishes this, and the only thing he gives up is the possibility of making a large short-term profit if for some reason the price of the stock shoots up.

This is the mental outlook of the perfect covered call writer—and covered call writing is the almost perfect answer to his needs. By selling calls on stock which he owns, he is transferring to the buyer of the calls much of the speculative nature of the stock which he owns. What he retains is the stock itself with the right to all cash dividends, and of course whatever profit he has obtained from the sale of the call. Since he receives the money from the sale of the call at the beginning of the transaction, that money is his to keep whether the stock goes up or down or stays at the same price. For this reason, the seller of a covered call has freed himself from some of the normal vulnerability to day-to-day price moves.

The option seller's maximum profit is known at the outset. The potential risk of loss is not known, and in theory it is limited only by the price of the stock (assuming the worst case of the company's going bankrupt and the stock's dropping to zero) minus the amount of money taken in for the sale of the option. Thus, if you buy a stock for $28 and sell an option on it for $3, the maximum amount of money you can lose is $25. But in real life there is a probability that the stock will decline by only a limited amount within the time period of the option, so that while one can't say precisely what the downside risk is, there is a high probability that it may not be too much more than the amount you receive for the option.

### EXAMPLES OF COVERED OPTION WRITING

Let's work through an actual example to see how covered option writing works in practice. Let's assume that you have studied a certain stock and that you have confidence in the company and would not mind owning the stock at its current level of $38. You also are not a speculator and are not trying to make a profit from guessing that the stock will suddenly move up in the next few months. In fact, you would rather not have to make any market predictions at all and would be very happy if you could make some money even if the stock stays still. Therefore, you decide to sell the call option with the 40 strike price which has four months left to run.

You buy the stock for $38 and sell the option for $3. Thus, your net cost for putting on this position is only $35. Now, there are two different things which can happen to your position. The first is that the stock can either stay still, go down, or move up to 40 at the option's maturity date. In all of these cases, when the option expires, there will be no reason for the owner of the call to demand the stock from you for $40 a share. If he can buy it on the floor of the New York Stock Exchange for $38, he is not likely to ask you to sell it to him for $40. Even if the stock moves up to $40 exactly, there is still really no advantage to the owner of the call to buy it from you. So in all of these cases, the owner of the option will not exercise his call and will not buy the stock from you for $40. This means that since the option has expired, you are now left owning your stock free and clear.

Whether your position shows a profit at that moment depends upon the price of the stock. Since your actual cost in putting on the position was $35, you will be ahead if the stock is selling for more than that and showing a loss if it is selling for less. Note that if the price of the stock remains unchanged at $38, you have made a profit of $3, which is the amount you originally received from selling the call. If the stock has gone up to $40, then you have made not only the $3 profit on the sale of the option, but a profit of $2 from the increase in the value of the stock.

In any event, you could then sell another option on the stock as soon as this one expired. You can see that as time went on, it might be possible to pick up a large percentage profit on the stock over the course of a year.

The other possibility is that the stock will move up over the option's strike price of $40. In this case the owner of the call option will exercise his option and buy the stock from you for $40 a share. Usually this is done at the very last day just before the option expires, but it can be done at any time and often is done the day before a stock goes ex-dividend. You are then left owning $40. Since your original cost of getting into the position was $35, you have a profit of $5 in four months on your investment of $35, which comes out to 14%. This is not your actual profit, unfortunately, because you must first deduct brokerage commissions charged when you bought the stock, when you originally sold the option, and then if the option is assigned, when you sold the stock for $40. However, if the stock pays dividends, you may have received a dividend which would add to your profit. In any event, if the stock has been called, you now have your money and are able to start in another position.

There is a method by which your percentage return on selling options can be greatly increased, and this is through the use of margin. When you buy stocks *on margin,* the brokerage firm you are dealing with will lend you part of the money to purchase the stock. They are willing to do this because you leave the stock with them as collateral for the loan, and they have the right to sell the stock at any time they believe it is necessary to protect their investment. At the present time brokerage firms are allowed to lend you 50% of the price you pay for stock. So in our example, when you bought the stock for $38, your brokerage firm was willing to lend you $19, which means that you have to send in only $19 to buy the stock.

At the same time that you bought the stock, you also sold the option for $3. This $3 is your money, and you can apply it against the $19, meaning that your cost for putting on this position is only $16. Once the position is paid for, it is treated exactly the same as if you had paid the full price of the stock. The only difference is that the brokerage firm will charge you interest on the amount of money that you owe them, in this case $19. This interest cost must be deducted from your profits to determine your net profit. Furthermore, if the price of the stock declines substantially, you will get a request from your broker to send in more money.

There is, however, a big advantage to you in using margin and in paying this interest. Your percentage return on selling the option can be substantially higher, because you are still making $3 a share profit from selling the option, plus the additional $2 a share if the stock moves up to $40. Since your initial cost was only $16, this gives you a gross percentage return on your investment of 31%, which compares very favorably with the 14% profit you got when you paid for the stock in full. Of course from this must be deducted the margin interest, but usually the percentage return will be substantially higher even after this interest is deducted.

The type of covered call writing described above is probably the most common form. It is called *writing out-of-the-money options*, because the options which you sell have an exercise price above the current price of the stock. The advantage of this type is that you can make a profit both from the price of the option and from the increase in the price of the stock up to the exercise price. This second part may be small, but if you are very bullish on a stock you may be able to sell options which have strike prices quite a distance above the current price of the stock. In this case you will be able to capture for yourself a much larger portion of the profits if the stock moves. The countervailing disadvantage is that an option which is far out of the money is not going to be nearly as high priced, so you will not receive as much money when you sell it.

As we noted above, you will make money in a covered writing program whether the stock stays still, goes up, or goes down by less than the amount of money you originally took in from the sale of the option. Your protection from a decline in the price of the stock is naturally limited to the amount of money you take in from the sale of the option. In the example we have been using, you took in $3 on a $38 stock. Anyone with experience in the stock market will tell you that it wouldn't take much of a decline in the market to bring this stock down by more than $3. In fact, the argument against covered option writing is that you give up the occasional large upside profits in exchange for a relatively small amount of downside protection. Is there anything which can be done to give more downside protection, since that is the one Achilles' heel of covered option writing?

The answer is yes, there is. Instead of selling out-of-the-money options, you can sell in-the-money options, with the strike price below the current price of the stock. In our example, with the stock selling for $38, you could have sold the option with a $35 strike price. Since the stock is already worth $3 more than the exercise price of the option, it has a current value of $3. In addition, speculators are willing to pay for the future time value of the option, and they might be willing to pay an additional $3 for that, which would give the option a price of $6.

As we mentioned before, the amount of downside protection which you get from selling a covered option is the amount of money you get for the option. Here you are getting $6 of downside protection for each share, which is exactly twice the $3 from the out-of-the-money option. You have thereby achieved your objective of doubling the amount of downside protection. Now the stock can decline by $6 from $38 down to $32 and you will break even, before transaction costs and any interest expenses. In the previous example you had break-even protection only down to $35, and we said that it was pretty easy for the stock to fall below $35. But now that you are protected all the way down to $32, it is less likely that you will suffer a loss.

Mission accomplished. And you might wonder why anyone would ever sell an out-of-the-money. There is a reason, because here, as in every other segment of Wall Street, there is no such thing as a free lunch. What one gains on one side is usually accompanied by a loss on the other. And here what one gains in downside protection, he loses on the potential profit side. While with the out-of-the-money, a covered call writer could have made a gross profit of $5 before transactions and interest costs, the most that he can make with the in-the-money option is $3.

An example will show why this is so. Suppose you buy the stock for $38 and sell a call with a $35 strike price for $6, giving you a cost of $32 to put on this position. If the stock closes at anywhere above $35, it will be called away from you for $35. Your profit will be the $35 you receive less your original cost of $32, for the $3 profit. But it doesn't matter how high the stock goes; you will never be able to get more than $35 for it, because you have sold all your rights in the stock for all the value in excess of $35. With the out-of-the-money option it was possible to make an extra $2 from the increase in the value of the stock up to the strike price of $40, but this is not possible here.

In summary, an in-the-money option can give you more downside protection, but it cannot give you the additional profit which is possible from selling an out-of-the-money option. Many times on less volatile stocks it will not be possible to make a very large profit at all from an in-the-money option; and you may have no choice but to sell an out-of-the-money option.

Naturally there are various degrees of both in-the-money and out-of-the-money options. The further above the price of the stock the strike price of the option is, the more potential profit there is if the stock goes up, the less profit there will be from the option if the stock stays where it is, and the less downside protection there is. On the other hand, the in-the-money option gives more and more downside protection as the strike price of the option is deeper and deeper below the price of the stock.

For example, a stock may be selling at 104. You might be able to sell a 100 strike price option for $8, which would give you $4 profit; or you could sell the 90 strike price option for $16, which would give you a possible profit of $2; and there could even be an option with an 80 strike price selling at $25, which would give you just a one point profit, and that might not even be enough to cover your commission costs. You can see that as the amount of money you receive for the option increases, giving you more downside protection, the amount of profit you can make decreases.

Therefore, one of the biggest decisions you will have to make as a covered option writer is whether you should try for a large profit by selling out-of-the-money options, or shoot for more risk protection and less profit by selling in-the-money options.

Now that we've covered the theory of option writing, let's get down to the practicalities of actually investing in such a program. There are a number of decisions and we'll discuss them in the order in which you have to make them.

The first question is whether you want to use margin, and if so, to what extent. As mentioned above, by borrowing money from your brokerage firm, you can substantially increase the potential profit you can make by leveraging your investment, expecially with deep-in-the-money options. The reason for not using margin, at least to the fullest extent, is that it makes you more vulnerable to large losses if the market declines. Let's consider the plus side first. As a simplified example, consider this: You buy a stock for $12 and sell the 10 strike price call for $3, obtaining a profit of $1 before transaction costs. Without margin your original cost is $12 for the stock minus the $3 from the option, for a net cost of $9. Your $1 profit comes to an 11% profit. Using margin, you buy the stock for $12 and then borrow half the cost, which means that you put up $6. You sell the option for $3, and the entire $3 can be subtracted from your cash requirement, so you only have to put up $3 to do this position. Your profit is still $1 before costs, and a $1 profit on a $3 investment is 33%, which is exactly triple what you could have made without any margin. It must be noted that the interest you will have to pay on the $6 you borrowed will reduce your net profit appreciably, but the additional dividends on the extra stock you buy may help to offset this cost.

That's the good news. The bad news is that if the price of the stock goes down far enough on margin, you could be asked to send in more money to cover a margin call, and if you fail to do so, then your positions might be partially closed out and you would suffer a serious financial loss. The reason for this is that brokerage firms are closely regulated as to the amount of collateral which they must have for the money they lend out on margin. The collateral is the current value of the stock which you bought, so when the stock declines in value the amount of collateral declines and the firm must ask you for more money. If you have already invested all the money you have or you intend to invest and do not want to send in any more, then the firm will have to sell out all or part of your position.

Now a strange quirk of the margin rules comes into play to your disadvantage. Let's say that you get a margin call for $1,000. You tell the firm that you don't want to send in any more money and ask that they take whatever action they must in order to bring your account up to margin requirements. They will sell some of the stock and of course buy back in the options which you have sold. If the stock is now worth $8 and the options have declined to $1, you would expect that for every share they sell for $8 and buy in one option for $1, you would have $7 left to apply to your margin call. Wrong, and by a large amount.

The reason is that you don't own the stock outright. Remember that when you sell the stock, you are now taking away the collateral for part of your loan, and therefore they must use a part of that $7 to repay the loan that was being collateralized. Only 30% of the amount of money received can be applied to reducing your margin call, or can be taken out of the account, for that matter. Therefore, when you sell a share of stock for $8, 30% of that or $2.40 is made available to fill the margin call. But you also had to buy back that option for $1. Do you think that you are charged only 30% of that amount? Sorry, the entire amount you paid for the option is deducted from the $2.40, so that you release only $1.40 toward your margin call by selling $8 worth of stock. In other words, if you ever get a margin call on a covered option writing program, it is very difficult to meet it by liquidating part of the account.

This problem can be avoided by using only part of the margin which is available to you. Instead of borrowing the maximum amount from your brokerage firm, borrow perhaps half that amount. This will give you far less likelihood of getting a margin call.

## WHICH STOCKS?

Once you have decided whether or how much margin you should use, the next step is to decide which stocks you wish to select for your covered writing program. This is the most important step in any covered writing program because how well you do in this program is determined about 75% by how well the stock does and only 25% by how well the options do. There are two methods for deciding upon the stocks. The first is to use some stocks which you may already own, and the second is to purchase stocks specifically for the option writing program.

The advantages of using stocks which you already own are that you have already made the major decision that you like the stock, have faith that its price is not going to crash, and believe in the company. Second, you do not have to pay any commissions to purchase the stock. The disadvantages are also twofold. First, the price of the option may be so low that there is really little point in taking it in when you consider the upside potential profit you are giving up. For example, many people own American Telephone & Telegraph but the premium of its option is so small that selling options on it really amounts to nothing more than picking up a small increase in the dividend. The second and more important reason is that when you own a stock for a period of time you begin to have a psychological attachment to it. Or perhaps it is because you have an attachment for a stock that you own it. Either way, the result is the same. You suffer through the declines in the stock's price and you exult in its climbs, and when it goes up you believe that you have earned that profit by right of your having owned the stock for so long and suffered so much. If after this you decide to sell an option on it, all may be well if the stock stays still or goes down. But what if it goes up? In exchange for a few dollars you have given away forever the right to make a profit from this big move. For example, there were people who owned Boeing and sold an option at the 45 level for $5, believing this to be a very good price. When the stock went up to 66¾ they were kicking themselves and vowing never to write another option as long as they lived.

If you decide to buy stocks just for the purpose of writing options, you have the benefit of not having any emotional attachment to the stock. Suppose you had bought Boeing at $44 and sold the 45 option for $5. When you did this you knew that the most money you could possibly make was $5 from the option plus the $1 increase in the price of the stock up to strike price, for a total of $6. Therefore, no matter how high the stock went, you were prepared to make just that $6. If the stock went up to $66.75 you were perfectly happy because there was no psychological disappointment. You were making exactly the money you wanted, and if the option buyer was able to make a lot of money also, so much the better! That only meant that he would be back to buy more options in the future and make the prices of options even higher, so the next time you decided to sell some calls you would make even more money than you did this time.

The second advantage in selecting the stocks specifically for writing options is that you can pick the precise stocks which offer exactly what you are looking for in terms of option price, quality of the stock, and stock price in relation to the strike prices of the option. The primary consideration should be the quality of the stock. It cannot be overemphasized that for a regular covered writing program such as we are discussing here, the quality of the stock is *by far* the most important aspect of the success of an investment program. If the market goes up, everyone will be making money whether he sold options or not. Suppose you took all kinds of chances by selling options on the most risky stocks. If the market goes up, your results might to 10 or 20 percentage points higher than if you used a more solid stock, but when the market turns down, or when that particular stock comes crashing down, you will be in deep trouble.

Unfortunately, there is always a trade-off between selecting those stocks which have the highest quality, that is, are the most resistant to a downturn, and those which have the best option prices. Naturally it is always the stock which has just recently gone up the most and is hence quite likely to come down the most which commands the highest premiums. The really good quality stocks which you would feel very comfortable owning often don't have premiums worth selling. Choosing between these counterbalancing factors is where the judgment comes in.

There is no scientific way to make such a decision, but one quick rule of thumb is, "Would you be willing to own the stock if you were not planning to write options against it?" If your answer is "Maybe not," then perhaps you can get enough downside protection from the option to justify the position. But if your reaction to the question is that you wouldn't be caught dead owning the stock, then you shouldn't buy it for the purpose of selling options on it. As we've said before, options offer you only a limited downside protection, and when the market crashes down it is never enough.

The second criterion is to select a stock which has an option price high enough to give you a good return on your money. Although you can figure this out, most brokerage firms prepare computerized reports which show what the annualized return on an investment will be for the various options, either in the money or out of the money and on both a cash and margin basis. By scanning one of these lists, you will quickly be able to discern what the range of option premiums is in relation to the price of the stock and amount of downside protection offered.

The final weighing of high-quality stocks against high-priced option is an individual decision. In the accounts I manage for my clients I usually end up selecting those stocks which are just below the top blue chip investment grade but are still large, well-financed, successful companies in which I have full confidence. They are usually companies which are leaders in their fields and have been around for many years, so there is no concern that they will be survivors. Also I usually spurn stocks which have had dramatic run-ups in price. As the main theme of this book points out, there are still a great many stocks around which are selling at very low prices. By studying a computer printout, you will be able to find a number of stocks in this "second from the top" category which also offer surprisingly high option premiums.

Of course, you will be able to select stocks which are just where you want them in relation to the option strike price, that is, just out of the money or just in the money or whatever. The rule for selecting the stike price is that if you want to get a lot of downside protection, you will select an option with a low strike price, but if you want to make the maximum profit and believe that the stock will go up, then you would write an option with a high strike price. The on-the-money strike price is the happy medium; it should give you some downside protection and the possibility of making a good profit if the stock stays at about the same price.

Having selected the stock and the option strike price, the next step is simply to pick the duration of the option. To compare which option duration you will select, it is helpful to have a computer list which gives the annualized rate of return. Generally you will find that the shorter duration options, that is, three to six months, offer the highest annualized rates of return. On the other hand, the longer options give you more downside protection. Generally, I select options in the four- to six-month range because they usually give the blend I am looking for of high annualized rate of return and some meaningful amount of money taken in from sale of the option.

Having selected the stock you want to buy and the option you want to sell, you are now ready to put on the position. If you are giving your broker a large order, he should be able to execute it for you on a "spread" basis. This means that you can tell him the gross amount of profit you want to make from the position and he is then free to fill your order at any prices, provided he gets you that amount of profit. You might say that you want to buy 1,000 shares of XYZ and sell the November 20 strike price option with a spread of 3. This means that if he buys the stock for 21 he must sell the option for 4. But it is also all right with you if he buys the stock for 21½ provided that he then sells the option for 4½. By giving your broker a minimum on the spread you want, you are assuring yourself of the potential profit you anticipated and still giving him the freedom to execute the order at prevailing prices.

## MANAGING THE OPTION WRITING PROGRAM

The basic strategy in managing an option writing program is to strive at almost all times to have options written which have the potential to produce profit. This is done by writing new options as soon as the ones you have already written have expired, or else buying back the ones you wrote when they are no longer capable of producing profit for you and then writing new options.

The simplest example is a case when a stock stays at about the same price and the option you wrote expires. Let's say that you want to write out-of-the-money options, and you buy a stock for $48 and sell the 50 option with five months to go for $4. Five months go by and the stock, having moved up and down in the intervening time, is now back at 49. You wait for the option to expire and on the very next day you sell the option, which then has six months to go, for $4.25. As long as the circumstances remain like this you can go on doing this forever, taking in your $8.25 a year and making a very tidy profit.

The one variation you might want to consider is that in the few days or weeks just before the expiration of the option when it doesn't have much value, say perhaps 50 cents, you are quite vulnerable to any downside movement in the price of the stock. Here you are with a $49 stock which is supposedly part of an option writing program, and the only protection you have against its moving down is a mere 50 cents. To rectify this you can buy in the old option for 50 cents and sell the further out one at the same time. This way you will always have more option premium outstanding to protect you. It will also somewhat decrease your potential profit, but you may be willing to pay this price for more downside protection.

## WHAT TO DO IF THE STOCK GOES DOWN

Unfortunately, instead, these nasty stocks insist on making life difficult for option writers by moving up and down, usually just at the wrong time. Let's take the worst example, when the stock you have bought for $48 goes down to $44. Depending upon how much time has elapsed since you sold the option, it will have decreased in price from $4 down to almost nothing if there is just a short time left in its life, or perhaps down to $1.50 if there is still a great deal of time. The paper loss on your position would be the $4 on the stock, minus the gain from the option. The gain on the option is the $4 you sold it for, minus its current price of $1.50, giving a $2.50 profit. Subtracting this from $4 gives you a paper loss of $1.50. What should you do now?

First, you can do nothing and hope that the stock stays where it is. If it does, then your option will become worth nothing and you will be breaking even on the position, at least on paper. Then you can make the big decision of whether the next option you write will be the 50 level option or the 45 level option. With the stock at $44, the 50 level option is only going to be about $1.50 whereas the 45 level option would be about $4. If you follow the strict rules of logic, your thinking should be guided by the fact that you originally set out to sell out-of-the-money options on this stock with the objective of taking in a meaningful amount of money from so doing. Obviously, taking in $1.50 for a six-month option on a $44 stock is not taking in a meaningful amount of money. So you would go ahead and write the $45 option, even though it means that by rolling down the strike price by $5 your position is going to be worth that much less. But for the short term there is as much chance that the stock will continue to go down as there is that it will go up, and you are trying to protect yourself on the downside by taking in a meaningful amount of option premium. Since the only way that you can do this is to write the 45 option, that is what you should do.

On the other hand, I must admit that it is tempting to write the 50 level option and hope that the stock will move back up to 50. If this happens, you will be better off having written the 50 option. With the stock at $44, if you sell the 45 option for $4 you have a chance to increase the value of your position by $5 (the option price plus the $1 move up to the strike price), whereas if you write the 50 option for $1.50 you can get a $6 move up in stock price plus the $1.50, for a total of $7.50 improvement in your paper value.

The disadvantage of writing the 50 option is that if the stock continues to move down, you have so little protection. Let's say that the stock moves down to $40. You are losing $4 on the stock, offset by the $1.50 you took in from the option, which leaves you with a loss of $2.50. If you had written the 45 option, your paper loss of $4 on the decline in price of the stock would be exactly offset by the money you took in from the option. You would then be able to write the 40 level option, and if the stock finally stayed still or went up you would be making money.

The answer to the question of what to do depends upon your point of view. While from the strictly logical Random Walk point of view you should be rolling to the 45 level, if you believe that the stock is likely to come back up to 50, it may be difficult for you to "lock in" a loss by rolling down. But at least you should be aware of what the proper thing to do is.

## IF THE STOCK MOVES UP

The other possibility is that the stock moves up, let's say to $57. This is fine. You originally bought the stock for $48 and if you do nothing it will be called away from you for $50. This $2 profit plus the $4 you originally got from the option gives you the total profit you were hoping for of $6, which is a very nice percentage gross profit of 13% in five months on your original investment of $44. So if you do nothing you will be left with $54 and be ready to look around for something else to do with your money. A happy ending.

If you want to continue to write on this stock, you will have to buy in the 50 option you originally sold and sell another one. The question now becomes which option to sell. The option you buy back will cost you at least $7, but if you wait until the last week or so it shouldn't cost you much more than that. Your dilemma is that you would like to rewrite the 50 option further out, but when you figure out what your profit on that will be you are disappointed to find that it will be very small.

With the stock at $57, the 50 option with six months to go is probably going to be selling for about $9. This means that after you buy in the old option for $7 you will have a potential profit of only $2. That is not very much gross potential profit to make on a $57 stock for six months. In fact, it is just half of what you originally received, at a time when you also had the possibility of an additional $2 profit because the stock was out of the money. You would probably conclude that it simply did not pay you to tie up your money in this stock for six months if the maximum amount of money you could make were only $2.

The strategy you can use to increase your potential profit is to "roll up" and out to the next six-month option on the 60 level. Since the stock has gone up, it is very likely that the 60 option with six months to go is selling for $6. Buying back your old 50 option for $7 and selling this 60 option for $6 will produce a loss of $1. Normally we try to take in money from selling options, because that is what profit is all about, but here we are actually going to be paying out money. Why? Because for a cost of only $1 we are able to raise the strike price level of our options by a full $10. This means that the potential value of the position is going to be $10 higher, and the $1 we pay out to roll up the option is a very small price to pay.

If the stock continues to go up to the 60 level or higher, your position has gone in value to $59 (the 60 strike price minus the $1 it cost you to get there) versus a paper value of $50 when you started out. So by rolling up, you are paying out a small amount of money and obtaining the potential to increase the value of your position substantially.

Once again there is a negative. Once you have paid out that $1, you are now quite vulnerable to a downturn in the price of the stock. If it goes back below $50, you have not only paid out that $1 in vain, but you have also foregone the opportunity to take in the $2 which you could have made by reselling an option on the $50 level. In fact at any level below $53 you would have been better off writing the $50 option. Rolling up can therefore be viewed as a way of buying your way up to a higher level of stock price at the cost of laying out some money in order to roll up the option. The way to decide whether this makes sense is to compute the benefit you receive in the higher stock price versus the cost. For example, if it costs you $7 to buy in the 45 option which is about to expire, and you can sell the six-month option at the 50 level for $6, then it will cost you $1 for the possibility of increasing the value to you of your stock from $45 to $50.

To pay out $1 for a potential increase of $5 seems like a pretty good bet, and indeed it might be, but not necessarily so. In the first place, if everything goes right for you, you will have made $4 on this position. If you bought the stock for cash, this means that you are tying up approximately $45 of your money for the purpose of gaining $4. This may be a good return on your money, but maybe it isn't so wonderful either. To help you decide, you should certainly compare the return available from other new positions on other stocks, and also compare the return which you would have been able to get if you had not rolled up the option, that is, if you had just sold the six-month option at the $45 level, in which case you are taking in money.

The real risk which you must weigh in rolling up is: What if the stock doesn't move up, or comes down to $45? Then you are a double loser. First, you have paid out money for the privilege of having your stock be worth $5 more to you, and you are getting nothing from that privilege. Second, you have given up the right to make money from selling options at the same level. So the real question you must ask yourself before ever rolling up an option, is: Are you willing to take the risk that the stock will stay at the higher level? This is the key question, and if you believe strongly that the stock is going to stay up, then you are probably better off rolling up.

Now you know the basic principles of writing covered options. It is a conservative program in that, by its very nature, it helps to take out some of the ups and downs which are characteristic of the stock market. If the market really goes straight up, then you will not do as well as if you had just bought stocks and not written any options. But in a moderate bull market you have every chance of doing as well with a covered option program as the person who does not write options, and the big payoff will come if the market stays still or goes down. In that case there is no question that you will be substantially ahead of a similar stock portfolio on which no options had been written. The only reason people stay away from the stock market is the risk that stocks will go down, and a program of covered option writing takes away some of that risk. It is therefore an excellent method for someone to enter the stock market.

While some of the methods outlined here may seem complicated, they are really quite simple. You are basically buying stocks and selling options against them. The initial selection of the stock takes a lot of judgment and must be made with the idea in mind that you are going to sell options. Therefore you must look at the combination of the stock and the option in order to decide whether the risk you are taking in buying the stock is offset by the percentage return you hope to get by selling the option. Once you have decided upon the stock, then you select the option strike price which gives you the combination of the amount of downside protection and potential profit that you want. Then it is just a matter of deciding which maturity option to select.

After the position is in place, if all goes well you can just let the option expire and write another option, or let the stock be called away if it is above the strike price of the option. If the stock moves down, then you should consider buying in the option you wrote and selling a further-out option with a lower strike price so that you will be taking in more money as a way of at least partially offsetting the loss in the stock. If the stock runs up, you can consider rolling up, which means buying in the option you sold and selling a further-out option at a higher strike price; this trade is usually done at a cost to you. You hope, however, that the stock will stay at the higher level and therefore more than make up for the small cost it took you to roll up.

While these methods are basic, applying them can be complicated. If you like the principle of taking some of the risk out of the stock market and taking in money from selling options, but find that you don't want to get involved in all the details of managing the account or don't have the time to devote to the constant supervision of such an account, then you can find certain stockbrokers, like myself, who are willing to undertake the complete management of such a program for you. There are also a number of money managers specializing in option management, who will do this for you for a reasonable fee.

# 14

## CONCLUSION: A BULL MARKET IS COMING AND IT COULD BE THE BIGGEST EVER

In this book we have reviewed the recent history of the stock market and seen how the varying forces of supply and demand create the cycles of bull and bear markets. In the early forties investors were so afraid a depression would return that stock prices were at a historic low. When the depression did not occur, investors began to buy more stocks, and the prices of good stocks gradually increased. Encouraged by their gains, they began to invest more. Others, seeing the profits that had been made in the stock market, began to take their money out of the bank or bonds and put it into the market. As more money began flowing into the market, the prices of stocks went even higher. The Dow Jones average tripled from 1950 to 1960, and when the blue chip stocks got fully priced, the more adventurous investors began to buy the second- and third-tier stocks, pushing them up too. Finally, the really speculative issues got hot, and even junk stocks made money for their owners.

But all good things must come to an end. When everyone has already invested all his money in the stock market, when stocks are selling at P/E's of 30, 40, 50, or even higher, when dividends are so low that they are considered a joke, when stocks are selling at so many times book value that no one even pays any attention to that figure any more, then the market is near its top and can only go down.

That is exactly what happened in the late sixties and early seventies. As prices came down, more and more investors became disillusioned with the market and sold out. Fortunes were lost for those who had jumped into the new hot stocks, and even many of those who had stayed with the blue chips suffered losses of over 50%. The effects of this massive bear market were substantial and long lasting. Millions of investors and would-be investors had "learned their lesson," never to go near the stock market again.

Institutions had learned their lesson that you made more money with a dull bond that paid just 6% a year then you did with a stock portfolio that went down 33% a year.

Therefore, it didn't matter that stock prices by the late seventies had declined to a point where the stocks were extremely attractive based upon any analysis of their fundamental economic strengths. When people don't want to buy stocks, nothing is going to keep them from abstaining.

Being the articulate and clever creatures that they are, it was easy for investors to come up with rational reasons for why they were not buying stocks. Inflation was too rampant, interest rates were too high, there was going to be another severe recession, the energy shortage made it impossible for America ever again to be a truly great industrial power, the profit ratio of corporations was down and was going to stay down, government regulations made it impossible for corporations to be profitable, confiscatory taxation made it unappealing for investors to even think about the stock market, and the number of shareholders had permanently declined.

But we looked at all these arguments in an earlier chapter and found that not one of them could stand up to closer inspection as a valid reason for keeping the stock market down. Inflation meant that, at least in terms of unadjusted dollars, the profits of corporations would continue to increase, and that with those increases the prices of stocks would have to go up, unless P/E ratios reached absurdly low levels. High interest rates come and go, but people do not invest in the stock market for the dividends, but rather for the potential capital gains, which can outperform almost any interest rates. Recessions come every three to six years with surprising regularity, but stock prices always have snapped back in the past and they will most assuredly do so again. The energy shortage has turned out to be not so much a shortage as simply a major price increase, which is a serious problem but one which can be overcome just like any other problem. When the profit ratios of American industry are adjusted for inflation's effect on liabilities as well as inventory profits, profit ratios are at about the normal levels now. Government regulations are indeed burdensome, but many of them produce economic benefits which must be subtracted to determine their true net cost, and even if they are as expensive as the most adamant critics maintain, their cost is only 4% of gross national product, hardly an amount which can permanently cripple the industrial might of America. Taxation hits corporation profits when they are earned and again when the dividends are taxed as income to the shareholders. But the profit made from an increase in the price of the stock is taxed at highly favorable rates, not more than 28%, provided that the stock is held for over a year. For high-bracket taxpayers this is a bargain tax rate. Furthermore, there is no taxation on this increase in value until the stock is sold, so that a certain amount of tax planning is available. The number of shareholders has indeed shrunk dramatically, but it can easily increase again just as it did in the fifties and sixties.

What our study of these arguments showed is that not one is a reason why the stock market is dead, and that in fact many of them are reasons why the stock market is actually going to go up in the future. Inflation means that there is no future in bonds and other fixed income investments. But stocks by their very nature are free to float up in value as the earnings of companies increase. Therefore, if one is pessimistic and believes that there will be no future growth in the U.S. economy, and one assumes that corporations are only able to maintain their real profits, their dollar profits will increase by the rate of inflation each year. Since P/E's cannot continually go down, the prices of the stocks must increase each year. History shows that over any substantial period, stocks have kept up with inflation, and there would seem to be no reason to think that the 1980's are going to be any different from the many periods which have preceded it. In fact the very fact of inflation is perhaps one of the strongest reasons to have your money in the stock market rather than in bonds, T-bills, or C.D.'s.

Interest rates on long-term bonds are higher than dividend yields of most stocks, admittedly, but the interest on these bonds is never going to increase by as much as one cent. Dividends on stocks have been going up at a rate of 8.6% a year, which means that even if you are getting a few percentage points less in dividends now, in just a few years you will be getting the same yield as those bonds are paying, and you will also face the possibility of getting even more dividends in the future, plus the very real possibility that your stock will increase in price. So the high interest rate of bonds merely reflects the fears people have about inflation, and the more inflation there is the more the prices of stocks should go up.

Now that we've disposed of the arguments as to why it is impossible for the stock market to go up, we should take a look at the fundamental economic facts about stocks and see if the stock market is really so cheap, and then consider whether this means that prices are likely to go up or whether stocks may simply get even cheaper in the future.

The most important factor to look at is the P/E of stocks, since what the shareholder is buying is the right to his portion of the earnings of the company, and we want to know how much is being paid for $1 worth of earnings. In the summer of 1980 the P/E of the Dow Jones was just at 7. This is very close to the lowest that it has ever been. As Chart 3 shows, at the start of the all-time great buying opportunity of the last thirty years, namely 1949, the P/E was higher than it is today, and even in the depth of the 1973–74 bear market the Dow P/E was only slightly lower than it is now. Both of these were, of course, terrific buying opportunities. In fact there is no time during the past 45 years that the P/E of the Dow Jones averages has been significantly lower than it is today. Therefore, we can draw one of two conclusions. One is that this low P/E will continue because the times right now are so much worse than they were in previous times that a low P/E is justifiable for a long period of time. This would mean that times now are significantly worse than they were in the 1930's, when we had a depression the likes of which has never been seen since; or worse than the period after World War II, when it was expected that the depression would return; or worse than they were in 1974, when the stock market had almost fallen in half, the country was in the worst recession in 30 years, and the price of oil had just tripled. At all of these times the P/E of the Dow Jones was close to where it is now, and in each of those times the P/E's subsequently increased so that stocks made small fortunes for those who had the foresight to buy them. But, the argument goes, times are so much worse now that it is not likely that prices will bounce back this time.

Are times really worse than they were then? If they are only equally as bad, then we should be in for a big rally as we were every other time they reached this level. It is my conclusion that not only is the economy no worse off than it was in those previous times, it is actually much better off. This should mean that the stock market will recover sooner and perhaps go farther than it did even on the previous occasions.

Another fundamental measure of a stock's value is the dividend yield. The higher the percentage yield, the better bargain a stock is. As Chart 5 indicates, current yields are now higher than they have been in 30 years. With interest rates coming down in the summer of 1980, the yield alone of stocks made them attractive. With the 8.6% increase they have been having every year for the past few years, the yields not only make stocks attractive for themselves, they are also an excellent indication that stocks are now underpriced. There is no reason why stock yields should not return to their normal levels of the past three decades, which was in the 3% to 4% area. If this comes to pass, then taking into consideration the increases in dividends, stock prices would have to double within the next few years.

In addition to buying a share in the earnings of the company and its dividends, a stock purchaser is also buying a portion of all its assets. The way to measure whether he is getting a bargain in this respect is to find out what the price of the stock is in relation to the book value of each share. Here again, stock prices are near their all-time lows, as Chart 4 indicates. Only twice before 1973 have the prices of the Dow Jones industrials been lower than their book values. In both other times prices soared shortly thereafter.

So there you have the three fundamentals, P/E ratios, dividend yields, and relationship of stock price to book value, all pointing to the fact that stocks are now at an outstanding bargain level. But if it is so obvious to me, why isn't everyone buying? Most people aren't buying because they believe the arguments we discussed earlier.

But there are a number of professional investors and corporate finance people who dispute these arguments. These are the people who engineered all the corporate takeovers, the going private buy-ins, the corporate spinoffs for cash, and the purchases by corporations of their own stock on a massive scale. These very knowledgeable professionals and insiders agree with me that stock prices are too cheap—and they have put their money where their convictions lie.

So there is the proof that many others believe stock prices are too cheap. But will they stay cheap forever? After all, they have been almost this cheap for five years. The answer is that a share of stock is not an inherently worthless piece of paper like a modern pop painting, but it is a dynamic money-making asset. This ability to generate money is a valuable one, and one which has been assessed for years. The weight of history says that now we are evaluating these shares too cheaply.

A share of stock is analogous to an old Roman catapult. You could pull the throwing arm back further and further. A person watching this might think that pulling the arm back was simply like pulling a cart backward. The further backward you pulled it, the further back it was and the further back it would stay. But these catapults had a unique property: The further back you pulled the arm, the higher the torsion in it became. When it was pulled back far enough and then released, the arm would thrust forward with tremendous momentum and power. The further the arm was pulled back, the stronger was the throw at the end. This is similar to what the stock market is. The longer stock prices are held down, the more tension is built up. When the pressure is finally released, the market is going to shoot upward, not unlike the Roman catapult, hurling stock prices upward like rocks thrown at enemy soldiers of old.

Exactly how is this power going to be released? It will come about slowly at first, and then build up into a crescendo. The rise will come about through the application of the basic economic laws of supply and demand. Right now there is very little supply of stocks. The public has sold out long ago, and institutions are basically ready to buy rather than sell, after having underbought for almost six years. This means that a small increase in net purchases will have a major effect upon prices.

But I also foresee a major increase in demand for stocks. First, foreigners are ready to buy as soon as they see the stock market stabilizing and the dollar firming against their currencies. Europeans and Japanese are already buying U.S. stocks, and it is probably only a matter of time before the rich oil countries of the Middle East begin to load up on American shares. (Note, for example, the Kuwait purchase of $1 billion of Getty Oil shares recently.) This surge in foreign buying will pull up prices, and this increase will be noticed by the American institutions.

Institutions have been buying fewer stocks than normal for over five years. Their ratio of stocks to bonds is now about as low as it has been for years, and they have plenty of cash sitting around in short-term money instruments waiting to invest. Once they see the market make a move up, the investment managers who have not bought stocks will be afraid that they are going to be left behind, and they will scramble to buy them. As the mighty flow of institutional funds hits the market, it will pull stock prices up tremendously. This could continue for a number of years, because the annual net increase in institutional funds is about $30 billion a year.

Finally, the increase in stock prices will be noticed by the individual investor. Granted that most of them are not active in the market now. But it happened in the twenties, it happened in the sixties, and it will happen again in the eighties. When their neighbors and friends begin to make significant amounts of money in the stock market, the people who have been left out will come back in. And the people who are not now in the stock market have so much potential buying power that it is almost stupefying. There is $80 billion alone sitting in money market funds, there are billions more in real estate which could be realized by selling or simply by more financing. There is the large discretionary amount of income which so many professional people have.

In short, all the ingredients for a super bull market are now in place. Stock prices are low, and there is plenty of potential buying power around. The one factor which has prevented a bull market so far is simply the psychology of losing in the market which is basically a carryover from the 1973–74 bear market. Now that several years have passed since that debacle, and the market has a firmer feel to it, potential investors are already beginning to lose their fears. Once those fears turn to pride in the money they have made, they will be investing more, and their sense of security will grow. That in turn will lead them to invest even more.

Wall Street is basically very simple. When demand exceeds supply, the price of the stocks moves up. Today there aren't many sellers left. There are plenty of potential buyers around who have the cash to be big buyers. What motivates these potential investors either to buy or not to buy stocks? Again it is very simple. The desire to make money. When they become convinced that once again the way to make money is through the purchase of stocks, then get out of the way of the coming bull market. It will be bigger, be stronger, and make more money for more people than anything we have ever seen before.

# GLOSSARY

**Asked**  As used in the phrase "bid and asked" is the price at which a potential seller is willing to sell: the price he is asking. If a market order to buy is entered, it will be executed at the asking price. Also referred to as the offering price.

**Bear**  A person who believes that stock prices will come down. He will sell all his stocks, and then sell stock short, and buy puts or sell calls without owning the underlying stock.

**Bear Market**  When stock prices tumble down.

**Beta**  A figure which indicates the historical propensity of a stock to move with the stock market as a whole. The lowest theoretical Beta is 0, which indicates no movement, and the highest is 2, indicating wild gyrations for small movements in the market.

**Bid**  The price at which a potential buyer is willing to buy; he is bidding that amount to purchase the security offered. A market order to sell a security will be executed at the bid price, which is below the asking price.

**Bond**  A debt instrument issued by a corporation. A bond pays a fixed amount of interest, whereas a stock pays dividends out of the profits of the corporation. Furthermore, a bond will be repaid at its full amount on its maturity date. Due to these factors, the prices of bonds cannot fluctuate as much as the price of stock.

**Bull**  A person who believes that prices will rise. He buys stocks, perhaps on margin, buys calls and sells puts.

**Bull Market**  When stock market prices rise.

**Call**  An option giving its owner the right to buy 100 shares of a given stock for a given price within a given period of time.

***Cash Value***   As applied to options, the value which an option would have if it were exercised now. It is the amount by which an option is in the money. For example, if a stock is now 22, the call with a 20 strike price has a cash value of 2. Also known as intrinsic value. Out-of-the-money options do not have any cash value. Compare future time value.

***Common Stock***   Stock in which the dividend is entirely at the discretion of the board of directors. Common stock holders usually are entitled to vote for directors. Since the dividend may vary greatly, the price of common stock tends to fluctuate more widely than that of preferred.

***Convertible Bond***   A bond which the owner, at his election, can convert into a predetermined number of shares of common stock of the corporation. Because of this conversion feature, the price of convertible bonds can go up to a theoretically unlimited price along with the price of the stock. This is in contrast to the prices of straight bonds which move only in a limited range in response to changes in interest rates and the financial status of the company.

***Convertible Preferred***   Preferred stock which can be converted at the election of the owner into a predetermined number of shares of common stock. Because of this feature, the price of convertible preferred stock can rise along with an increase in the price of the common stock.

***Cover***   To close out one's position. A person who has sold some options will cover his position by buying them back in.

***Covered Call Writer or Seller***   A call writer (seller) who owns the stock underlying the calls he sells. By owning the stock he is protected from any loss from an increase in the price of the stock. His risk of loss is if the stock price declines by more than he received from the sale of the option.

***Deep in the Money***   An option which has a large value because the stock is substantially beyond the strike price. A call option is deep in the money when the stock is well above the strike price and a put option is deep in the money when the stock is substantially below the strike price.

***Dividend***   The payment by the corporation of its profits to the owners of its stock. The dividend on preferred is usually fixed at a set amount, i.e., $1.00 a year, but the dividend on the common stock is determined by the board of directors based upon the amount of profit the company has earned and the needs it has to retain part of that profit for its future financial requirements. By law a corporation cannot pay out dividends unless the money comes out of current or past profits.

***Ex-dividend*** The date on which the purchaser of a stock does not receive a dividend. For example, if a stock goes ex-dividend on the 15th, anyone purchasing the stock on the 14th will receive the dividend, but those purchasing on the 15th will not. Usually the opening price of the stock on the 15th will be reduced by the amount of the dividend. A call owner who exercised the day before a stock goes ex-dividend is entitled to the stock and the dividend, notwithstanding that the call writer will learn of the assignment only after the stock has gone ex-dividend.

***Exercise*** To do what a stock option gives one the right to do, i.e., to purchase stock for the exercise price in the case of a call and to sell stock for the exercise price in the case of a put. Exercising an option requires paying a commission as if the transaction were a regular purchase or sale of stock.

***Exercise Price*** The price at which the buyer of a call can purchase the underlying stock during the life of the call, and the price at which the buyer of a put can sell the underlying stock during the life of the put. Also called the strike price.

***Future Time Value*** In the case of an option, this is the part of the option price which does not represent cash value. Future time value is the excess which option buyers are willing to pay in order to obtain leverage and to limit exposure. In the case of out-of-the-money options, the entire option price is future time value.

***Good Till Cancelled (GTC)*** An order to buy or sell that remains in effect until it is executed or is cancelled. For example one might enter a GTC order to buy a stock for 63 when the stock is now selling for 65. Your order will remain in effect until the stock falls down to 63 and you buy it at your price, or the stock goes up and you decide to cancel the order.

***Hedge*** A transaction consisting of two or more separate transactions with the objective of providing a greater chance of making a profit, although perhaps a smaller one, than a single transaction.

***In the Money*** An option that is worth money because of the current market price of the stock. If the option were to expire today it would be worthwhile to exercise it. A call is in the money if the stock is above the exercise price, and a put is in the money if the stock is below the exercise price.

*Intrinsic Value*   Synonym for cash value.

*Long*   To be long is to own something. Opposite of being short.

*Margin*   When applied to buying stock it means borrowing part of the purchase price from the brokerage firm and leaving the stock certificates with the firm as collateral for the loan. At the present time you may borrow up to 50% of the purchase price. Thus with $5,000 you can purchase $10,000 worth of stock. The disadvantage is that if the stock declines to $5,000 you would lose your entire investment.

*The Market*   The market for a particular stock is the current bid and offering (asked) prices on the floor of the stock exchange.

*Market Order*   An order to buy or sell a security placed at the market, rather than for a specific price. When the order hits the exchange it will be executed immediately at the best current price. For example if a stock is bid 37 and offered at 37½, a market order to buy that stock will be executed at 37½, and a market order to sell will be executed at 37. The advantage of a market order is that if the price of the security is changing rapidly, your order will be executed no matter what the current price is, whereas specifying a price may mean that you will not get what you want. The disadvantage is that you may pay more than if you specified a price and were willing to wait and take the chance that you will not get an execution.

*Naked Option Writer or Seller*   One who sells (writes) a call without owning the underlying stock, in contrast to a covered call writer. The naked call writer faces a theoretical unlimited liability if the stock increases dramatically in price. Also, one who sells a put without being short the stock.

*Option*   A legal right allowing the owner to buy or sell 100 shares of stock at a specific price (exercise price) within a specific period of time. A call is an option to purchase stock, and a put is an option to sell stock.

*Out of the Money*   An option which would be worth nothing if it were to expire today. A call is out of the money when the stock is below the exercise price of the call, and a put is out of the money when the stock is above the exercise price. An out-of-the-money option will usually still have some value because of the possibility that the stock will move before the expiration date of the option. This value is called future time value.

*OTC (Over the Counter)*   Any security which is not traded on an exchange. Also called unlisted securities. They are traded by a network of dealers, and generally certain dealers will make the market for specific securities.

*Point*   One dollar

*Preferred Stock*   Stock on which a company must pay a dividend before any dividend can be paid on the common stock. Frequently the amount of the dividend is fixed, as for example a $2 preferred will pay a dividend of $2 a year regardless of how high the profits go. Of course the dividend can only be paid if there are enough profits to cover the dividend. Since the dividend is often limited, the price of preferred stock tends to move more like the prices of bonds rather than common stock. With cumulative preferred if there is not enough profit to pay the dividend, it must be paid later. Noncumulative means that if a dividend is skipped, it will never be paid.

*Put*   An option giving the owner the right to sell 100 shares of the named stock for a specified price within the specified period of time. The purchaser of a put expects the price of the stock to go down.

*Short*   To be short a stock or option means that you owe it to someone. Whereas the regular investor buys a stock or option and hopes that it increases in price so that he can then sell it at a profit, the short seller reverses the order. First he sells the stock or option, then he hopes that the security will decline in price so that he can buy it back for a lower price.

*Spread*   A combination of long and short positions in options of the same underlying stock, which options have different exercise prices or different expirations.

*Stock*   Stock is a share of the ownership of a corporation. The stock is issued by the corporation in return for a contribution of capital. The main right of a stock owner is to vote for the directors of the corporation, and they in turn elect the officers and decide upon dividend payments. The two divisions of stocks, common and preferred, are defined earlier.

*Writer*   The seller of an option.

# INDEX

222